DATE			

IMPROVING SCHOOL
PERFORMANCE

IMPROVING SCHOOL PERFORMANCE

How New School Management Techniques can Raise Learning, Confidence, and Morale

Fredric H. Genck

PRAEGER SPECIAL STUDIES • PRAEGER SCIENTIFIC

Library of Congress Cataloging in Publication Data

Genck, Fredric H.
  Improving school performance.

  Bibliography: p.
  Includes index.
  1. School management and organization.   2. Academic
achievement.   I. Title.
LB 2805.G38   1983   371.2   82-18127
ISBN 0-03-062477-0

*REF
LB
2805
.G38
1983*

Other Books by Fredric H. Genck

*Effective Schools Through Effective Management
with Allen J. Klingenberg*

*Northwestern University School Management Course
Case Study Book*

Published in 1983 by Praeger Publishers
CBS Educational and Professional Publishing
a Division of CBS Inc.
521 Fifth Avenue, New York, New York 10175 U.S.A.

© 1983 by Praeger Publishers

3456789   052   987654321

Printed in the United States of America

FOREWORD

This book will help you improve the performance of your schools, whether you are a school board member, administrator, or teacher, or a parent, taxpayer, or student.

It explains why school performance has been declining. Traditional authoritarian administration, suited to an earlier era, has not yet been replaced. Continued application of old techniques in the face of new circumstances — not anything wrong with teaching talent or techniques — is causing school performance to decline by demoralizing teachers and administrators, eroding test scores, and reducing public confidence. It is also spurring the taxpayer revolt, and encouraging vouchers and tax credits.

The new but practical and proven school performance and management concepts and techniques described in this book have already been implemented successfully. The results are improved student learning, increased public confidence and staff morale, and better control of costs in a variety of districts.

This book emphasizes the human side of school management: communication, participation, relationships, and teamwork, coupled with recognition and reward for good performance based on fair and effective evaluation, information, planning, and responsibilites.

Teachers will no longer tolerate unfair practices, and are in a position to defend themselves successfully through unions. Parents and school boards are not prepared to accept assertions of good performance without evidence in the face of national indications of decline.

Consequently, past practices no longer work today. Traditions of secrecy and authority must be replaced by communication and participation, information and evaluation, and recognition and reward.

The new management techniques that work — invented and used successfully by school boards, administrators, and teachers — are described in this book:

Why participation, communication, and responsibility for performance are essential in schools today.

Practical planning and evaluation that is simple and straightforward.
Using performance information — e.g., test scores and parent/teacher surveys — to build confidence and morale, and improve performance.
Compensating and evaluating administrators based on fairness and performance.
Evaluating and developing teachers in a way they can accept and support.
Cost control and financial planning to build public confidence and support.

Part I of the book describes and explains these new management concepts and techniques in detail. The causes of declining school performance (i.e., decreased test scores, confidence, and morale) are made clear. The policies and practices working to improve performance are set forth. The connection between school performance and management is explained.

In Part II examples of good school management are presented, in case studies developed for the Northwestern School Management Course, based on the author's extensive consulting experience. These are specific practical examples of school management techniques that work to improve performance, with descriptions of implementation and results as well as hazards and pitfalls.

If these new school management techniques are more widely understood, and the skills required to implement them are developed, the downward trends of school performance in the past decade will be reversed. Student learning will increase, public confidence will rise, teacher morale will be lifted, and costs will be controlled.

ACKNOWLEDGEMENTS

I am most indebted to the teachers, administrators, board members, and others whose creative perception and successful action are defining by example the kind of management that can improve school performance. I hope this book will result in the wider communication and application of the ideas they have pioneered and successfully applied. I want to express appreciation to three particular groups who have made a special contribution to my understanding of education and its management requirements:

My clients — the thousands of board members, superintendents, administrators, principals, teachers, and other staff members, as well as parents, students, and taxpayers — from whom I have learned what good school management is, and how it can help to improve school performance.

My colleagues on the board, and the staff of Lake Forest School District #67, where school performance and management have been exceptionally well developed, and where I've had the opportunity to learn as a participant.

The faculty at Northwestern University's School of Education and School of Management, and the board and staff of the Illinois Association of School Boards, who have supported and encouraged my efforts in public management writing and teaching as well as consulting.

And it would be inappropriate not to mention my personal gratitude for their guidance, encouragement, and support in a variety of ways to Jim Allen, John Barr, Ralph Westfall, David Wiley, Barbara Schneider, Hal Seamon, Jerry Glaub, Al Klingenberg, and Peter Warner.

CONTENTS

LIST OF EXHIBITS

LIST OF CASE STUDIES

IMPROVING SCHOOL
PERFORMANCE

PART I
SCHOOL PERFORMANCE AND MANAGEMENT CONCEPTS

This section examines why outdated authoritarian school administration is causing performance to decline and why new school management techniques are needed. These techniques are identified.

1

INTRODUCTION:
Why a New Kind of
School Management is Needed
to Improve School Performance

Declining school performance is not usually recognized to be caused by the inadequacy of traditional school administrative practices to meet today's requirements. We usually look for something wrong with teachers, with children and parents, or with teaching techniques and materials. Seldom do we look for the cause on the human side of school management: changes in the internal operations and outside circumstances of schools, and how these are impacting on the people involved — teachers, administrators, board members, parents, and students.

Yet my firsthand experience in nearly a thousand schools during the past ten years demonstrates clearly that the cause of declining performance lies in challenging circumstances combined with inadequate management. Changes during the past decade — teacher unions, public concern, the taxpayer revolt — have in effect disconnected many schools and districts internally. Traditional, authoritarian, informal administrative practices just aren't working anymore.

This old style of school administration seemed to work well enough in the 1950s and before. Superintendents who were forceful leaders and articulate spokesmen for public education persuaded Americans to support schools with a breadth and quality unequalled elsewhere in the world. But that authoritarian style of leadership no longer works, because of new circumstances. A general climate of public concern with schools, sustained by continuing media attention and evidence of actual declines in key indicators of school performance

3

has influenced school management policies. Also, the advent of teacher unions, and the ability to demand fair, participative management, has played a major role in this area. These two key changes, as well as declining enrollments, the taxpayer revolt, and other challenging circumstances, have dramatically expanded school management requirements.

In the absence of management techniques suited to these new circumstances, and to the nature of education, most school districts are in a situation of internal disruption that is demoralizing, and damaging to performance and productivity. The internal communication and teamwork essential to good schools is made difficult, sometimes impossible. There is no means of pulling together the efforts of the many people involved. So naturally performance drifts lower. In spite of the widely documented and perceived decline, neither complaining nor setting higher standards will help schools improve, without the internal management practices that are required.

Yet some schools are performing well in spite of these circumstances. Districts and schools are functioning successfully, in every kind of community. What do these schools and districts have in common? They have created a more participative and humane process of management that emphasizes performance and results as well as people and relationships. What are the key features of their management process? They evaluate performance, using information wherever possible, even in a field like education that sometimes defies any quantitative indicators. They accept responsibility for performance, organizing teachers and administrators to strive for and achieve good results. They maintain teamwork and constructive working relationships among teachers, administrators, and board members, in spite of universal pressures toward conflict and fragmentation.

As a result, these districts are realizing the ultimate objective of all education — the academic achievement and development of students. They sustain high levels of public confidence, parent and community satisfaction, and staff morale, productivity, and job satisfaction. Costs are reasonable and under control. They are accomplishing these things whether their communities are black or white, rural or urban — and whatever their position on the socioeconomic scale.

This book describes these performance standards and achievements and the school management philosophies, policies, and practices that contribute positively to them. It also explains how the combination of adverse circumstances and inadequate traditional administrative practices in schools is causing performance to decline. The goal is to stimulate and contribute to wider understanding and application of management appropriate to schools.

READER AUDIENCE

The book is designed to be useful to those responsible for the performance and management of education — school board members, superintendents, administrators, principals, teachers, and other staff members. Obviously their success in fulfilling these responsibilities determines how well our schools serve us. The book should also be useful to those who receive the services of schools (i.e., parents and students) and to those who pay for them (i.e., taxpayers and citizens). Understanding the connection between school management and performance and knowing the key requirements for improving the latter by means of the former should enable all of these groups to make a more constructive contribution to improving school performance through better management. In a democracy, for an institution as huge as public education, widespread understanding of what needs to be done is essential to accomplishing it.

Most people lack the opportunity for enough contact inside schools to understand what is really going on. They see only the external indicators — a teacher strike, school closing, or national media reporting of declining test scores. Even inside schools, teachers, administrators, and board members often have little understanding of management and how it can be a positive, constructive process. School management is not well defined. School administrators have had little or no management training. And board members often lack management experience, or have it in a field other than education.

The board of education and administrators of the district are primarily responsible for the quality of management and its contribution to good school performance. Teachers, however, are also now in a position to influence this, through collective bargaining. There are districts where they have successfully taken the initiative toward better management. And they certainly have good reason to, if the board and administrators won't act responsibly on their own, since the professional satisfaction and performance of teachers is directly affected — for better or worse — by the quality of management in the schools and districts where they teach.

In an era of public concern, the obligation of teachers, administrators, and board members to find an approach to accountability, evaluation, information, and management that is fair and effective and actually works to improve school performance is their most essential responsibility. Education is the largest and some think the most important of our public services. It is the first public service to recognize the need for new management techniques, and take action to design and implement them in practice. While each public service is a little different in the specific information and management requirements it presents, many of the techniques described in this book also indicate directions in which the management of other public services should be developing. In this sense the book should serve a broader audience than education — the providers and consumers of all public services, a group that includes virtually everyone.

BACKGROUND

The basis for this book is my firsthand experience during the past decade — visiting schools, classrooms, and district offices, interviewing board members, administrators and teachers, and conducting management studies for school districts — in more than 100 school districts, 200 management studies, and thousands of interviews. For almost 20 years the purpose of my work as a general management consultant has usually been the overall improvement of performance, strategy, and organization. This work has generally focused on the human side of management — corporate strategy, plans, organization, and personnel policies, selection, development, evaluation, and compensation. The orientation has been to problem solving and decision making, helping make organizations more successful and effective in the satisfaction and productivity of staff as well as products and services to customers.

Like an itinerant anthropologist, I've had the opportunity to observe firsthand the inner workings of thousands of organizations, of virtually every size and type, in a number of countries. Many have been businesses — some small, others large multinational corporations. Over the years, my consulting practice has gradually shifted from business to public management. I've worked with more than 100 school districts as well as federal, state, and local governments, universities, hospitals, private agencies, foundations, and associations, mostly in the United States and sometimes in Europe. I also serve as a school board member, and teach school management. As a result, I have observed firsthand the relative weakness of public management in the United States as one of our most serious national problems at this time. To make our public services as effective as industry and agriculture in serving us must be one of our paramount national objectives.

I have seen the turmoil inside districts caused by the challenging circumstances education faces today. School boards are fighting among themselves, firing superintendents, and making adversaries of parents and teachers. Administrators are confused and unsure about their authority and responsibility in the face of public concern, aggressive boards, teacher unions, and less respect for authority on the part of parents and students as well. Teachers are confused and demoralized by declining enrollment, reduced mobility, threatened job security, and more challenging students. Finally, parents are concerned about declining school performance, and usually blame teachers for this problem. Not surprisingly, performance declines under these circumstances. Traditional school administrative practices are informal, unprofessional and, as evidenced by teacher unionization, considered unfair by teachers. Thus, they have simply broken down in the face of today's pressures.

I have also seen districts and schools performing with great success today, in spite of these same circumstances. In these districts and schools, I have observed and consolidated, from firsthand experience, those management policies and practices that contribute to good school performance. This connection between management policies and practices and their effect on school performance is the key to turning around school performance trends. Through management research and teaching I've had the opportunity to pull together this experience into the conceptual framework described in this book. This is a model of school management that I believe will work anywhere, and this book should make it easier for educators and others concerned about school performance to access, understand, and apply these findings.

An outline definition of good school performance and good school management (performance information, planning and evaluation, organization, the development and compensation of administrators and teachers) is shown in Exhibit 1.1 following this page. Each of these concepts is defined in some detail in Chapter 4.

EXHIBIT 1.1
A Concept of School Management and Performance

Good School Performance	*Good School Management*
Student learning	*Performance information*
Academic progress and	Student progress
general development	Parent opinions
Parent satisfaction	Staff opinions
Public confidence and support;	Cost analysis
student opinions	*Planning and evaluation*
Staff satisfaction	Board
Program quality and performance;	Administration
working conditions; productivity	Staff
and morale	*Organization*
Cost control	Responsibilities, relationships
Includes financial planning	Communication, participation
	Administrative evaluation and
	compensation
	Based on performance; fair to staff
	Teacher evaluation and development
	Operational, fair, and effective

Source: Compiled by author.

HOW TO USE THIS BOOK

If you understand the management principles and techniques described in this book, you will be able to participate in and contribute to the management revolution of our public services. This will eventually result in as much productivity improvement for public services, with benefits for staff and public alike, as we have achieved in agriculture and industry through better management there. It will restore the public respect and contribution of schools to our national democracy and economy. It will also improve all of the key indicators of school performance — student learning, public confidence, staff morale, and cost control.

Of course the performance of schools is extremely difficult to measure, subject to intense personal feelings, pressures, and opinions on the part of various constituents. Management and evaluation of performance under these circumstances are necessary but difficult.

It is important not to add time or cost burdens, but rather to seek a relatively simple, economical, and straightforward system of practical value.

Because school management is at an early stage of development, the concepts and techniques in this book will be improved upon as the years pass, but they will presently work in practice to improve performance. Their widespread application is essential for success. While no concept or technique of management can be applied in a simpleminded way in every situation, these work in a sufficient variety of circumstances to be worth considering everywhere. Using this model, we have the opportunity to turn around the performance of our schools.

The deterioration of educational performance could be the early warning sign of national decline. If we are unable to turn around negative school performance trends, they may be compounded by further declines in confidence and support that reduce funding and thus performance, confidence, and support in a downward spiral. Designing and successfully applying management practices in our public schools and other public services that work to improve performance is one of our most challenging and important national priorities. You can contribute to improving the performance of public management whether you are a teacher, administrator, or board member, or a parent, taxpayer, citizen, or other interested party. But don't expect the understanding and application of management to be easy. Making an organization purposeful and effective is one of the most challenging of human arts. It involves analysis and action in a complex human setting where results are difficult to measure and attitudes are never quite certain.

Depending on your point of view, before you read this book you may need to put aside some preconceptions. One is that adversarial relationships among teachers, administrators, and board members are appropriate or even unavoidable in schools. This is not the case. On the contrary, based on extensive consulting, research, and teaching experience in schools, I am convinced that teamwork is essential to good performance. And this experience has also convinced me that teamwork and positive, productive working relationships are still possible in schools and that they help to improve performance. This doesn't ignore the existence or the valuable functions served by unions, not only in protecting the rights of teachers but in highlighting the need for better management in schools. Good management is as important and useful to teachers as it is to parents and students, since their performance and satisfaction partially depend upon it.

Another preconception you may have to put aside is that school performance can't, or shouldn't, be measured. In working with organizations of all kinds in several different countries I have found that some indicator of performance is a prerequisite of good management. This holds true even when that indicator is as judgmental and abstract as a scientist's view of his or her latest creative efforts, or artistic and critical views on the quality of a painting, play, or music, or the impact of teaching on a student. While the ultimate results of education in human development over a person's lifetime may never be measured, short-term indicators described in this book are helpful, indeed I believe essential, to improve performance.

I hope this book will help you learn about school management, but it can only initiate the process. Your own practical experience and learning by actually applying these techniques will be more important. Like most education, the teaching of school management cannot be compressed into a simple "cookbook" that will produce a competent manager or even an understanding of management as a result of a few hours of reading. Testing and applying these ideas for yourself will be far more important. This is a process that may well take years, perhaps decades. Don't expect results overnight.

Within this context of cautions and caveats, the book does try to accomplish two things. The first is to provide a general concept or framework for thinking about school management, along with criteria for judging good school performance and the management that is required to achieve it. These concepts are necessarily a little abstract at times. But they are based on extensive real-world experience; and I hope to make them as tangible and concrete as possible. Second, the book explains a number of very specific and practical techniques of management used successfully in schools. These are not borrowed from other fields or suggested on the basis of theory, but rather from actual firsthand observation of their success in improving school performance.

2

DECLINING SCHOOL PERFORMANCE:
Circumstances that are Causing It

Education seems always to have been the most important public service to Americans. Perhaps it should not be surprising that we have reacted with alarm to the mounting evidence that school performance is declining. Lower test scores and literacy, reduced public confidence and parent satisfaction, teacher frustration and concern evidenced by unions and strikes, and rising costs contrasted to declining enrollment and student achievement are frequent topics of national magazine coverage and television specials. The declines in these key indicators of school performance may be slight, and to some extent explained by the more challenging circumstances educators face today. Still, they raise disproportionate levels of concern; and, in light of the size of public education and its importance to Americans, well they should. There is no question that the performance of schools has declined, seriously in big cities and to a lesser extent in many other districts as well.

Declining test scores and literacy are well known by now, and no attempt has been made to further document or analyze them in this book. The situation is somewhat complicated, and in all fairness educators are being asked to shoulder responsibility for many social trends that certainly were not their fault. Nonetheless, student achievement seems clearly to be down. This is documented extensively in such excellent books as *The Literacy Hoax* by David Copperman and *Less Than Words Can Say* by Richard Mitchell, among others.[1] Educators must not pretend that there isn't a problem, even though it hurts a little to analyze and react positively and constructively to negative performance trends in the industry, trade, or profession for which you are responsible. Statistics on declining school performance receive frequent national media attention.[2]

Beyond student achievement, it is also obvious that parents are dissatisfied with schools in many districts and that the general level of public confidence is low. While educators rightly complain that this may reflect more media attention to the negatives of education than the positives, public confidence is still a key indicator of school performance. Concern is evident in national surveys, media attention, and the taxpayer revolt. The latter, while reflecting the current condition of the economy and the inherent complexity and perhaps inequity of property taxes, also reflects the relatively low level of public confidence in school performance and the feeling that schools are not as cost effective as they might be.

Equally important to the low level of public confidence is the widespread and I believe correct assessment of teacher morale as being under serious pressure. Threatening and adversarial staff relationships, high levels of frustration and concern on the part of teachers, and widespread talk about burnout and low morale are evident in schools today. The rapid unionization of teachers indicates underlying dissatisfaction.

In our major urban areas, there is little question that the problems and costs of crime, welfare, and unemployment are growing in part from inadequate school performance. This focuses on the weakest part of U.S. education, accounted for in part by organizations that are simply too big to be effective in a field which is so hard to measure and sensitive to human relationships. Yet it is important to acknowledge the seriousness of this problem. It could offset the United States' great accomplishment in the political and social attitudes that have led us to policies of racial integration that would seem naive and impossible in virtually every other country.

Simply listing the challenges to teachers today as the causes of performance decline — family difficulties and distractions of television and drugs, for examples, or declining respect for authority — does not explain the decline. These challenges are no less real in districts and schools performing well than in those that have declined in performance. Successful schools can be found in both urban and rural areas, with every racial mix. Nor is the talent of teachers inadequate, nor is the explanation to be found in faulty teaching techniques. On the contrary, the relationship of supply to demand for teachers has improved the quality of teachers in the last ten years. And educational innovations, so often criticized, are evidence of a healthy profession, even though not all have worked.

The principal cause of decline in educational performance over the last decade or two does not lie in the talents or technology of teaching but in the superstructure of education — that little understood area of board policies and administrative techniques, practices and skills. Although the smallest part of the educational structure, these elements of education are historically weak, tremendously important in their impact on the productivity, morale, and job satisfaction of teachers, and presently inadequate to meet the challenging circumstances with which educators are confronted. Instinctively, most of us look for something wrong with teachers or teaching methods in trying to explain the decline in school performance. The real cause is inadequate school management. With these negatives reviewed, it is only fair to note and acknowledge the strength and competence of U.S. education before proceeding further.

Based on my personal experience over the past 20 years in working with education in the United States and Europe (as well as government and industry in both places) I believe that U.S. education is unequalled throughout the world in terms of its breadth and quality. This is an accomplishment that American educators can and should take pride in. Even the downtrends in indicators of performance discussed above, while serious and important, certainly don't go so far as to offset this fundamental accomplishment.

Public education can be proud of the greater number of children today who graduate from high school. Programs developed during the past decade or two in special education are beginning to correct a basic inequity in our society that existed up until very recent times. Many schools and districts are performing well in spite of the difficult circumstances facing educators today.

Contrasting to negative national trends are the positive, constructive achievements of a few districts who have sustained and improved school performance, even though dealing with the same circumstances as districts experiencing decline. Teachers and administrators in these districts have pioneered to find management techniques that work, in spite of the limited training and tradition of management in education. The rest of this chapter is organized around the three subjects outlined in Exhibit 2.1.

EXHIBIT 2.1
Circumstances, Characteristics, and Management Requirements*
(overview)

New Circumstances	Characteristics	Requirements
Changes in education, expanding management requirements.	Characteristics of education, determining management requirements.	School management requirements today, based on characteristics and changes.
• Unions	• Multiyear, multiparty	• Performance
• Public concern	• Hard to measure	– Evaluation
• More divergent goals	• Schools important to participants	– Information
• More aggressive school boards	• Close to communities	– Compensation
• Traditional authoritarian administration	• Teacher independence	• Teamwork
• Taxpayer revolt	• Feelings and attitudes	– Management responsibilities
• Contentious decisions	• Dedication and time	– Communication and participation
• Intervention	• Job satisfaction	– Decision making

*Three exhibits showing each section of this exhibit in more detail will be found later in this chapter.

Source: Compiled by author.

New Circumstances:
Changes in education and expanding management requirements have been too rapid to allow school management policies and practices a chance to catch up. Consequently, performance is going down.

Characteristics of Schooling
The nature of teaching and learning determines the management requirements of schools. Failing to recognize these characteristics leads to management practices inappropriate to schools, and negative in performance impact.

Management Requirements
School management standards must be established to meet these circumstances and characteristics.

NEW CIRCUMSTANCES

The principal causes of expanded management requirements in public schools are the changes that have occurred over the last decade or two. While generally known individually, the cumulative extent and significance of their impact on education is not widely recognized.

In my experience with many industries in several different countries, I have not seen any subjected to such dramatic changes over such a short period of time. An analogy could be made with the impact on industry of the muckrakers, the Depression, and unionization during a period of some 30 or 40 years. Schools have been put through a similar process — media attention to public concern with school performance, rapid unionization of teachers, tough decisions and negative impact on morale of declining enrollment, financial constraints, and the taxpayer revolt. As industry did many years ago, education is turning to a new management philosophy to deal with these pressures and demands.

These changes have created tougher management requirements in schools that are not being met by the traditional administrative practices of education. The conflict between these traditional practices and the new management requirements of schools is causing morale to decline, conflict and fragmentation to develop within districts, and consequently student learning to receive a lower proportion of the energy and effort available. The result is declining school performance.

EXHIBIT 2.2
New Circumstances

New Circumstances	Characteristics	Requirements
Changes in education, expanding management requirements.	Characteristics of education, determining management requirements.	School management requirements today, based on characteristics and changes.
• *Unions*, thrusting schools suddenly into an era of teacher power, leaving superintendents without traditional internal support.	• Multiyear, multiparty	• Performance
	• Hard to measure	– Evaluation
• *Public concern* about school performance, fanned by media attention.	• Schools important to participants	– Information
	• Close to communities	– Compensation
• *More divergent goals* and interests versus congruent goals articulated by authoritarian superintendents – respected, successful community leaders.	• Teacher independence	• Teamwork
	• Feelings and attitudes	– Management responsi-bilities
• *More aggressive school boards*, overinvolved, firing superintendents, adversarial.	• Dedication and time	– Communication and participation
	• Job satisfaction	– Decision making
• *Traditional authoritarian* administrative models colliding with demands for participation and communication.		
• *Taxpayer revolt*, economic difficulties, inflation.		
• *Contentious decisions*: school closing, budget cuts, negotiations.		
• *Intervention* of state and federal governments.		

Source: Compiled by author.

16

In the long run, these changes will provide the foundation for improving school management. But in the short run, they are the cause of declining school performance. They are summarized in Exhibit 2.2.

In the past, school districts typically were under the control of a long-term superintendent, who was likely to be authoritarian and patriarchal in image and practice. His stature in the community, personal leadership, and the respect accorded his educational experience and academic credentials enabled him to run the district largely according to his own desires – at least so long as he met community moral and ethical standards. He satisfied both the school board and the community without pressure to document success. Typically, he dealt with a conservative board of leading citizens, more often than not unified in their ideas of what education should be, and thus able to provide both stability and experience.

Teacher groups at the time were organized around professional goals and made little effort to dispute the superintendent or board. The personal commitment of teachers was primarily to teaching, and minimally on improving their financial and working conditions. The community generally was passive in its relationship with the schools. The board and superintendent had wide latitude in deciding how to run the schools.

In the 1950s, education entered a period of enrollment growth that strained school financial resources to the fullest. The dollars involved in providing more buildings, staff members, and learning materials thrust education into the "big business" arena. It was not until the early 1970s that declining enrollment began to ease the demands for new facilities and expanded staffs in most districts.

The superintendent today operates under new and more intense pressures. No longer the captain of his own ship, he increasingly is buffeted by pressures from parents, demands from teachers, and criticism from the public and the press – all often seeking conflicting goals.

Teachers and Unions

Unionization of teachers probably has had the most dramatic impact on the need for management in education.[3] Teacher unions today demand input into the decision-making process of running a district. The development of professional management in business and industry also occurred in tandem with unionization.

Many superintendents who served in the 1950s and 1960s have explained to me that the one constant they could always count on in the political process of running a school district was the support of teachers. The National Education Association had room within its membership for teachers, administrators, and even board members. The sense of teamwork was reinforced by common college educational experiences and the comradery of a profession with a high sense of identity, considerable contact with other educators as well as some isolation from other people.

Contrast this with the situation today. In the 1960s the National Education Association became a union, with a ready-made membership that no doubt contributed to the speed and extent of teachers' unionization, unequalled in virtually any other industry. As a result, teachers have been organized — and separated from their administrative and board colleagues. Anyone observing a teacher strike has seen the sharpness of the change. Typical bargaining strategies and employee actions, indeed ones that seem mild by comparison to the early history of industrial labor relations, nevertheless have had a startling impact on teachers, students, and parents in districts that have experienced strikes. Teachers marching on picket lines have strained relations that are difficult to put back together afterward. Handling negotiations and the adversarial relationships that are involved is difficult. Many superintendents have found themselves so angered by teacher unions, and the confusing and distressing nature of strikes and related actions, that they simply took early retirement.

The complex demands of negotiating add directly to the management requirements of schools. More important, the existence of unions gives staff members an opportunity to communicate, either across the bargaining table, through strikes or within the union organization. The need for internal channels of communication, especially from the staff to administrators, is heightened. A participative management process that gives the staff an opportunity for expression and participation becomes absolutely essential.

These requirements for more staff communication and participation came to school districts that had been perhaps the last refuge of authoritarian management practices in this country. School administrators enjoyed an unusually free hand, and collegial relationships with the staff. I have seen many examples of the extent of their authority. No doubt these practices were an underlying cause of the rapid unionization of teachers. But they also created a situation in which it was difficult for such authority-oriented administrators to respond positively and constructively to the more participative and communicative management demands being made by unions.

Public Confidence and Parent Concern

A close second to the importance of the unionization of teachers would be the growing public concern about school performance. This started in the 1960s with the revolutionary behavior of many young people, in the era of the Vietnam war and the increased use of drugs by the youth in our country. But the concern really seemed to be compounded when evidence of declining test scores and literacy, noted earlier in this chapter, began to receive media attention. Such publicity often focuses on the most troubled school districts in the larger cities.[4]

The public is no longer compliant. Generally its attitude reflects criticism and demands for change rather than support. The public knows that test scores of college-bound students have been getting lower, as have standardized achievement test scores in the elementary schools. While the causes are yet to be fully understood, low achievement test scores fuel public concern about education and provide ammunition for any person or group that seeks to attack the current system, muckrakers and internal dissidents included.

Public concern and media attention have led to a widespread, general feeling that all schools are in trouble. This tends to put parents, taxpayers, and board members in a frame of mind that encourages aggressive behavior. This is not an inappropriate response, but it is one that creates additional problems inside school districts. Again, the traditional structure was not equipped to deal with this concern. For example, it was customary for superintendents to limit the amount of information given to school boards. This tradition has made it difficult for schools to respond to concern about performance with evidence – documenting results where they're good, and identifying problems so that action can be taken to correct them.

Because schools are naturally located within the immediate communities they serve, a national image of declining performance interacts with any local problems that may exist. Parents become uneasy about their own school because of national media attention to the negatives of school performance, even though these might be occurring elsewhere. And any local problems that do arise, and some are inevitable, tend to be magnified in a general climate of concern and suspicion. The need for even the best school to defend its performance to its community increases. For schools with performance problems, the negative impact of these problems is increased, and the risk of a deteriorating cycle of confidence, morale, and performance is enhanced. The problem is further compounded by the unavailability of information on learning, parent and teacher satisfaction, and costs with which boards, administrators, and teachers can defend the performance of the districts, schools, and classrooms for which they are responsible.

More Aggressive School Boards

Boards are changing in composition and attitude. Members bring more diverse experiences and viewpoints; increasingly they represent special interests. A substantially larger proportion of women and members of minority groups serve on school boards. Board members also serve for fewer years. Perhaps most important, school boards have become more aggressive in recent years. Many of them are overinvolved in district administration, no doubt in some cases with good reason. But everyone who has experience with boards in all fields knows that they cannot run an organization. Overstepping board responsibility can only be temporary, to solve a problem. The high turnover rate of superintendents and many early retirements reflect this aggressive board behavior.

That school boards should respond actively to the general climate of public concern about school performance is neither surprising nor inappropriate. And school board members today are different from those of 20 years ago, at least according to most superintendents. While sociological evidence and documentation is not readily available, there is a widespread impression that board members 20 years ago tended to be leading members of their community, predominantly male, and in relatively senior managerial positions themselves. They tended to be busy, eager to delegate to the superintendent, and respectful of his authority. In contrast, school board members today are a much more diverse group. They include a larger proportion of women, fewer people from senior managerial positions, and more professionals, perhaps just reflecting the balance of the work force today. Some women on school boards have a great deal of time available to devote to their duties. And many of these people were elected on a platform of concern about school performance or, as noted below, taxation.

Divergent Goals and Contentious, Divisive Decisions

Another important change in schools is the divergence of goals and interests, contrasted with more congruent goals successfully articulated by authoritarian superintendents who were respected community leaders. Today, demands from special education, gifted, civil rights, and other groups have created a more fragmented political constituency for school districts. And the authority of superintendents to give leadership within the community has declined. The impact of national news media, and the negative performance indicators available to them, is much more important than just a few decades ago. The result is fragmentation and confusion of goals, with outside forces much more challenging to local confidence and support. Less respect for authoritarian leadership makes it difficult for superintendents to respond in the traditional style. And of course declining performance in an institution located within the community it serves, and so important to Americans, naturally invites public outcry. It's easy to find your local school, and democracy works in most communities so that complaints are focused on the locally elected and responsible school board.

Schools today also face more contentious, difficult, and potentially divisive decisions. An era of declining enrollment brings about the need to consider closing schools. Americans are quite attached to their schools; in many communities they provide the main focus of community identity. Many districts have found in school closing that the entire community can agree that a school should be closed — but no one wants it to be his school. Educators have sometimes overemphasized the cost aspects of school closing decisions and underemphasized the human relations and attitudes of local attachment to schools. But apart from this need for a sound and practical analytical viewpoint, deciding whether to close a school and then doing so is a very difficult issue with which schools must deal today.

Budget cuts brought about by costs rising through inflation, and tax rates and revenues that may not be so flexible, are another example of difficult issues. Negotiations also belong in this category. The existence of such difficult issues and decisions creates the opportunity — sometimes unavoidable — for dissension and conflict. And they can easily lead to a general feeling of decline, frustration, dissatisfaction, and loss of morale. I have seen many communities in which the following series, or a variation of it, has occurred: closing a school, losing a referendum, having a teacher strike, firing the superintendent. Sometimes this cycle repeats itself every few years.

A more recent phenomenon that has had great impact on schools, and probably will continue to do so, is the taxpayer revolt. Frustration over a tax system not designed to be functional and defensible in an era of inflation, compounded by the feeling that schools aren't performing very well, has led to a taxpayer revolt. This seems to be continuing, and perhaps still accelerating. Obviously public perceptions of schools present a more difficult situation today than they did 20 years ago.

Finally, these trends have encouraged many state governments to intervene in school matters.[5] Even assuming the best of intentions, many of these interventions have compounded the problem. States have forced upon schools impractical program budgeting systems, revenue sharing plans greatly complicating financial planning, or demands for accountability that have added to the perception of declining performance. They have offended and alienated teachers, and in most cases not helped performance. Without being overly critical of these interventions — some have probably been helpful — they have certainly added to the difficulty and challenge of managing schools.

Changing parent, teacher, and student attitudes are part of a generally lower level of respect for authority in all of our institutions. In schools, where traditional authoritarian practices survived longer than practically any other institution in our country, this change has been particularly dramatic. This trend can be traced back for centuries; it seems unlikely to be reversed.

Another change is the attitude of teachers toward administrators and the board. Unions now provide for participative involvement whether management wants it or not. Also important is the loss of the traditional respect by the school board and community for the superintendent, looking up to the degrees that followed his name and rarely challenging his decisions and opinions.

The widespread breakdown of families, and to a lesser extent communities, in the United States has also affected schools. Teachers are well aware that they're working with children who have pressures and circumstances at home today that are much more difficult than was the case 20 years ago.

To summarize these changes is a little frightening. Inflation has put every industry into a position of needing to defend its costs and prices, and schools are no exception. Teacher unions have turned upside down traditional staff relationships, replacing an implicit assumption of teamwork and professional comradery with adversarial and combative relationships that are confusing and disruptive, whatever their value. Federal and state governments have imposed obligations on school districts, perhaps rightly, in light of the competence of schools indicated by national performance trends, but nevertheless adding to the job they are asked to do. Declining enrollments have added to the problems of schools, creating conflict by requiring consideration and in some cases actual closing of schools, and threatening staff job security, adding to the frustration of teachers. Perhaps we should be surprised that school performance has not declined further under these circumstances.

It seems increasingly to be recognized by educators and others that these threats to school performance seem likely to continue or expand in the future:

Continued low levels of public confidence in school performance invite action by various outside groups.

Low levels of teacher morale and poor personnel policies discourage good performance and limit career and personal development.

The apparently still growing taxpayer revolt threatens to cut programs, diminish the ability of education to produce results, and contribute to further loss of public confidence.

Schools are being drawn further into the provision of social services, while funding continues to flow through big centralized social service agencies that are ineffective and unproductive.

Continued interest in tuition tax credits and/or vouchers, to fund private alternatives to public education, could further diminish the ability of public education to respond effectively to parent demands.

Virtual elimination of local control over major decisions such as funding of schools has happened already in California, and now in Massachusetts.

Many of the negative trends noted above will be extended to those states where they haven't yet occurred.

The changes that have occurred in the circumstances of schools demonstrate that their management requirements today are considerably different, and more difficult, than those of 20 years ago. Equally important is the need to recognize the peculiar characteristics of schools that determine their management requirements, and explain why some management techniques applied during the last few years, especially those borrowed from industry and government, have not worked very well.

CHARACTERISTICS OF SCHOOLING

The characteristics of education — summarized in Exhibit 2.3 and discussed below — put it among the most difficult organizations to manage successfully.

Responsibility for the development of students is unavoidably shared among many people — the student, parents, and teachers in several years, grades, and subjects, for example. Who gets credit or blame for the development that occurs? Many years are involved in a person's education. It's almost impossible to tell how an event in one year might influence learning in the next. Or how the student's progress is affected by his or her own physical or mental development or readiness to learn at a particular time. Responsibilities can never be so sharply separated as to avoid the need for teamwork and a shared sense of responsibility and accomplishment, always hard to achieve.

As an example of this shared responsibility, consider the pride typically reflected in children's marking of their growth every few months on a convenient door edge in their home. Their sense of pride is in no sense diminished by sharing it with their parents. But who gets the credit or blame in academic subjects, when the parties

EXHIBIT 2.3
Characteristics

New Circumstances	Characteristics	Requirements
Changes in education, expanding management requirements.	Characteristics of education, determining management requirements.	School management requirements today, based on characteristics and changes.
• Unions	• *Multiyear, multiparty* — many individuals involved in teaching a child over many years; responsibility, credit and blame unassignable with precision.	• Performance
• Public concern		– Evaluation
• More divergent goals	• *Hard to measure*: human development uneven, human nature mysterious.	– Information
		– Compensation
• More aggressive school boards	• *Schools important* to participants — staff career, parents' concern for children's future, community quality, property values, tax dollars, the American dream.	• Teamwork
• Traditional authoritarian administration	• *Schools close to communities*, available for complaints; subject to conflicts in community, family difficulties.	– Management responsibilities
		– Communication and participation
• Taxpayer revolt	• *Teacher independence*, closed door, now protected by unions.	– Decision making
• Contentious decisions	• *Feelings and attitudes* vital to good performance, motivation, etc. Hard to be effective while angry, frustrated.	
• Intervention	• *Dedication and time* required by good teaching.	
	• *Job satisfaction* related to performance.	

Source: Compiled by author.

25

include many teachers as well as the student and parents. Obviously clear lines are hard to draw.

Another charming if somewhat quaint example of shared respon sibility came up in my work with the National PTA a few years ago. From reading their archives one can find that the original concept related not so much to home/school relations between parents and teachers, but rather to the fact that the functions of parents and teachers could never be fully segregated, and thus overlapped inevitably and unavoidably.

The characteristic of shared responsibilities in education is, I believe, one of the reasons that fine-tuned incentive and measurement plans will never work effectively. Experiments trying to do so have widely failed, with both contract teaching based on test score achievement and merit pay plans with salaries tied directly to specific indicators of performance.

Human development is hard to measure and uneven in progress, for reasons that are often inexplicable. While some factors can be sorted out analytically, the measurement of education will always be subject to judgment. I have spent a great deal of time over the past decade trying to find measures of school performance, with some success, as explained in this book. Yet ultimately human development in its most important respects probably will always continue to defy measurement, much as human nature will always remain to some extent mysterious.

The importance of schools to the diverse groups who participate actively in them, and their close physical proximity, is another important feature of schools from a management point of view. Obviously the professional impact and career of the staff is involved. Parents are naturally concerned for their children's education. The community is concerned about the quality of schools and their financial impact — directly on taxes and indirectly on property values. The American dream is importantly involved with education. And schools must keep all of their constituents reasonably satisfied, unlike most businesses who need to cater successfully only to their own customers. Unlike a university whose paying customers (parents) are typically a long way away, schools exist right within their communities and are readily available for complaints. They are subject to conflicts in the community and directly affected by whatever family difficulties may be occurring.

The independence of teachers is well known. They feel that they should be in charge, and our traditions of academic freedom rightly protect this. Furthermore, a teacher has only to close the door in order to largely preclude observation. These rights are now protected by unions.

The feelings and attitudes of teachers are highly relevant to performance, motivation, and morale. One might be able to work in a production line or drive a truck while angry or frustrated, but it's hard to be a good teacher under those circumstances. While these human dimensions are vitally important in any organization, in a performing art like teaching they are even more important. The intensity of human relationships in schools compounds this situation. And the dedication and time required by good teaching adds to the complexity as well. Today, the generally reduced mobility of teachers in an era where supply exceeds demand, coupled with declining enrollments, is causing a rising average age of teachers in most districts.

These characteristics are not without their counterparts in other fields. Many parallels exist between the performing arts, teaching, and other professional fields including law, accounting, consulting, research, and even the corporate staffs of companies that support selling and manufacturing activities. Many of the features listed above can be found in some or all of these other fields as well. And many of the management techniques developed there have their counterparts in education. But there is no question in my mind that schools present some of the most challenging management requirements today, because of these difficult characteristics. Failure to adequately recognize these features of schooling can, and has, led to the development or application of inappropriate and dysfunctional management techniques in schools. Management by objectives[6] for example, when applied to schools has tended to generate excessive paperwork in a setting where performance measures are difficult and generally unavailable. Industrial-type compensation plans in public organizations have tended to inflate salaries and diminish morale because they fail to recognize the difficulty of measuring performance and the hazards of tying compensation to inadequate measures.

Some of the management techniques being developed in education to suit these characteristics may well find their way back into industry. You are likely to see parallels between the ideas in this book and two important developments in industrial management. One is the continuing effort to find ways to be more participative, communicative, and satisfying to employees in business management, even though efforts in this direction have been going on for at least half a century and probably longer. Second is the effort to define the objectives of business in a more comprehensive and socially productive way, including impact on customers, employees, environment, and long-run economic consequences as well as just short-term profitability. This trend has also been going on for a long time, and by no means reverses the position taken by many companies. Both developments seem important and likely to benefit from the human relations and performance measurement ideas developed in education and other public services.

MANAGEMENT REQUIREMENTS

Changes in the circumstances of education have expanded its management requirements.[7] These changes are conditioned by the character of education, in order that management can be related to the function and character of schools and the nature of the teaching/learning process. These key school management requirements are summarized in Exhibit 2.4 and discussed below.

Emphasizing Performance and Results

Increased emphasis on performance and results is a common feature of successful industrial management and farm management that I believe also applies to schools. Efforts to evaluate performance analytically and judgmentally, using information wherever it is relevant, and tying performance to rewards, including compensation, are key elements in successful management in any field, in my opinion.

Evaluation needs to be operational, fair and effective, and in three distinct areas: programs, administrators, and teachers.

Performance information is needed to indicate success, sustain and support confidence and morale, and identify improvement opportunities. Information on four specific categories of

EXHIBIT 2.4
Requirements

New Circumstances	Characteristics	Requirements

Changes in education, expanding management requirements.
• Unions
• Public concern
• More divergent goals
• More aggressive school boards
• Traditional authoritarian administration
• Taxpayer revolt
• Contentious decisions
• Intervention
	Characteristics of education, determining management requirements.
	• Multiyear, multiparty
	• Hard to measure
	• Schools important to participants
	• Close to communities
	• Teacher independence
	• Feelings and attitudes
	• Dedication and time
	• Job satisfaction
		School management requirements today, based on characteristics and changes.
		• *Evaluation* that is fair and effective.
		  – Programs
		  – Administrators
		  – Teachers
		• *Performance information.*
		  – Student learning
		  – Parent satisfaction
		  – Teacher morale
		  – Financial planning and cost control
		• *Compensation* contributing to job satisfaction.
		• *Teamwork* emphasized, in spite of pressures toward conflict and fragmentation.
		• *Management responsibilities* and relationships.
		  – Board
		  – Superintendent
		  – Principals
		  – Teachers
		• *Communication and participation.*
		  – Staff
		  – Public
		• *Decision making.*
		  – Curriculum
		  – Finance

Source: Compiled by author.

performance — student learning, parent satisfaction, teacher morale, and cost control — is described at length later in this book.

Compensation is the most tangible aspect of an employee's relationship to the organization of which he is a part. Failing to use it to reward good performance lowers job satisfaction, reduces morale, and damages performance. Those responsible for organizations of all kinds, whether professional managers or responsible board members, contribute to poor performance and productivity and authorize expenditures without adequate foundation if they do not tie compensation to performance. There simply is no alternative. Doing so in a field such as education, where teamwork is so important, holds special challenge. That more school districts have failed than have succeeded in their efforts to tie compensation to performance should not discourage board members, administrators, and teachers from recognizing the essential importance of doing so, and from drawing on successful experiences to find out how.

Emphasizing Teamwork

This concern with the human side of organization and management is also one of the fundamentals that I have seen in every field of activity and country where I have been involved.

Management responsibilities and relationships need to be defined, with a clear-cut sense of direction and purpose, and indicators of achievement. This applies to the board, superintendent, principals, teachers, and all staff members — in other words, throughout the organization.

Requirements for communication and participation — both staff and public — are much greater today than they used to be, and are perhaps the most challenging of school management requirements. Communication with the staff is made more difficult, and more essential, by the existence of unions. Some superintendents have responded to these requirements by closing the door on communication with teachers; most who have done so haven't kept their jobs very long.

Equally important, especially in an era of public concern about schools, is the opportunity for parents to become involved in and to learn about their schools. The techniques and practices of doing so are well developed in schools, but their application in each new situation is always challenging.

Unions also emphasize the importance of teacher participation in decisions made in schools. Actually, schools have a rather successful tradition of doing this, using teacher committees to decide curriculum and textbooks, for example. But this participation has often broken down in the early stages of collective bargaining and needs to be reestablished in many districts.

Making decisions in schools with respect to both curriculum and finance is challenging. Getting the right decision is always difficult, and good management doesn't necessarily guarantee the right answer. Issues such as school closing, setting tax rates, considering individualized instruction, for example, are always difficult decisions in schools. Decisions that suit the needs and character of a community, consistent with the attitudes and feelings of staff, parents, students, and others who may be involved, are important. Then balancing of the financial side of decisions with physical structure and educational impact is challenging also. With good management most districts can handle these decisions successfully. Without it, any one of them can become so controversial as to disrupt the basic stability and integrity of the district's operation. Then, the task of rebuilding management is even more challenging.

Public school education in the United States has gone through a period of dramatic change — moving from widespread respect to growing criticism; from rapid growth to declining enrollment; from compliant teachers to organized unions; from adequate financial resources to severe budget constraints; from passive school boards to aggressive ones. No simple, single, or short-term solution can solve these problems. But the situation is not hopeless.

I believe from intensive experience in school districts that a turnaround has begun in the performance of education, at least in those districts healthy enough to do so. But whether that turnaround can be sustained in the face of continued heavy burdens imposed on schools over the past decade and those which seem likely to be coming in the future is a question about which it is hard to be completely optimistic. It will be difficult even in those districts most able to shoulder such burdens successfully. In those districts already incapacitated by the negative trends of the past, not only big cities but many small and medium-sized cities as well, turning around declining performance will be extremely challenging.

Development of management at district, school, and classroom levels, and involving the entire management team of board, administrators and teachers, can return school performance to a level that satisfies students, parents, public, and staff. In the final analysis, the success of boards and administrators depends upon their ability to make the work of teachers in the classroom more effective. And all of these participants in education must satisfy their constituents if the teamwork and satisfaction essential to good school performance is to be achieved.

NOTES

1. Paul Copperman, *The Literacy Hoax* (New York: William Morrow, 1978). Richard Mitchell, *Less Than Words Can Say* (Boston: Little, Brown, 1979).

2. "The Plight of U.S. Secondary Education: Why Are Today's High School Students Learning Less and Disliking It More?" *Time* 110 (November 14, 1977): 62-75. "Help! Teacher Can't Teach: The Multi-faceted Crisis of American Public Schools." *Time* 115 (June 16, 1980): 54-63.

3. An excellent survey of this subject is presented in *Teacher Unions and Collective Bargaining* (Berkeley: McCutchan, 1980) by Anthony Cresswell.

4. Changing public attitudes toward education can be traced in the Gallup poll reported annually in the *Phi Delta Kappan*, (Bloomington: Phi Delta Kappa, annually).

5. This change and some of the others discussed in this section of the book are insightfully discussed in Michael Kirst's section of *Changing Politics of Education* (Berkeley: McCutchan, 1976).

6. This is the common industrial management practice of setting goals and reviewing results by supervisors.

7. These school management requirements were first documented by Fredric H. Genck and Allen J. Klingenberg in *Effective Schools Through Effective Management* (Springfield: Illinois Association of School Boards, 1978).

3

THE CONSEQUENCES OF
INADEQUATE MANAGEMENT:
Chaos and Conflict in Schools

As a result of traditional administrative practices, inadequate to meet the new management requirements of today, many school districts today are in turmoil. They look like a revolution in which traditional authoritarianism is thrown off suddenly, without a sound replacement. Some school districts are so deeply mired in conflict and fragmentation that one could reasonably despair of ever turning them around.

Whole states are witnessing a downward spiral of school performance. California and Massachusetts, for example, with their taxpayer revolts, have cut back school funding in the face of dissatisfaction with performance, and have probably damaged performance further in the process, perhaps setting up a downward spiral.

Most of our major cities have lost any connection between the wishes of the people and the capabilities of school management to see them carried out through staff efforts. They are disconnected internally, incapacitated in direction and purpose, and are failing terribly in the basic indicators of student learning, parent satisfaction, teacher morale, and cost control. Worse yet are the long-term costs in crime, welfare, and unemployment.

In Chicago, for example, schools are virtually free from any positive, constructive impact from the central office. They are influenced only by the overlay of bureaucracy and paperwork that is gradually strangling them. Student learning is 20 percent less and costs 20 percent more than in suburban districts. The dissatisfaction and frustration of parents and teachers is obvious. The schools are unmanaged. Only about a half dozen (1 percent of the 600 schools) are efficiently managed and successful, usually due to extraordinary talent and perseverence of their principals.

In a smaller city district, to take another example of conflict and fragmentation, the board is being sued by one of its members. New board members are campaigning on the basis of firing the superintendent. The board is intensely preoccupied in an adversarial relationship with the teaching staff. The administrators are forming a union in order to protect their own interests. They fear that in the midst of conflict the board will single out one of them for disciplinary action, fail to make any upward salary adjustments, or take some other foolish and unjustified action. Not surprisingly, administrators feel they need to protect themselves in advance. All three levels of district management responsible for performance – board, administrators, and teachers – are so busy fighting among themselves that there is hardly any time left for teaching or running the schools.

In another district the superintendent has given up any hope of measuring performance or evaluating personnel. He has come to exist entirely in a political frame of mind in which simply maintaining an equilibrium that keeps his job is the primary objective. No consideration of student learning, parent satisfaction, or teacher morale is possible. All efforts are devoted to surviving.

In another, the teachers have taken over control of the board of education through political action. But what do they do now? Sound management policies and practices that build staff morale and productivity are the only answer. I have found that in most districts where teachers have won control over the board their receptivity to these techniques is high – a hopeful turn of events.

These examples are not universal but they are common. Fortunately, schools don't stop functioning completely, even under these difficult circumstances. Only on rare occasions do they go bankrupt. Somehow, teachers struggle on, but performance declines, student learning decreases, dissatisfaction of parents and staff rises, and taxpayers revolt. No wonder national performance trends are down. Management is both the cause and the solution of this problem.

Recently I had the opportunity to study the membership decline of the National PTA, falling from about 10 million members in 1960 to about 5 million today. While the reasons for the decline are complicated, and include the alternatives available to women today and the time demands on all of us, one major factor is the conflict and turmoil in schools. When the PTA was at its membership peak, schools were the focal point of communities and an excellent choice as a base of operations for the PTA. Today schools are battlegrounds of conflict — collective bargaining with teachers, divisive issues such as school closing, tough budget decisions forced by unforeseen financial circumstances, and so on. The PTA has generally tried to be helpful and has often succeeded. But sometimes the battle becomes so heated that there are no winners. In Ohio, for example, it is said that the PTA supported bargaining for teachers, and then supported all but a few teacher positions. Teachers then turned against them for the positions they failed to support, and administrators did the same for those positions the PTA did support. As a consequence, PTA membership in Ohio has fallen sharply.

Disorganization, confusion, fragmentation, and conflict — caused by a management inadequate to meet the circumstances — are the reasons school performance is declining. In this chapter I will share with you my observations from visits to hundreds of schools over the past decade, from thousands of personal observations and discussions with boards of education, administrators and teachers, from studies of school management in every respect, and from surveys of parents, teachers, students, and communities. First, we'll turn to the perceptions of board members, teachers, and administrators and then to some of the tough issues and challenges that are causing conflict and fragmentation.

DIFFERING VIEWS OF BOARDS, TEACHERS, AND ADMINISTRATORS

Compounding the downward pressure on school performance of new and challenging circumstances are the attitudes, concerns, and feelings of school board members, administrators, and teachers.

School Boards

Traditionally one of the primary examples of effective democracy at work, school boards have successfully linked schools with their communities and provided citizen guidance of educational policies in the United States. Their roots, in the oldest traditions of democracy in England and the Anglo-Saxon customs from which English local government grew, serve to remind us of the importance of the institution. It has, I believe, served us well.

In the face of this impressive and important tradition, school boards today are under considerable pressure. In some states they have virtually lost their job, for example, in California where local financial decision making has been elevated almost entirely to a state level by Proposition 13. State and federal initiatives to improve school performance are not complementary to the effectiveness attributed to local boards.

Boards have become concerned, uneasy, and more aggressive today, not always to the benefit of the educational institutions for which they are responsible. They are rightly sensitive to the widespread criticism of education. And most recognize that the basis for their decisions and actual control of education may be very limited. But as part-time amateurs in the field of education, they have had difficulty marshalling the resources needed to solve the problems they face.

Spurred by their uneasiness with school performance, many boards today are meddling in the operations of the district for which they are responsible, to the detriment of performance. Yet they are motivated by well-intentioned concern over publicity about declining national school performance trends. The performance information and evaluation techniques specified in this book are the answer boards need to control without meddling.

Boards have become a conduit for the inherent conflict between pressures for accountability and reactions of staff protectionism. Recognizing and understanding this fulcrum of the inner dynamics of education today is vitally important to a positive and constructive solution. If boards attempt to move toward needed accountability in ways that are adversarial and combative in their relationships with administrators and teachers, further declines in performance will result. Combining effective staff relations of communication, trust, and confidence with practical accountability, fair and effective use of information and evaluation can turn the situation around.

School boards have also become more representative of the communities they serve today. They are less likely to be limited to business executives or owners of local industry. There is a larger proportion of women and workers from various fields including professionals, teachers, and laborers.

The combination of public concern, more aggressive boards, and wider community representation accounts for the rising rate of superintendent turnover in school districts. But the longevity of school board members in their tenure on boards also seems to have declined. Many districts report difficulty in getting citizens to serve, partly because boards have become overinvolved and the job more demanding and time consuming than is appropriate.

This overinvolvement is a serious problem because school boards cannot function effectively on this level. They must learn to delegate responsibility to the management team and hold the superintendent accountable for performance. This must be documented with information and fair and effective evaluation, as described later in this book. In this way, they can fulfill their responsibility for accountability to the public without becoming overinvolved in district operations. Equally important, boards must understand that teamwork and good working relationships are essential in schools. The collective bargaining process cannot be allowed to overshadow this key requirement.

The other dramatic impact of collective bargaining, however, is that many boards, particularly in cities, have found themselves overwhelmed by the strength of the union in bargaining. Often they didn't appreciate that this was an adversarial process in which management needs a position and strategy and the fortitude to stand by them. Many districts today are saddled with contracts so complicated and negative in their impact on teacher morale and productivity that, particularly in big cities, the board and administration have little or no influence on school operation or performance.

School boards have very little time available in which to do their jobs. They must avoid being drawn into detailed involvement in district management or into any time-consuming aspect of district operations. Yet, they need confidence in district performance.

Many school boards today are frustrated at their inability to really find out how well their district is performing. Since this is a principal need addressed in the later chapters of this book, it's worth quoting a few school board members:

I know that test scores in my district have declined over the last few years, but what does this mean? What should I do about it?

I know that my district conducts standardized achievement tests annually, but I can't get the superintendent to share these with the board in a form that we can understand. The reports are so long and complicated that the board doesn't have the time or the technical expertise to make sense out of them.

How are we supposed to know whether the district is doing a good job when education isn't really measurable in the same way that business is? And if we don't know that a good job is being done, how can the board serve to support and encourage good performance rather than just carrying forward the adversarial process of collective bargaining?

I know how to read and understand a corporate financial report, but school finance seems impossibly complicated. The more one looks into the situation the more confusing it seems to become. I wind up depending on trust in the school business manager, rather than having any bottom-line figure that I can point to with confidence as an indication of whether or not we're solvent and how long we're likely to stay that way.

School finance seems to contain many unnecessary complexities, perhaps reflecting the lack of any intention to be comprehensible. This compounds the problems of school boards who must defend school finance to the public, and of administrators who must defend it to the board. A simpler system with more readily understandable indicators of a district's financial situation would be helpful. This would make the financial situation more understandable, avoid inappropriate tax increases as well as bankruptcy, and make financial control more practical.

Often the first problem to surface in a school district's internal administrative relationships is unwillingness of the board to fund increases in administrative salaries justified by inflation. This often arises out of underlying uneasiness about district performance and the lack of a sound basis for understanding it. Many districts lack any formal salary plan to justify administration compensation. Board assertiveness on this issue puts immediate pressure on the superintendent in terms of the loyalty of his management team. While a useful step to get attention, by itself this only makes the problem worse. Some administrative unions have resulted, and more will, unless practices for administrative evaluation and compensation like those recommended in Chapter 10 are more widely applied.

Boards are particularly vulnerable at the time of selecting a new superintendent. They are not doing as good a job of this as they should, thus contributing unnecessarily to superintendent turnover. Because little evidence is usually available on the results achieved by a candidate in his or her last position, and boards typically interview as a group, they are very susceptible to someone who articulates past accomplishments effectively, whatever actual results may have been. While superintendents are no more prone to self-laudatory comments than other executives, their presentation to boards of amateurs gives them a better chance of success.

Teachers

America's teachers have also changed over the past two decades. In some ways the changes are positive, but in other ways the ultimate impact is not yet clear.

On the positive side, the changing balance between demand and supply for teachers has clearly favored staffing selectivity. Administrators responsible for employing teachers today often seem to feel that they are obtaining a higher level of talent. The graduates of leading schools of education are reportedly better prepared and more capable today than they were 20 years ago.

On the other hand available evidence, or at least conversation in education, would seem to indicate that there may have been some deterioration in the average level of teachers being prepared by schools of education. An entire recent issue of a leading professional journal, the *Phi Delta Kappan*,[1] was devoted to an excoriating series of articles on the quality of typical graduates of education schools, following more popular coverage in *Time*[2] magazine.

The most conspicuous trend among teachers today is their rising average age. As enrollments have declined, fewer beginning teachers have been employed. In many districts, the average age of the teaching staff has gone up by practically one year with each passing year. Older teachers aren't necessarily better or worse performers than their younger counterparts. But some lose interest and enthusiasm for the job. Not all of us retain the ability and stamina to keep up with the energetic demands of a teaching career. In many districts the opportunity to preserve a balanced staff — with representation of both older experience and younger enthusiasm, energy, and new techniques — has been lost to the effects of declining enrollment.

Teachers used to enjoy considerable mobility. If they found themselves disliking circumstances in one district, it wasn't impossible to find a job in another. Today, because of declining enrollments, most teachers find themselves essentially trapped in the district where they are currently employed. While it is not impossible to find a job elsewhere, there are not many available, and a considerable risk of losing tenure is taken by changing districts in an era of declining enrollment. Consequently, teachers who are frustrated and dissatisfied in the district of their present employment, for whatever reason, are likely still to be there.

Of course, teachers recognize the challenging nature of the students today. The problems children bring to school now, that exceed those of an earlier generation, are obvious. These are most often cited in our discussions with teachers as: divorce, single parents, working mothers, drugs and alcohol, television. Teachers feel they are receiving the blame for declining school performance without recognition of these more challenging problems and without the credit they deserve for dealing with them. They are often the first to feel public concern and suspicion about educational performance.

Compounding this frustration is a tendency in many school districts over the past ten years to close down traditional channels of communication and to lose the relationships of trust and confidence that once were typical. Often the precipitating cause is the response of administrators and teachers to initiation of collective bargaining. In many cases, administrators are offended at the adversarial and combative stance being taken by teachers. For this reason, or because under these circumstances it becomes more difficult to visit schools and communicate with teachers, they simply allow these practices to fall by the wayside. Consequently, teachers may find that their opportunities to communicate upward in the organization are severely reduced. The effects on morale are obvious. Teacher unions, capitalizing on this phenomenon, have used it to strengthen their own communication role on teachers' behalf. Internal communication is perhaps the single most important aspect of management that must be strengthened to remain successful in an era of unions.

Teachers have also been encouraged by the advent of unions to express complaints. These concerns seem to center especially on policies and practices for evaluating teacher performance. This has traditionally been done in an authoritarian, and probably also unfair, fashion. Today unfair practices can be effectively objected to by teachers. These are typical comments:

Teaching is a performing art and the application of rigid standards will damage its effectiveness.

For teachers to be evaluated by any other one individual creates an impossible situation in terms of the influence of personality and style.

Defining educational performance is difficult, and yet also essential. Certainly it's not just academic learning, but the social and emotional dimensions of child development and the role of the school in the community. The district must decide who is accountable for what, although teachers should be involved in this decision. If this isn't done, how is the teacher to know what the job responsibilities are?

Teachers today are having to spend more time dealing with children's emotional problems rather than with academic learning — divorce is becoming epidemic, working mothers are the rule rather than the exception, and schools are suffering from our changing lifestyles.

Schools can't be measured in the way a product or business can, and perhaps too much measurement will detract from higher goals. On the other hand, some things can and should be measured — 50 percent dropout rates in New York and Chicago, for example.

Teaching is complicated by administrators who do not always appreciate the scope of the issues involved, and seem to be concerned only with costs or just responding to the community.

Teachers want to be evaluated, but don't consider present practices fair or effective but rather threatening, intimidating, frightening and demoralizing.

Teachers complain that most administrators are incompetent evaluators, perhaps not good teachers themselves, or lacking the observation skills and communication abilities needed to coach other people to be good teachers. Teachers should have the opportunity to evaluate the evaluators.

Because of attitudes like these, teachers have effectively subverted the evaluation process in most school districts today. Most districts can set forth their policies and procedures on teacher evaluation at a school board meeting or in written form. Few have actually applied them in practice, based on actual internal documentation and description of the process by teachers and administrators. This, coupled with the unwillingness of many administrators to subject themselves to the discipline of due process requirements, has created a situation where many districts have simply stopped trying to get rid of teachers who may for whatever reasons no longer be effective. In many cases teachers themselves, while rightly defending due process procedures, have been aggressively outspoken in asking that district administrators with the support of the board take the action that is needed to get rid of teachers when required. Books on urban schools written by teachers have made this point, and I have heard it personally on many occasions.

Administrators

I have saved the description of administrative attitudes for last, because they arise importantly out of the middle position in which administrators naturally find themselves — between teachers on the one hand and boards on the other. In some cases administrators have been so pressured by this squeeze that they have retired early, resigned, or been fired. The situation differs somewhat between district and school levels, so it makes sense to discuss superintendents and principals separately.

Board pressures to demonstrate good performance, evaluate personnel, and provide a solid rationale for compensation have been targeted first at superintendents. Some have responded with admirable inventiveness, creating with little or no precedent management policies and practices as good as their industrial counterparts, in many cases borrowing from that field. Others have resisted the need to develop documentation or to deal with their board in a way that provides the necessary basis for decision making. Some of them are still surviving on this technique; others are not. It is a much more difficult job for a superintendent to provide staff support to a board making decisions, rather than just to make the decision and expect approval.

As superintendents look around for models on which to base their own administrative style, most of what they find is, unfortunately, not very relevant to the circumstances of education today.

Traditionally, school superintendents have been authoritarian, and thus have had little need for formal, professional management policies and participative management practices. There is little on which superintendents can draw in the way of well-documented management techniques proven to work in school districts today. And neither superintendents or their staffs have any management training.

While many of the principles and practices of industrial management have relevance in schools, they require translation and must be applied very cautiously, in a setting where it is so difficult to measure performance. The management approaches that work in service organizations generally work equally well in schools. But they are not yet very well documented. Most industrial management developed out of manufacturing concerns, and much of the descriptive and training material still relates to these kinds of enterprises. Simplistic application of these practices in schools usually does more harm than good.

School principals find themselves in an equally difficult position. Particularly because their staff is in most cases protected by a complicated written contract, they are often frustrated. Even finding the opportunity to converse with staff members, much less supervise them, can be challenging.

Traditionally in school administration, many principals have found themselves able to fulfill the requirements of the job by effectively managing not the instructional program, curriculum, and faculty in their building, but rather handling the difficult children and parents, saving the teachers the difficulty or supporting them in dealing with these problems. Or the principal's attention was concentrated on making sure that various supporting services were satisfactorily handled — sweeping floors, serving lunches, keeping records.

School districts today that are seeking to demonstrate and develop good performance are finding that the people and instructional management side of the school principal's job must weigh more heavily, in responsibilities and performance. But many principals took the job under the old circumstances, where keeping parents and teachers happy was sufficient, and teachers were responsible for academic performance. Obviously these changes create tremendous challenges for principals, and it's not surprising to hear them say things like:

The Board will have to let us know what they expect or we won't be able to do it.

I really don't know what the principal is responsible for anymore.

How can I manage the staff without any sanctions – rewards or punishments?

My hands are tied by the negotiated contract and teacher tenure laws.

I don't know whose side the board is on.

In some districts, principals have looked with envy on the working conditions, salaries, and protection won by teachers, and have taken the route of unionization themselves.

In the face of these challenging circumstances, some school administrators have simply backed away from any real responsibility. They have encouraged the board to negotiate directly with teachers. They have refused to assemble information that is reasonably indicative of performance, like test data, or have presented it in such a confusing form that no one could make any sense out of it. This era of school administrators refusing to share performance information is quickly drawing to a close as school boards become more aggressive. And it is becoming increasingly apparent to school administrators that public concern and the taxpayer revolt are not likely to disappear overnight. Still, the turnaround in basic administrative strategy – from an era of secrecy and authority to one of openness, participative management, and aggressive use of information and evaluation to improve performance – is a major transition. Obviously the stresses and strains personally, professionally, and organizationally are considerable. It took nearly a century to go through the process in business. School administrators have been asked to accomplish it in little more than a decade. That they are still struggling to do so is commendable.

CONFLICT AND DECREASED PERFORMANCE

Education faces some of the most difficult and challenging circumstances and attitudes of any industry or institution in our country today. In this challenging context, traditional school management practices are proving inadequate. The combination of challenging circumstances and new attitudes with management policies and practices geared to a more authoritarian and less challenging era is causing the decline of performance.

Perhaps the greatest management challenge is the many pressures toward conflict and fragmentation in school districts today. The internal operations of school districts — and the traditional supportive and collegial relationships between administrators and teachers — have been torn apart by the advent of unions, collective bargaining, and strikes. In my work recently with the National PTA, I discovered their founding belief of the impossibility of completely distinguishing between the roles of parent and teacher. Supportive, constructive working relationships between parents and teachers, community and schools, are essential. Their membership decline is occurring partly because the circumstances of conflict and fragmentation in schools make this supportive function more difficult and less satisfying.

Compounding the problem are the changing attitudes toward authority, parents who are less respectful of educators, family problems, the negative morale impact of declining enrollment, attitudes of concern and suspicion on the part of taxpayers, and continuing media attention to performance problems. These negative factors exist in virtually every district. In some they have reached a downward spiral. These trends interact to cause a more serious decline than any one of them might alone.

Teacher unions, for example, have created the opportunity for teachers to effectively complain about unfair evaluation of personnel policies. Obviously it's more challenging to evaluate performance once unions are available to protect the staff. There is no alternative to doing so in a way that is fair and effective, rather than arbitrary or excessively subjective. Yet traditional school practices for evaluating teachers have been highly unfair and ineffective. Typically they have included checklists of behavior and even personality, comportment, and dress. These inappropriate standards have been applied in ways that offer little protection against the whims of personality, often with little documentation, or supervision of those doing the evaluating. Teachers complain that traditional practices aren't fair; their complaints are well founded.

As a result, however, in many districts no evaluation at all is going on. In education, as in most other personal service fields, a certain number of individuals find themselves unable to carry on or perform effectively every year. Sometimes this reflects personal distractions, a loss of interest and enthusiasm, or the many other factors that affect human performance in any personal service field. From my experience, the rate of this inadequate performance appears to be about 1 percent per year, quite a small proportion. This is manageable, and traditionally handled by simply dismissing these people. But where evaluation has stopped and the weeding out does not occur over a period of a decade or two, incompetent personnel accumulate. Teacher productivity is adversely affected both directly, and indirectly by the impact of incompetent teachers on the morale of others. In some districts incompetent teachers have accumulated, over the years, to as much as 10 percent to 20 percent of the total teaching staff. That student achievement is low should not be surprising under these circumstances.

Unions have contributed to the welfare of workers in our country, and in the long run to the development of more fair, responsible, and participative management. However, in the short run their tactics can be disruptive, to say the least. The history of industrial labor relations contains many examples of these consequences of union development. In schools the same phenomena can be observed.

Unions have stimulated an adversarial relationship inside many districts. While nowhere nearly as violent as early industrial labor relations, these circumstances have led the various parties — board members and administrators as well as teachers — to assume a combative, adversarial attitude that sometimes pervades all relationships in the district. Consequently, some superintendents are unwilling, perhaps in some cases even afraid, of talking to their staff and visiting schools. Boards criticize administrators and teachers to the point of undermining any feeling of support. And the staff can behave during negotiations and strikes in ways that make it difficult for the district later to resume cordial and cooperative relationships essential to good educational performance.

Parents and taxpayers concerned about school performance or costs can also contribute to the downward spiral. Complaining excessively, sometimes when there isn't any cause, or cutting back funding of schools and therefore causing performance to decline further add to the problems.

State and federal governments sometimes seek to impose solutions, again usually acting out of a belief that there is something wrong with the schools. Generally these government initiatives have not proven to work very well in practice, in terms of their impact on local performance. Federal paperwork, not just reports but applications and administrative time required, is excessive. States have imposed programs on schools that have distracted local attention from the basic job, and compounded the performance problem.

NOTES

1. "A Kappan Special Section on Teacher Education," *Phi Delta Kappan* 63 (October 1981): 106-33. n.a.
2. "Help! Teacher Can't Teach." *Time* 115 (June 16, 1980): 54-63. n.a.

4

THE SCHOOL PERFORMANCE
AND MANAGEMENT CONNECTION:
A Concept of School Performance

Instead of the chaos, conflict, fragmentation, demoralization, and decline of performance described in the preceding chapter, schools can and should achieve good performance through good management. Some schools are. The purpose of this chapter is to establish this connection, between school performance and school management.

CHALLENGING CIRCUMSTANCES + UNDERDEVELOPED MANAGEMENT = POOR PERFORMANCE

Challenging trends and circumstances do not, by themselves, explain the school performance decline. These challenges are no less real in districts and schools performing well than in those that have declines in performance. Successful schools can be found in urban, suburban, and rural areas and with every racial mix.

Instinctively, most of us look for something wrong with teachers or teaching methods in trying to explain the decline in school performance. Some observers of education and some educators blame teachers or teaching techniques. Either the talent of teachers is inadequate and declining or there is something wrong with teaching techniques, causing educational performance to decline.

My experience, on the contrary, is that educational performance is not declining because of weakness in either the talent or technology of teaching. The relationship of supply to demand has improved the quality of teachers in the last ten years. The educational innovations so often criticized are evidence of a healthy profession, even though not all of them have worked. Some of these innovations have failed and rightly been abandoned: new math, modular scheduling in high schools, and some open classroom experiments. But others have produced substantial improvements in teaching techniques and educational programs, for example in individualized instruction, special education, and vocational education.

What then is causing the problem? From observation of relationships and operations inside school districts today, the problem is arising from internal organization — how schools are managed. The main cause of decline in educational performance over the last decade or two lies in the superstructure of education, that little understood area of board policies and administrative practices and skills. Although the smallest part of the educational structure, these elements of education are historically weak, tremendously important in their impact on the productivity, morale, and job satisfaction of teachers, and presently inadequate to meet the challenging circumstances with which educators are confronted.

Difficult circumstances confronting educators today are being dealt with organizationally in ways appropriate 20 years ago but not today. Negative circumstances previously discussed are colliding with inadequate management practices to compound the decline. Districts that have recognized this and adopted management policies and practices appropriate to the new circumstances are succeeding in spite of the challenges. Those that have not are declining. Unfortunately, the latter outnumber the former. But, the solution is straightforward: those districts that have not yet found these new management techniques need to learn about them, and how to apply them successfully in practice. A few examples of negative pressures on school performance colliding with inadequate management policies and techniques might help to clarify the current state of affairs.

The loss of public confidence in schools is reinforced by the absence of any documented performance information to offset this concern. Education lacks the analytical and management skills to use performance information. Indeed, it has been customary to keep any such information secret, to water down questions in surveys and provide only academic analyses of test data, thus avoiding even raising questions about performance. In an era when performance was good and the public was satisfied, this worked. Now that dissatisfaction and concern are widespread, education is without the tools it needs to defend itself. We must show proof where performance is good, identify improvement opportunities and act upon them.

The trend toward more challenging students, many of them experiencing difficulties at home, is also colliding with the inadequacy of performance measures in education. In this case the impact is more direct. Most schools have not been equipped or inclined to analyze performance trends. Consequently, they don't recognize the composition of each classroom or school in ability and achievement, nor are they able to monitor student learning performance. The declines reflected clearly in national statistics have often gone unnoticed in the very schools and districts that are causing the downward trends.

And concern about performance declines tends to compound the problem. The time and inclination to invent measurement techniques, when performance is under pressure, are naturally limited. It's a little like being asked to design the M1 while on the battlefield. Only those districts with unusual foresight, perception, responsibility, and perhaps ambition, have recognized and acted to meet the need to analyze student learning. They are performing well.

Adding to teacher frustration over more challenging students, combined with lower levels of public confidence and respect, are the many other pressures toward fragmentation and conflict in school districts. School closings, declining enrollment, and budget problems add to these pressures toward conflict and fragmentation, making it difficult to build teamwork, raise morale, and improve performance. Collective bargaining and combative relationships provide less communication and feeling of mutual involvement. Yet teachers naturally want fair personnel policies, communication, and participation.

There is no question that the challenges confronting education today require extra effort to overcome. But the differences between those districts that are performing well and those contributing to the decline are principally in the use of relatively straightforward management techniques. The key management requirements resulting from these circumstances are listed below. These requirements identify the missing elements of school management needed to meet these new circumstances. These are the needs addressed by the management policies and practices recommended in Chapter 5.

Circumstances	*Resulting Management Requirement*
Public skepticism and concern about school performance, spurred by evidence of decline and media attention.	Evidence of good performance and identification of improvement opportunities so that they can be acted upon.
Pressures for conflict and fragmentation in schools (i.e., unions, strikes, concerned parents).	A fair and effective internal process of planning and evaluating performance that aids communication and builds teamwork.
Difficult circumstances confronting teachers (i.e., more challenging student attitudes and family situations).	Evaluation and compensation for administrators and teachers to improve performance in a positive and constructive way; recognizing and rewarding good performance and encouraging the hard work required to meet difficult circumstances.

SCHOOL MANAGEMENT WEAKNESSES

These negative pressures and circumstances come into a situation in education where management policies and practices have never been well developed. School districts have traditionally been small, most beginning with one room schools. Obviously the management requirements in these circumstances are minimal, and internalized within the classroom teacher. A useful and appropriate tradition has developed of teachers being independent and self-sufficient. Within this context, administration came to be considered as merely supplementing the teacher in the classroom. Care was taken not to abridge the traditional autonomy that teachers had come to enjoy, dealing rather with those things that could be provided outside the classroom — materials and supplies, business matters in the district, handling troublesome parents and children. These features of educational administration, perhaps appropriate at the time, now weaken its ability to deal with broader issues of purpose and performance as well as people and personnel policies that are essential today.

Historically, even in larger districts, any formalized, professional, documented, explicit process of management was usually rendered unnecessary by a strong authoritarian superintendent. He simply took the action that was required and made the decisions that were necessary. A cordial, supportive relationship was maintained with both board and staff. Men of integrity and a philosophical bent were attracted to these positions. They did a good job of convincing Americans that education was the key to the American dream. They succeeded in obtaining funding and support for public schools that no other country has achieved. Teachers and administrators felt a common professional tie, exemplified by their membership in a single national association.

But these superintendents of an earlier era left behind little in the way of documented concepts, policies, and practices of management. They didn't develop ways to measure such a difficult field as education. Personnel policies and practices depended mainly on the personal authority of the superintendent. Many of these superintendents took early retirement close on the heels of the first teacher strike, school closing, or lost referendum in their districts. And they left behind no tradition of management on which to build to meet the more professional and participative requirements of evaluation, performance information, and communication today.

The concepts of participative management, staff involvement, and job satisfaction that developed over the past several decades in industrial management have no counterpart in school districts. This accounts in part for the rapid influx of unions. Techniques for measuring performance, understanding customer needs and desires, evaluating staff performance, motivating productivity, developing skills, and rewarding good performance were not developed. The whole field of management as it has been defined and developed in industry for more than 100 years, and especially intensively during the past 50 years, has been ignored or avoided by education.

Perhaps surprisingly, in a field so inherently humanistic in character, schools were one of the last bastions of authoritarian administrative practices. When the transition came, it was forced by unions with a suddenness that left many districts without the internal relationships needed to even hold themselves together. These pressures toward fragmentation and conflict have led some districts to the point where they're just holding on to solvency and continuity by a thread. Others have slipped over the edge, as Chicago did recently, following on the pattern of New York, Cleveland, Detroit, Boston, and Philadelphia.

The inadequacy of school management is especially reflected in policies and practices for evaluation and personnel matters. Schools make little or no investment in staff development, either financially or in staff time allocated for this purpose. Compensation is geared to factors that have nothing to do with good performance — college credits and years of service — rather than serving to reinforce a teacher's natural motivation to teach effectively and productively. Evaluation has been oriented to checklists of personality, style, and even dress rather than the real product of education: student learning, parent satisfaction, public confidence, staff morale. Greater attention to these key aspects of the people side of good school management is a pressing need in education as well as in other public services in our country.

These failures to develop fair and effective policies and practices for personnel evaluation, development, compensation, communication, and teamwork are causing the evident stresses and strains in the internal relationships of school districts. The other major missing element in school management is performance information needed to instill objectivity and fairness in the evaluation process at all levels. Information routinely available to industrial managers in the form of financial reports, sales and market analyses, market share data, market research information, and statistical reports doesn't exist in education. Consequently, faced with the need to find a more fair and effective way to evaluate performance, educators have been thrown back on rigid authoritarian models and charismatic leadership rather than the management techniques of information and evaluation as well as communication and participation that are required.

The academic support for educational administration from schools and colleges of education has also been limited. The literature of school administration tends to be naive. It is 50 to 75 years behind its counterparts in business schools, where management has found a more fertile field in which to grow. These limitations now hold back the development of management in education. Most superintendents and principals report that there is little in their educational training that helps them cope with the real and practical problems of managing schools today. Consequently, the managerial competence required to deal with the disruptive organizational impact of today's trends simply isn't available. Educators are having to invent the management policies and practices they need and test them in practice under adverse battlefield conditions.

The problem is further complicated because, as in any professional field, teachers must be considered as part of the management team; they have the most direct impact and responsibility for performance. Collective bargaining makes this difficult, but not impossible, and no less required for good school performance.

Under these challenging circumstances, only the strongest and most successful districts have been able to move forward. Even their progress is limited by the fact that management is a very hard thing to invent and apply.

AN EXAMPLE OF INADEQUATE MANAGEMENT: THE CHICAGO PUBLIC SCHOOLS

As an example of how management contributes to declining school performance, Exhibit 4.1 highlights a few key characteristics of poor management in the Chicago Public Schools. And the following paragraphs describe the connection between these management practices and the poor school performance these schools are achieving.

One of the most important but little recognized contributors to poor school performance in Chicago is the administrative compensation plan developed by an industrial consulting firm during the 1960s. It ties administrative compensation to the achievement of specific measurable objectives. In industry, such plans have been relatively successful because ample performance information is available. It's easy to tell whether a business is successful economically. Sales indicate customer satisfaction with products, staffs who are unsatisfied leave to work elsewhere, and even the public contribution of an industry is generally definable.

In schools, where few measures are available, such compensation plans simply reward the achievement of trivial objectives. In Chicago, for example, a principal received a salary increase because he achieved the objective of improving relations with teachers in his school by holding seven staff meetings during the year compared to an objective of four. You can readily see how such a compensation

EXHIBIT 4.1
Declining School Performance in Chicago

Key Management Mistakes

- Overpaying administrators on the basis of trivial objectives.
- Eliminating the principal's responsibility for teacher selection.
- Rigid teacher salary schedules that preclude any feeling of reward for good performance or even that compensation is being fairly earned and thus publicly justified.
- A complex contract requiring a rigid bureaucracy and limiting local flexibility to respond to parent and staff needs, to do the right thing under whatever circumstances exist locally, and to sustain the communication and teamwork needed for good school performance.
- Practical elimination of teacher evaluation and thus of any opportunity for principals to reward, develop, and assist teachers.
    - Consequently, accumulating teachers whose performance becomes inadequate, in my experience about 1 percent a year, or 10 percent to 20 percent of the staff over a period of a decade or two.
    - Demoralizing the rest of the staff, who observe incompetent teachers damaging children and receiving the same salaries and increases as competent ones.
    - Discouraging the hard-working, dedicated teacher whose rewards are identical to those of minimum effort and accomplishment.
- Overstaffed central office out of touch with the schools, tolerating excess costs and not lack of responsibility for performance.
- Public perceptions of poor performance precluding adequate funding and support.
- Substantial investment in facilities and renovation making little difference without adequate management.
- Federal funding confusing and reducing local performance responsibility.

Source: Compiled by author.

plan would demoralize administrators. To the extent it has any effect, energies may even be directed away from school performance and toward measurable activities like staff meetings. An additional result of this compensation plan, although it may be more a tribute to clever implementation by administrators rather than the plan's design, is that Chicago school administrators are paid substantially more than their suburban counterparts (in reverse proportion to the performance of the systems for which they are responsible).

Another contribution of poor management to poor school performance in Chicago arises out of the elimination of principals' responsibility for teacher selection. Under the practically computerized staff assignment policies in Chicago, principals have no choice over their staff. Consequently, any matching of teacher talents and desires to the needs and circumstances of individual schools is impossible. This alone could account for the poor performance, since in any big city, particularly in Chicago, neighborhoods vary dramatically from one to another in many characteristics including what is required of teachers. Eliminating teacher and principal choice in this assignment process almost guarantees poor performance. Building that choice back in would enable teachers to select schools on the basis of where they thought they could be most satisfied and productive, and permit the district to hold principals accountable for results.

Most suburban, small town, and rural districts have avoided this mistake by recognizing the crucial importance of staff selection in any personal service activity. While districts vary in the extent to which they hold principals responsible for staff hiring and firing decisions at local school levels, I know of none that have totally precluded both teacher and principal choice in the process, as Chicago schools have. While some of the blame may lie with federal requirements for staff desegregation, the implementation and performance impact have fallen on Chicago and are clearly the fault of local management policies and practices.

Rigid teacher salary schedules in Chicago preclude any feeling of reward for good performance on the part of teachers. They make it impossible for teachers to feel that their compensation is being fairly earned and thus publicly justified. While this is also true of most suburban school districts, it is especially discouraging in a situation where performance is declining and the challenging circumstances faced by teachers require an exceptional sense of dedication to the work at hand.

A feature that Chicago schools have in common with many suburbs and other cities is a highly complicated negotiated contract with the staff that tends to establish a rigid, inflexible bureaucracy, as unresponsive to staff needs as to those of parents and students. Such contracts are commonplace in education today. Only a few districts have recognized that good staff relations, communication, participation, and fair, effective evaluation supported with information can create a situation where unions are unnecessary for staff protection. Some contracts have locked school boards and administrators into such inflexible positions as to practically eliminate their ability to manage the district effectively. This is not to blame the unions; obviously in a situation like Chicago, where teachers periodically fail to receive their paychecks, the union is valuable, perhaps essential, to the protection of teacher rights and benefits. Management has been inadequate to cope with these circumstances successfully.

Partly as a result of the contract, and teacher objections to traditional unfair evaluation practices, teacher evaluation has been virtually eliminated in Chicago schools. And this is also true in many suburban districts. Consequently, those teachers whose performance becomes inadequate accumulate in the system. In my experience such teachers amount to about 1 percent of the staff each year. A variety of reasons account for this: for example, personal problems that distract from teaching effectiveness, people who tire of the rigorous demands of a teaching career after a number of years in the field, and those whose interests simply move in different directions over time. In any professional field some practitioners remain good performers and continue to improve throughout their careers, while others lose effectiveness or change interests over time. If performance is not monitored so that these individuals can be counseled in other directions or if necessary terminated in employment, they accumulate in the system. Since it has been a decade or two since any effective evaluation existed in Chicago schools, it might be calculated that roughly 10 percent to 20 percent of the staff is incompetent. That Chicago test scores are 10 percent to 20 percent below national average may be not an accidental correlation.

Perhaps even more important than the accumulation of these incompetent teachers in the system is the demoralizing effect they have on the rest of the staff. As one can see from many books written by urban school teachers, the observation of incompetent teachers damaging children with no one taking action to remove them from the system, especially with compensation plans that guarantee these teachers the same salaries and increases as the competent ones, is extremely discouraging to dedicated teachers who aim for more than minimum effort and accomplishment.

While the virtual elimination of teacher evaluation is about equally common, although not quite as extreme, in suburban, small town, and rural districts as in large cities, the overstaffed central office in the Chicago Public Schools is practically unique to that system and other large cities. Well over half of the central office staff positions could and should be eliminated; even better would be discontinuing central staffing with decentralization to independent local districts. These central office administrators have little or no connection with the operation of schools, virtually no responsibility for school performance, and a history of tolerating excess costs in the supporting services of schools that channel funds unnecessarily away from teachers and classrooms. I believe decentralization would improve public access and responsiveness of schools as well as learning, confidence, morale, and support.

Chicago also provides a good example of how the public's perceptions of poor performance in schools exacerbate financial constraints and limit public support. Because the schools are seen not to be performing well or to be cost effective, the public's willingness to fund them at adequate levels is naturally constrained. This has a further negative effect on performance and morale in a potentially catastrophic downward spiral that seems to have gone furthest in cities like Boston and Philadelphia. But it exists to some extent in virtually every large city in our country today. The impact on our most precious national resource in human development and the long-term costs in social services, welfare, and criminal justice are tragic and unaffordable.

Perhaps in concluding this discussion it's worth noting three erroneous arguments often made about large city school systems. One is that the urban population cannot achieve any better in schools than what is now being accomplished. My experience with urban districts outside of major cities who achieve satisfactory school performance argues to the contrary. It is also sometimes suggested that urban schools do not spend enough money to achieve good performance; again my experience is contrary. Chicago schools spend more than their counterparts in the suburbs, and achieve less. Finally, it is worth noting that a substantial investment has been made in Chicago school buildings over the past couple of decades with impressive results obvious to anyone who visits these schools. Yet the contribution of these excellent facilities to good school performance means little without the management required for teachers to be effective.

The substantial federal funding contributed to the Chicago schools has, in my opinion, helped to deflect responsibility for school performance away from teachers and principals and into a centralized bureaucracy and specialized field staff. On balance, I suspect the contribution to school performance may even have been negative, in spite of the cost.

HAZARDS AND PITFALLS

Some hazards and pitfalls of school management development are outlined in Exhibit 4.2 and discussed in the following paragraphs.

Perhaps the most disappointing management practices have been those elaborate systems that are simply too expensive to be practical in schools. Some of them also overwhelm administrators with paperwork, don't have any impact on performance and results, or involve such substantial projects as to preclude their practical application. These ideas have used many different names, making it difficult to be specific in identifying them. Very often these titles have also been applied to management approaches that have been made to work successfully, further complicating the situation. Another example of overly elaborate and expensive yet ineffective management is the application and reporting procedures for federal grants. They require detailed reporting that has been expensive in its own right and contributed little to performance improvement or any real control of the effective application of funds.

A second set of mistaken notions about school management can be grouped as adversarial, threatening, and combative with respect to the relationship among boards, administrators, and teachers. These techniques seem implicitly to assume that management/staff relations are inherently adversarial and combative. They seem to have grown up in response to hard bargaining, and a legalistic approach in which an adversarial relationship is assumed. They have failed to recognize that communication, participation, and trust are essential to good management in any organization, especially one so full of and sensitive to human relations as schools.

A third group of inappropriate school management practices are those that fail to emphasize performance and results with information to document this wherever possible. Academic approaches to

EXHIBIT 4.2
Pitfalls of School Management Development

- Techniques that are too expensive, with too much paperwork, not enough payoff in performance and results.
  - Management by objectives.
  - Program budgeting.
  - Application and information procedures for federal grants such as Title I and 94-142.
- Techniques that are adversarial and threatening to teachers.
  - Without adequate communication, participation, trust, and confidence.
  - Perceiving management/staff relations as inherently adversarial and combative.
- Inadequate emphasis on performance and results with information to document it wherever possible.
  - Academic approaches to teacher evaluation that skirt the issues of performance, results, and measures.
  - Overly quantified approaches that don't leave enough room for judgment and interpretation.
  - Gearing rewards too closely to performance, in a field where teamwork is essential and measures can never be completely accurate.
- Technical errors in design and implementation of new school management techniques, usually through underestimating the complexity and challenge of implementation. Many merit pay plans, for example.
  - Tying salaries too closely to performance indicators on an individual basis.
  - Failing to build in adequate controls to keep salaries from excessive escalation or unwarranted staff expectations.
  - Failing to appreciate the delicate and sensitive human relations of compensation based on performance.
  - The essential requirement for fair and effective evaluation and adequate communication, trust, confidence, and teamwork at all levels of the organization.

Source: Compiled by author.

teacher evaluation, for example, seem to intentionally avoid issues of performance, results, and measures. Consequently, they concentrate on the appraisal of means rather than ends, and therefore constrict creative teachers, focusing on inputs rather than outputs. This is particularly odd since education is in some respects highly measurable. It really isn't that hard to find out at lower grade levels whether students are learning in the basic subjects, or not. And ascertaining the opinions of students, parents, and teachers is very straightforward.

On the other hand, however, overly quantified approaches that do not leave enough room for judgment and interpretation have also failed. Some of the early efforts at contracting with teachers on the basis of test scores demonstrate this. It is almost impossible in education to completely separate the contribution of one teacher from other teachers or even students, parents, textbooks, and so on. And therefore any rigid, single indicator of performance is not likely to be suitable.

Another source of inadequate management practices in schools involves technical errors in the design and implementation of school management techniques that are, in a broader sense, appropriate. One of the best examples is merit pay. In principle, tying compensation to performance boosts staff morale and improves performance. But more than 90 percent of the merit pay plans that I have seen tried in education, usually with the best of intentions, have contained technical errors that doomed them to failure before they were even implemented. And these failures when they occurred have left many bad feelings that have made educators overly cautious about these ideas.

Underestimating the technical complexity of these management techniques and especially the human relations skills required for their successful implementation is a common mistake. The challenge of gaining staff understanding, communication, participation, and trust in schools is perhaps the greatest single management requirement. The very limited management training that has been available to school administrators almost guarantees that remedial management training and outside management development assistance will be needed by schools. Even then, with the best available teaching and assistance, the challenge of successfully implementing these techniques and practices is always substantial, requiring a period of

years and the perseverence, support, and encouragement of all concerned at board, administrative, and teaching levels.

Worst of all, however, is a situation where the board, superintendent, and/or administrators in a district are unwilling to accept
responsibility for performance and management. Virtually all of
the districts I have worked with are at the opposite end of the
spectrum. They have been eager to invest and implement new techniques of school management to improve performance, eager to
see performance improve and to see themselves as responsible for
it. There is another group of districts larger in number, but I believe
declining over time, where the board or administrative staff is not
eager to be responsible for performance and is willing to tolerate
or even encourage a general lack of performance information, evaluation, and accountability. It is in these districts that the public,
whether as parents or taxpayers, or the teachers may have to sieze
the initiative in forcing change if education there is to be managed
successfully.

The right management policies and practices are a prerequisite
to good school performance. Nevertheless, some failures of management in schools have rightly made educators cautious about
embracing and welcoming the need for management. These hazards
need to be understood, and avoided.

Management by objectives has proven inadequate in a field where
measures of performance are so difficult to find. I know only a
handful of districts who have made this work in practice. Many
others have found themselves overwhelmed with paperwork and
given up, or had objections from teachers so strong and effective
that any real application was impossible.

Program budgeting has met a similar fate. Unfortunately this
excessively detailed analysis of costs in a school district is not very
helpful in making decisions, although it can be of some value in
cost control. Unlike hospitals where sophisticated cost accounting
seems to pay off, it doesn't in school districts. For example, knowing
the per student cost of the music program doesn't really help very
much in making a decision about whether to teach this subject or not.

Systems management became fashionable for a while, but has
disappeared more recently. It seems to have grown up out of the
computer field and never to have had much relevance to such a
humanistic endeavor as teaching.

Business management is a term that has been around for a long time in schools, but relating to the support functions of overseeing custodial and food services, keeping books, and ordering supplies.

Naive attempts to apply industrial management techniques in the public sector have not succeeded. The Chicago Public Schools adopted an organization structure modeled after industry and abandoned it a few years later. They adopted a compensation plan prepared by an industrial consulting firm and found their salary costs rose 20 percent and performance declined as much. The industrialists didn't understand how hard it is to measure education, and designed a system that would have worked very well if a profit and loss statement had been available.

THE SCHOOL PERFORMANCE AND MANAGEMENT CONNECTION

Outlined in Exhibit 1.1 (page 8 in Chapter 1) is a concept of school management showing the connection with school performance. On the left of the exhibit are listed the key components and indicators of good school performance. This list reflects the results of our experience and research. And it is a common sense expression of the key constituent groups and what they have to gain from good schools, i.e., the learning of students, the satisfaction of parents and community, the morale and productivity of the staff, and cost control in terms of resource allocation and taxpayer funding. The political character of this equation is obvious.

On the right of the exhibit are listed the key components of good school management to be discussed in the next chapter. Developing and successfully implementing each of those components of school management, with the skills and talents required to make it work in practice, are the keys to good school performance. Many different approaches can work successfully, in a field like management, so subject to personality and human nature and variation from place to place, situation to situation, and time to time. But a concept of school management is essential, to establish its component parts and to provide a framework for continued development, experimentation, elaboration — and even departure from the model itself.

Educators do not usually have a concept of management within their mental frame of reference. Consequently, declining school performance is not perceived to be caused by the inadequacy of traditional school administrative practices to meet the circumstances of today. Those who do understand management, usually business-men or farmers, often don't know enough about education to appreciate how it can be applied there.

Naturally the public is concerned about evidence of declining performance and would like results to be higher. But without man-agement in school districts, there is no internal connection, no means of pulling together the efforts of the many people involved toward any objective. Therefore performance drifts lower. We can define and exhort higher educational performance, but this will never get through to the troops who must deliver this performance, without management.

CONCEPTS OF SCHOOL PERFORMANCE

Each concept of school performance deserves further explanation.

Student Learning

Obviously this is the main purpose of education. At lower grade levels, student progress is surprisingly measurable, especially in such basic subjects as math and reading.

Standardized achievement test scores are subject to inexplicable variations and need to be analyzed with great caution, as discussed later in this book. They are, nevertheless, a surprisingly useful indi-cator of student progress, in the lower grade levels and basic subjects. A high level of technical development and standardization over many decades provides a sound base for comparisons to national norms. Cautions are needed. For example, basic subjects such as writing are not covered. And teachers are only one ingredient in the equation that makes up student learning, with other obvious compo-nents being the students themselves, parents, materials, programs, finance, et cetera.

As students advance through the academic subjects, the avail-ability of such quantitative indicators declines. There are still some useful tests in math and science at high school level, and to some extent in languages. But by and large standards at this level become more philosophical, and they require more judgment. The A and O level examinations used in England to monitor student progress, with written examinations read by college instructors, suggest the kind of achievement measures and indicators that become essential. In higher education, of course, the problem is even more severe. But even at secondary level, judgment and ingenuity of department heads and management teams in finding appropriate indicators are essential. Some other more fundamental indicators of student progress are also relevant: dropout rates, attendance, and disciplinary actions.

At secondary school level, two examples of the successful development and application of academic standards are particularly noteable: the International Baccalaureate and Advanced Placement programs. The International Baccalaureate has succeeded in providing a curriculum and examinations with enough flexibility to be applied in many countries. Originally developed for overseas high schools, it is now being used much more widely. For example, one of Chicago's previously most troubled inner city high schools is using it to help convert Waller High School to Lincoln Park Preparatory School. Advanced Placement has enabled many students to earn college credit while still in high school. It is an excellent example of how high academic standards can be applied successfully in practice. And the growth of Advanced Placement during the past 20 years exemplifies the willingness of teachers to embrace and apply high standards.

Parent Satisfaction

One major indication of success available to a business is its sales statistics. They indicate not only customer demand but also, if the company makes a profit, that those services or goods were produced at a cost less than what was paid. Schools lack this basic indicator; they need to find a substitute for it. Of course, any good teacher or administrator is sensitive to the state of mind of both parents and students. Many will feel that they already know the level of parent satisfaction.

My experience is that surveys of parents are an extremely useful supplement to the firsthand knowledge of teachers and administrators. A survey can be revealing even to the most knowledgeable and sensitive teacher or administrator. Objective data can be used to build morale, confidence, teamwork, support, and a willingness to delegate responsibility by the school board to administrators that is essential to good school performance and effective management.

Students can also help assess the quality of programs and opportunities for improvement, especially at higher grade levels. And in addition to the district's most immediate customers — students and parents — the larger community including taxpayers without children in school also represents an important constituency. While their opinions are generally less useful as an immediate indicator of performance, since they are not as close to schools and thus are more dependent upon the community's general image of its educational establishment, their perceptions need to be known.

Staff Satisfaction and Morale

The third component of school performance is the satisfaction, productivity, performance, morale, and attitudes of the district's staff, particularly its teachers. Their opinions on the quality and effectiveness of programs and on working conditions, evaluation, and supervision in the district are of great value in judging performance and are essential to its achievement. The triangulation of these data with the results of a parent survey and test data analysis provide a particularly good basis for analyzing performance.

Cost Control

The final criterion of good school performance is a financial one, and is naturally difficult to balance with the more personal criteria previously discussed. We have found it essential to focus on a few key indicators: staff/student ratios, salary policies, detailed cost analysis in certain other key areas (such as busing, lunchrooms, maintenance), sound financial planning with projections of enrollment and finance, revenues and expenses, and a comparison of all these key indicators to the district's own history and to data from other nearby or similar districts.

By and large we have found this scheme to hold up well in practice. It is vitally important for management to have a concept of performance. The rationale of this framework is also useful in teaching educators and others the importance and relevance of management to public service performance. It demonstrates the connection between good school management and good school performance, and provides a basis for evaluating school performance and developing useful information that can be analyzed and used to improve performance.

5

THE ALTERNATIVE TO DECLINE:
Successful School Management Policy and Practices

The concept of management presented in this book is based upon research, practical experience, and teaching of school management during the past decade. It is relevant to the circumstances of today, but a marked departure from traditional school administrative practices. Consequently, its application in any district is challenging. New management skills must be developed.

It is important not to add time or cost burdens, but rather to seek a relatively simple, economical, and straightforward system of practical value in actually improving performance. The components of school management described in this book provide a starting point for each school district's management policies and practices. Included are evaluation of programs, administrators, and teachers, and the development, analysis, and use of performance information. These key management systems should sustain good performance — including delegation by the board to the staff based on well-founded confidence in good performance.

These essential management systems are counterparts of the key systems required for an automobile or human being to function. Trying to run a school district without them is like a runner whose circulatory system isn't working properly or a car without a carburetor. Simply trying harder in schools, or demanding more from them, won't help until the internal management systems that are essential to good performance are in place.

Of course school districts are not all the same. Each has its own traditions, values, and norms arising out of local history and personalities, both within the school and in the larger community. Obviously large urban districts are different from small rural and suburban ones. These differences require differences in management. For example, a certain toughness is needed in any large district, whereas more friendly, informal relationships are characteristic of successful smaller districts. But these are largely matters of style. The basic management policies and practices described in this chapter are needed in every district. Applying them successfully in any situation, however, requires adaptation and a management style appropriate to the unique circumstances there.

Exhibit 5.1 shows the key components of successful school management, with results listed at the bottom of the exhibit. Each of these components is discussed in the remainder of this chapter. First, however, it is appropriate to describe general policies of management as a framework for considering specific techniques.

SCHOOL MANAGEMENT POLICIES – PERFORMANCE AND TEAMWORK

Policies are not the dull, bureaucratic written documents that eventually seem to be needed and developed in any large organization. The real policies are the strategy and philosophy of the organization and how it is to work, whether in a business or a public agency. In this sense, many school districts have not really thought through their policies at all. If they did so, they would find many problems implicit in them. Relationships with staff and public that are adversarial and combative would be noted, as well as an absence of performance information and evaluation internally. In extreme cases, these schools would be adrift in terms of any management control, without much attention at all (except in the negotiated contract) to the most important human side of management needed to achieve good performance.

These implicit assumptions are characteristic of many school districts today, and contrast sharply to the policies that we think are essential for schools. Emphasizing performance, based on a practical concept of the purpose of schools, and using information in a fair and explicit evaluation process that is positive and constructive in

EXHIBIT 5.1
Key Components of Successful School Management

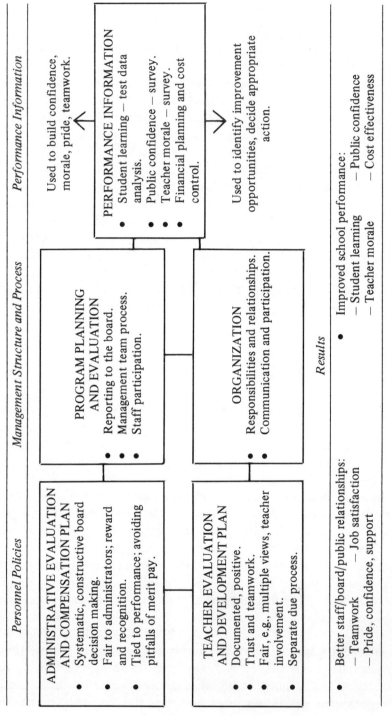

Personnel Policies	Management Structure and Process	Performance Information

PERFORMANCE INFORMATION

Used to build confidence, morale, pride, teamwork.

- Student learning – test data analysis.
- Public confidence – survey.
- Teacher morale – survey.
- Financial planning and cost control.

Used to identify improvement opportunities, decide appropriate action.

PROGRAM PLANNING AND EVALUATION

- Reporting to the board.
- Management team process.
- Staff participation.

ADMINISTRATIVE EVALUATION AND COMPENSATION PLAN

- Systematic, constructive board decision making.
- Fair to administrators; reward and recognition.
- Tied to performance; avoiding pitfalls of merit pay.

ORGANIZATION

- Responsibilities and relationships.
- Communication and participation.

TEACHER EVALUATION AND DEVELOPMENT PLAN

- Documented, positive.
- Trust and teamwork.
- Fair, e.g., multiple views, teacher involvement.
- Separate due process.

Results

- Better staff/board/public relationships:
  - Teamwork – Job satisfaction
  - Pride, confidence, support

- Improved school performance:
  - Student learning – Public confidence
  - Teacher morale – Cost effectiveness

Source: Compiled by author.

70

purpose and impact, is a vital aspect of this, as is encouragement of teamwork, morale, and productivity through staff relations and personnel policies designed to do so. Further, an important part of teamwork is communication and participation of the staff in management responsibility and decisions, and in planning and evaluating performance. And finally, management should develop fair and effective personnel policies for selection, development, evaluation, and compensation that are accepted and supported by the staff.

These relatively simple and straightforward policies make sense and are not hard to understand. Yet they are not operational in more than a few school districts today, for two reasons. One is that they differ markedly from traditional school administration practices. The second is that the techniques to implement them in practice have only recently been developed and have not yet been widely communicated.

Another way to position these new school management policies is to contrast them with more traditional school administration. In these policies the emphasis is on responsibility for performance and results and the practical use of information and evaluation to prove that schools are doing a good job (where they are) and to identify improvement opportunities that can be acted upon and realized. This contrasts to traditional school administration, where performance information is often ignored, kept secret, or complicated to the point of being uninterpretable. Consequently, the techniques essential for demonstrating good performance and identifying improvement opportunities have not been generally available.

Although a growing emphasis on performance and results is evident in recent writing on school administration, many of the proposals for how to do it have involved such complicated, expensive, and sophisticated techniques as to make the situation worse rather than better, or actually damage performance in the process. Both management by objectives and program budgeting are good examples. They have generated excessive paperwork and statistics in most situations where they have been applied, while doing little to help improve performance or make better decisions.

The second essential emphasis is on teamwork of teachers, administrators, and board — the human relations of school management essential to good performance. This includes communication, participation, and involvement as well as emphasis on a common effort toward good performance that is mutually satisfying. Again this contrasts to traditional assumptions in which administrators are viewed as a distinctly separate group from teachers, with authoritarian or adversarial relationships. Teachers are managers in the classroom, the most critically important position in terms of responsibility for and direct impact on educational performance. Traditional school administration has used evaluation in a negative and threatening way, paid little or no attention to staff development, and permitted compensation practices for staff that are not even designed to have a positive impact on performance, and in fact do not.

These traditional school administrative practices, particularly the assumptions about the distinction between teachers and administrators, have been reinforced by union negotiations. Some administrators, have even concluded that, as a result of unions, adversarial and even combative relationships in school districts are necessary.

Concern about school performance has also led many school boards to be more aggressive in asserting their authority, furthering conflict and controversy. Financial difficulties, school closings, strikes, and other conflict-oriented incidents have contributed to this atmosphere. The downward spiral of performance and pressures for fragmentation rather than teamwork are visible in practically every school district today.

In contrast, my experience indicates that a participative style of school management is essential to meet the basic character and requirements of good performance in education. Results in districts moving in this direction confirm the effectiveness of such an approach. An emphasis on the human side of school management in terms of staff relations, student learning, and teacher productivity pays off in improvements on all of these scores. Administrators and the board contribute to and support teaching effectiveness, and the resulting sense of teamwork pervades the district's staff as well as those it serves. An internally reinforcing upward cycle of good performance, confidence, and job satisfaction is established.

A final policy of such importance as to warrant special mention is delegation by the board to the management team and teaching staff of the district. This delegation only makes sense in concert with the performance information and evaluation procedures recommended in this book. Without it boards become overinvolved in school operations, reducing the effectiveness of their staff rather than helping to improve performance.

SCHOOL MANAGEMENT PRACTICES

These are the management practices that we have found most practical and effective in implementing the policies and meeting the requirements outlined above.

Positive Use of Evaluation

Evaluation is crucially important in two ways. One is building the confidence and morale of district staff as well as the support of board and public. The other is in achieving the actual performance of the district in terms of student learning and progress that is in turn the most essential ingredient for confidence and support. Correctly done, it is a positive, constructive, essential part of school management and good school performance. With communication, evaluation is the most vital prerequisite to an upward cycle of good school performance and staff job satisfaction.

In the view of a majority of teachers, administrators, and board members, however, and an opinion that I share, evaluation is not working satisfactorily today. Teachers find evaluation threatening, frustrating, and demoralizing, especially in an era of declining enrollments. With the power gained through unions, practices they consider unfair have been effectively subverted. Consequently, evaluation in most districts has little or no positive impact on teacher professional growth development or performance. And even inadequate teachers can't be fired.

Because education is so inherently difficult to measure, subject to different styles that can be equally effective, with staff resistant to authoritarian supervision, evaluation is extremely challenging and difficult. Unions and due process laws have made it impossible to use inadequate evaluation to get rid of even poor teachers. Perhaps, in an era of public concern and aggressive school boards, it should not be surprising that many administrators have opted simply to avoid any real evaluation. The following paragraphs offer some practices that have been used successfully to meet these challenges.

Evaluating Programs and Curriculum before Individuals

In evaluating program and curriculum performance, use at least some information, such as test scores and surveys discussed below. Assume a common responsibility for school performance that recognizes the essential need for teamwork among teachers, administrators, and boards as well as students and parents. Provide for reporting program and curriculum performance throughout the organization: summary reporting to the board, including personal presentations by teachers and administrators on all of the key programs in the district and more detailed analysis and planning internally involving teachers as well as administrators. Use a simple, straightforward process for this program evaluation, avoiding both the overly quantified accounting details involved in program budgeting approaches, and the excessive paperwork and time consuming character of most management by objective systems. Keep it simple.

A model for program evaluation showing its relationship to performance information as well as administrative and teacher evaluation is shown in Exhibit 5.2 and discussed in detail in Chapters 9 and 10.

Understand and Assess Performance with Performance Information

Even though education ultimately must rest on opinion and judgment in evaluating performance, some information to offset unavoidable subjectivity and personality and to provide a broader basis of judgment is an important step in strengthening school performance through better management. Unfortunately educators are usually not oriented or trained in the use of information and analysis to monitor performance and make decisions. The human relations requirements of teaching are high, so these skills naturally predominate. Most school districts are small, without planning and control positions that lend themselves to the analytical skills and organizational arrangements from which objective assessment of performance can be made. For these reasons, and because the tradition of educational administration has been not to provide much information on performance that might encourage the overinvolvement of board members or the public, too little use is made in schools of performance information.

Today, the general climate of public suspicion about school performance requires aggressive defense of that performance. This same circumstance also requires courage and high performance ambitions on the part of both administrators and teachers, and a supportive board/management relationship. Yet only in this way can good performance be recognized, demonstrated, and documented

EXHIBIT 5.2
The School Performance Accountability System

SCHOOL PERFORMANCE CONCEPT and PERFORMANCE INFORMATION	*SCHOOL PERFORMANCE EVALUATION COMPONENTS*
Student Learning	*Program*
Test data analysis	Planning
	Monitoring
	Reporting
Parent Satisfaction	*Administrative*
and Public Confidence	Evaluation
Parent survey	Compensation
Teacher Morale	*Teacher*
and Job Satisfaction	Evaluation
Teacher survey	Development
Financial Planning	*Financial*
and Cost Control	Planning
Staffing ratios, costs	Cost control

Results:
- A practical, affordable accountability system
- Board confident and supportive of staff
- Improved staff morale, public confidence, and student learning

Source: Developed from research conducted during the past three years — sponsored by the Illinois Association of School Boards, funded by a group of foundations, directed by Fred Genck — based on practical experience in 100 districts during eight years, and the perspective of a school board member and management consultant.

with evidence, and the staff thus provided with the satisfaction of success and public confidence.

Performance Information Centering on Common Sense Concepts

The concept of school performance and relevant information that I have found most useful is (1) Student learning — analysis of standardized achievement test scores and other indicators; (2) Parent satisfaction — surveys; (3) Teacher satisfaction — surveys; and (4) Cost control — financial analysis. A more detailed description of this essential school performance information follows.

Student Learning Indicators

Although rightly controversial in their impact on individual students, these data are extremely valuable as indicators of student learning, particularly at lower grade levels. They have been developed, tested, and proven over a period of many decades. Where these data are analyzed correctly and effectively, their threatening quality is defused and student learning levels improved, depending of course on the opportunities to do so.

The correct analysis of standardized achievement test scores is extremely important and relatively rare in schools. Perhaps the most important single analytical technique is to concentrate on annual growth, so as to adjust for the differing levels at which students may be starting each grade. I have found the most useful analysis to be historical comparisons within the district over a period of at least five to ten years. It is important to analyze performance at district, school, and classroom levels as well as by subjects to pinpoint improvement opportunities. And remember that these data are subject to inexplicable variations that make caution in analyzing them essential.

Summary reporting of district test scores in a simple, understandable pattern to the board is required in every district. Sharing this information with the public is also appropriate. Some districts also share test scores for each student with that student's parents, partly as a communication device and partly to be sure that these scores are seriously considered by teachers for individual students.

More important than this summary reporting to the board is a process of comprehensive internal analysis, and training for both administrators and teachers in how to use these data, as the basis to improve and maintain performance. Again the emphasis should be on simple interpretation and use of data, with the mounds of computer printouts and detailed statistics returned by test companies boiled down to much more simple and straightforward presentations.

Ultimately, every district should have the objective of making these test scores useful to teachers in the classroom. This applies not only to assessing the progress of individual students, but to reviewing the profile of the class at the beginning of the year, and then at the end of the year to have feedback on results achieved. This provides management information to the teacher in the classroom. It is useful in self-evaluation and judging the impact of alternative teaching styles, as well as making sure that performance information is utilized at the level of the organization closest to the classroom.

Rather than overemphasizing student learning, aggressive analysis of test score data helps to defuse this issue. It permits more attention to other important aspects of educational performance, such as social and emotional development of children, once satisfactory student learning is demonstrated.

While there is not room here to detail the many cautions and caveats essential in test score analysis, these essential requirements deserve to be highlighted: (1) Focusing on annual growth from year to year in analysis is essential; (2) Test score analysis cannot be used effectively without communicative and trusting staff relations; (3) Some basic skills are not indicated in standardized achievement tests (for example writing); (4) Testing relevance is greater at lower grade levels and thus the tests are more useful there; and (5) In high schools, test score analysis needs to be organized on a department by department basis, using a variety of indicators in the context of department plans and objectives. A specific example of test data analysis and student learning improvement is presented in Chapter 8. Exhibit 5.3 summarizes this analysis.

Survey of Parents, Teachers, and Students

School districts should survey parents at least every two to three years in order to provide ongoing information regarding satisfaction and concerns. It is essential that such surveys contain straightforward questions dealing with every important aspect of school performance, each academic program, relationships and communication channels to parents, and all supporting services.

Parent surveys help to ensure recognition throughout the entire school district organization that what parents think is important. Parents are usually pleased to be asked their opinions, and even those who may not respond will appreciate the opportunity to do so. Positively phrased questions imply that the district knows the importance of such things as basic skills and cost control, and this helps to communicate a favorable impression to parents.

Most important, of course, the survey can identify improvement opportunities that, when acted upon, will actually improve performance in those areas that are of greatest concern to parents. In some cases these may be misimpressions of the district's performance,

EXHIBIT 5.3
Summary of Annual Growth and Improvement in Annual Growth
(Brookdale School District)

School	Grades						Total
	2	3	4	5	6	7	
Annual Growth: 1978-79							
Lincoln							
Reading	1.3	1.9	0.9	3.0	0.9	1.4	1.6
Math	1.1	1.5	0.5	3.0	0.5	1.5	1.4
Wilson							
Reading	0.6	0.8	NA	NA	NA	NA	0.7
Math	1.0	1.1	NA	NA	NA	NA	1.1
Adams							
Reading	NA	NA	0.5	1.1	0.7	1.2	0.9
Math	NA	NA	1.0	0.7	0.6	1.5	1.0
Garfield							
Reading	NA	NA	0.5	1.3	0.8	1.4	1.0
Math	NA	NA	0.4	1.8	1.1	1.9	1.3
District							
Reading	0.8	1.0	0.5	1.5	0.8	1.4	1.0
Math	1.2	1.2	0.7	1.4	0.9	1.7	1.2
Improvement in Annual Growth: 1974-75 to 1978-79							
Lincoln							
Reading	+0.6	+1.0	+0.5	+1.4	+0.2	+0.6*	+0.7
Math	+0.4	+0.3	+0.1	+1.6	−0.5	+0.6*	+0.4
Wilson							
Reading	0**	+0.1**	NA	NA	NA	NA	+0.1
Math	+0.1**	+0.2**	NA	NA	NA	NA	+0.2
Adams							
Reading	NA	NA	+0.1**	0**	0**	+0.3*	+0.1
Math	NA	NA	+0.6**	−0.1**	+0.1**	+1.0*	+0.4
Garfield							
Reading	NA	NA	+0.1**	+0.1**	+0.1**	+0.5*	+0.2
Math	NA	NA	0**	+1.0**	+0.6**	+1.0*	+0.9
District							
Reading	+0.2	+0.1	+0.2	+0.1	+0.2	+0.6	+0.2
Math	+0.2	+0.1	+0.3	+0.5	+0.3	+1.2	+0.4

*1978-79 school compared to 1975-76 District total.
**1978-79 school compared to 1975-76 total for Bunche, Palm, and Woodland.

NA: These grades not at these schools.

Source: Compiled by author.

which can be corrected. In other cases, they will be accurate perceptions of poor performance that require adjustments in programs or practices.

A survey can identify these concerns well before they surface in the form of irate parents at a school board meeting. And it provides evidence to offset the unavoidable incidents that occur in school districts that otherwise raise board concern and reduce public confidence, such as a parent complaining inappropriately or one whose complaint is the exception rather than a widespread opinion. The evidence of a survey can offset these inappropriate indicators of performance and provide the confidence needed to take them as isolated incidents, or confirm that the problem is widespread and needs attention. In larger districts such a communication channel is practically the only way to be sure that parent opinion is monitored and made clearly available for response, and that necessary action to correct a situation is initiated by teachers or administrators.

A similar survey of teachers serves many of the same purposes as the parent survey with respect to teacher communication and identification of perceived or real problems. In addition, it supplements channels of communication from teachers in a useful way. Obviously the survey needs to be objective and anonymous in order to obtain realistic opinions.

In addition, the teacher survey provides an important complement to the results of the parent survey. Teachers' views are more professional and based on inside knowledge of the district. By combining these opinions with parent views, the places at which they coincide are very likely to be real trouble spots and well worth attention. Like the parent survey, a teacher survey says to administrators that what teachers think is important, and must be responded to constructively. The possibility of unfair teacher opinions must be acknowledged and cautiously regarded. However, in an era of unions, administrators must learn to manage schools in a way that is at least tolerable to teachers; the opportunity to object through grievances, bargaining, or strikes is always available.

While we have found the opinions of parents and teachers to be the most valuable source of performance information, students also have useful perceptions, especially at higher grade levels. There is a definite value in using surveys in this area as well. Another appropriate target group for surveys is graduates; their perceptions on reflection have value in pinpointing weaknesses from this perspective. Finally, surveys can be broader than just parents, reaching out to the majority of community members who do not have children in school. Their opinions are less relevant to identifying specific problems. But their perceptions are important in terms of overall public confidence in school performance, and specifically at the time of seeking funding approval from taxpayers.

Technical assistance — to develop questions that are straightforward, relevant, analyzable, and understandable and to use procedures that maximize the utility of the information gathered — is essential. Of the school surveys that we have observed, 90 percent have used watered down questions that are never actually analyzed and used to improve performance in practice. Don't bother with a survey unless you're prepared to obtain the technical assistance needed to make sure it's done correctly. You must also have available the training for your management team in how to use survey results constructively. With this assistance, the cost of surveys is modest and their benefits very substantial. Without this assistance it's better not to bother. Examples of effective parent and teacher surveys and how to use them in practice are presented in Chapter 9.

Staffing Ratios and Financial Planning

Obviously financial information is necessary to plan and control district revenues and expenditures and to ensure that taxpayers are receiving fair value for their investment in public schools. Particularly important is narrowing down the financial data provided to school boards to a few simple indicators.

One such indicator is a comparison of teacher/student and other staffing ratios over a period of five to ten years, particularly in situations of declining enrollment where reducing staffing levels in proportion to enrollment is somewhat difficult and requires careful monitoring. In high schools, this requires staffing analysis on a department by department basis.

Salaries are obviously another key factor — policies should be clearly specified, with analysis of how they compare to the district's actual situation. Comparisons of cost increases to rates of inflation is another useful and simple indicator of cost control in schools.

Financial planning in schools is complicated by the peculiar intricacies of local property taxes and state aid formulas. Simplification into a system that permits dealing with the most important variables involved, assessed valuations and enrollments for example, is important.

Some important decisions, school closings for example, involve both educational and financial issues, a difficult combination of quantitative and judgmental factors. The analytical sophistication required to deal with the many facets of such an issue is comparable to the complexity of almost any other situation that I have come across, and consequently is not always as well handled as it might be at either board or administrative staff support levels.

These challenging problems are discussed in detail in Chapter 12, with specific examples of financial planning, cost control and decision-making models. A summary school finance model is shown in Exhibit 5.4.

It is only fair to point out that financial planning and control in most school districts is well handled, Howard Jarvis and his tax protestors notwithstanding. Of the new management techniques discussed in this book, this is the one that is already well done in most school districts.

Use of an Efficient Administrative Team

District administrators provide the arms, legs, and machinery through which the board impacts on the actual operations of the district. Because most school districts are small, requirements of administrative organization are relatively straightforward. But evaluating administrative performance is difficult, because the character of education is difficult to measure. Therefore, gearing compensation to performance is not easy either. Yet good management is vital to good school performance. Administrative staffing has an important leverage on overall district performance, if responsibility is maintained.

Provide for enough administrators, with well-defined responsibilities, to achieve good performance. Definition of administrative responsibilities in school districts is more difficult today because of changes in authority brought about by declining public confidence and rising unionization. These circumstances require each district to rethink and redefine administrative responsibilities and staffing levels.

EXHIBIT 5.4
School Financial Planning and Cost Control Model

Cost Control	Financial Planning	Decision Guidelines
Key Board Policy Decisions	Projections and Assumptions	Cautions
• Staff/student ratios.	• Enrollment.	• High level of complexity and uncertainty.
• Salaries policy.	• Assessed valuation.	• Staff support from superintendent and business manager.
• Other costs.	• Timing of tax receipts.	• Positive rather than negative morale implications.
• Tax rate (referendum timing).	• State aid.	• The political/financial equation — parents, teachers, taxpayers.
• Cash reserve/debt policy.	• Inflation.	• Cost control and financial planning versus program and resource allocation decisions.
	• State school finance policy; taxpayer revolt.	• School performance information to support board confidence and delegation.

Source: Compiled by author.

82

The demands of fair and effective performance evaluation outlined above require a sufficient number of administrative positions to provide the time needed for communication, and interaction with teachers, and for sufficiently frequent observation and awareness of classroom circumstances. These responsibilities tend to center on the school principal at elementary levels and on department heads in high schools. Both positions are vitally important to fulfilling successfully management responsiblities for school performance.

Organization must be well defined in terms of specific responsibilities and working relationships with enough positions to provide for the policies and practices that are discussed in this book. These organizational requirements are ones that most school districts have met successfully. Some boards, however, failing to understand the importance of administrative staffing, have streamlined positions to the point where adequate communication and evaluation are not really possible. And there are also districts where administrative staffing may be unnecessarily extensive; in my experience these are relatively rare.

Tie administrative evaluation to program evaluation, taking into account individual contributions and circumstances. Every district needs documented policies and procedures for administrative evaluation that are constructive, as well as supported by the administrators concerned.

The program evaluation process outlined above, along with the performance information specified, should provide the two main components of administrative evaluation. Thus administrators should be judged mainly on the performance of the programs or schools for which they are responsible, in the context of the situation, circumstances, and objectives in each of those programs or schools, and using information as evidence of good performance as well as to identify improvement opportunities.

A simple format that we have used for implementing this kind of program in school districts is shown and the process in a particular district is described at length in Chapter 10.

Base administrative compensation primarily on performance evaluation. One of the most serious weaknesses in school administration today is the lack of well-defined policies and practices for administrative compensation. As a result, boards are often becoming overinvolved in these decisions, or refusing to decide them at all. The reaction of administrators to opt for union protection is understandable.

Using simple, proven compensation devices largely borrowed from industry is the first important requirement in providing a more rational basis for administrative compensation. These techniques include: (1) Analyzing responsibilities, to provide the basis for categories of positions ranked according to the overall importance, difficulty and scope of responsibilities, and impact on school performance; (2) Using these categories to construct a salary plan with ranges and target levels of compensation so that a structure is provided for board decision making, for administrators to understand the basis on which their salaries are to be set, and for objective analysis of how the district's actual salary practices compare to its intended policies; and (3) Gearing these salary categories to a predetermined position – decided by the board – compared to prevailing salaries in some appropriate sample of school districts.

The most important part of the compensation plan is that it should be tied to performance. This requires the kind of evaluation system, including performance information, outlined above. Without this essential link to performance, a compensation plan may do more harm than good.

A formal and well-documented evaluation and compensation plan for administrators is essential. Too often administrators see their performance being considered in an atmosphere of conflict at a board level, and note the uncertainty of their compensation compared with the security won by teachers through unions.

Design of Constructive Teacher Evaluation

Perhaps the greatest opportunity for improving school management today lies in policies and practices for teacher evaluation. Traditionally subject to authoritarian practices, teachers have rebelled successfully during the past decade or two through unions to practically stop evaluation in many school districts.

Teachers' assessments of traditional practices for evaluation are generally correct in judging them to be unfair and inadequate. Personal opinions, personality traits, superficial procedures, and checklists that focus on personal characteristics rather than results contribute to the frustration and dissatisfaction of teachers. With declining enrollments and the tendency of some boards to want to use evaluation as part of an adversarial relationship with teachers, the threatening quality of evaluation has in many districts practically cut off communication about classroom performance between teachers and administrators.

In order for teacher evaluation to be understood, accepted, and implemented by teachers, a well-documented plan designed to be fair and constructive is essential. It should encourage good working relationships, teamwork, trust, confidence and communication. Evaluation for dismissal — applying to only a small percentage of teachers, and appropriately requiring documentation, to meet legal due process requirements — should be distinguished from development-oriented evaluation. Teacher participation in evaluation is essential, in a spirit of teamwork and communication. Staff development should be individualized, and multiple views should be used to offset personality. Administrators should be trained and supervised to ensure consistency. These criteria for fair and effective teacher evaluation are listed and discussed in detail in Chapter 11, using a case study of teacher evaluation and development that has been working effectively for more than five years.

Merit pay plans for teachers provide the ideal way to reward good performance. But their demands in staff relations, evaluation, compensation techniques, and general management are extremely high. Wherever possible school districts should gear pay to performance, because this provides the maximum satisfaction to employees in feeling that their salary has been earned. This has proven extremely challenging in practice in education because the essential prerequisites of merit pay have usually not been met. They are effective and fair evaluation that is accepted and supported by the staff, good staff relations based on open communication and participation, and compensation plans that are technically adequate for the purposes and situation in schools.

Most merit pay plans in education have failed because districts have not first met these requirements. In some, performance has been tied too closely to compensation in a field where it is virtually impossible to isolate the contribution of one individual. Competent technical compensation know-how could have avoided these problems. In others, teacher evaluation was not first fully developed to be fair and effective and accepted and supported by teachers. Without this foundation for performance-based compensation, it will not work.

Obviously these are tough requirements. Most districts will need a few years to meet them before they even consider merit pay. In many, once those other requirements are met, the added benefits of paying teachers for performance may not be worth it. However, in the several districts that I have worked with where merit pay has been used, it has been extremely effective in rewarding performance, motivating the staff, justifying expenditures to taxpayers, and resulting in improved performance and better value for money. Everyone wins.

Emphasize Communication and Relationships

The glue that holds together any organization is the network of communication, participation, feelings of trust, and mutual involvement in the purpose of the organization and satisfaction in its accomplishments. It's almost impossible to describe these aspects of an organization in a way that truly reflects their intensely human and personal character. The evaluation process and performance information outlined above should encourage these attitudes of communication and mutual responsibility, as well as an orientation to good performance and the satisfaction of achieving it. But it is equally true that relationships of trust and confidence will be needed in order to move forward with evaluation and to use performance information, and thus these two key aspects of management are closely interwoven.

A spirit of cooperation must be encouraged and rewarded in public communication and behavior of the board, superintendent, and administrators. Board members can be especially helpful because of their position at the interface of the district and community, ceremonially at the top of the school hierarchy. This sense of teamwork is just as important today in an era of collective bargaining as it ever was. Boards need to understand these requirements as well as the adversarial character of collective bargaining and, assuming unions haven't been avoided, find a way to balance them in spite of their paradoxical nature. Insisting on fair and effective accountability using information and evaluation is one essential step to do so.

The opportunity for teachers to assess the policies and practices and performance of the district both in face-to-face contacts with administrators and periodically through a formal written survey is essential. Communication of problems, concerns, needs, and desires up and down the organization, especially from teachers to administrators, is essential. Boards and administrators should insist on and encourage relationships of trust and confidence between administrators and teachers because these are vitally important to good school performance.

Obviously also important are effective communication channels and relationships between school personnel and parents. Communication at a school level traditionally has been handled well. It is also obviously important, and requires the participation, support, and encouragement of administrators as well as teachers and other staff personnel.

The many devices available to provide communication and good relationships, and the human sensitivity and communication and relationship skills that are required, go beyond the space available in this book. However, perhaps a few examples of successful practices will illustrate the point.

One superintendent I know visits each school once a year to speak with all teachers individually about what they see to be the needs of that school and any problems that may exist in their classroom. This kind of open communication helps to assure that problems and concerns are communicated within the organization, rather than continuing to frustrate teachers. Frequent visits by principals to classrooms and by central office personnel to schools are essential to maintaining communication, even though they are time consuming.

School districts that lack media oriented to their particular community need to take special steps to ensure communication not only with parents but to some extent also with other members of the community. However, it also continues to be true that in some respects school performance is all too rapidly communicated to parents and community, since the children bring home each night their daily experiences. Good school performance is the essential ingredient to public confidence. However, communication of that performance in a spirit of confidence, pride, and teamwork on the part of teachers, administrators, and other staff members as well as the board is also essential.

School Board Operations: Delegation of Responsibility

I have saved school board operations for the last section of this chapter because they are at the same time the most and least important part of a school district. Least important in that they don't actually produce the work and ought to function in a way that makes them completely dispensable in the short run. But most important in that their policies have such a dramatic impact on the overall productivity and morale of the staff. Unfair policies or those that are conducive to adversarial relationships and a lack of emphasis on performance will not drive a school district into bankruptcy as might be the case with an industrial firm. But they can diminish performance, by as much as 20 percent in my experience. On the other hand, appropriate policies can have a similar impact on the plus side.

The oldest rule of board operations in business and government as well as education, and surely something of a platitude but still true nonetheless, is that the board should concentrate on policy and delegate responsibility for operations and performance to the administrators and teachers of the district. There is a natural tendency, like gravity, for boards to slip down into the operations of the organizations for which they are responsible. Perhaps operations are just more interesting than setting policy, more tangible, and even seem to some board members who don't understand the function of policy to have more impact on the district. Doing so, however, will obscure the responsibility and jeopardize and confuse the authority of administrators and teachers without actually helping the situation. One of the reasons for the strong evaluation and performance information recommendations earlier in this chapter is to give the board the confidence they need to delegate to their staffs and to support and encourage good performance.

One function uniquely belonging to the board is insisting that teachers and administrators demonstrate good performance, with documented evidence wherever possible. Only the board can insist upon this feature of good school management. While this book shows how to do so, the will to do so is something that the board itself will have to muster. While strong administrators will insist upon this kind of relationship with the board, others may prefer not to have evaluation and information used. We could all rest more comfortably on our laurels if performance were assumed to be good and relationships were supportive without evidence.

Boards must recognize and foster through their own behavior the teamwork that is essential to good school performance. Fair personnel policies on such matters as selection, development, evaluation, and reward of teachers are essential. A good deal of time at each board meeting should be devoted to reports from teachers and administrators on the performance of school programs. And finally boards should be careful not to become drawn too heavily into their responsibilities, limiting their time involved in board matters at most to one or two days per month unless exceptional circumstances arise.

TEACHING AND MANAGING

Teaching is a performing art, hard to measure, and subject to many of the imponderables common in other personal service fields. Needed skills are more likely to be learned on the job rather than in school.

Because teaching involves motivating other people, there is a great deal of confusion and uncertainty in specifying a particular style. Like other professional fields and the arts, a style that works well for one person may not work well for another. Or one that works in one situation may not work in another. Each school and each district develops patterns of behavior, values, and norms that would challenge even an anthropologist to understand and explain. Consequently, the requirements to be a good teacher in one school may be quite different from those in another. Different techniques are needed to perform well in different settings.

Managing has many similarities and some differences when compared to teaching. It also involves other people and questions of style that differ considerably from place to place. Learning how to get one's satisfaction out of the development and accomplishment of other people is crucial. Motivation and communication are obviously important. Standards of performance make a difference.

Perhaps the only really substantial difference between teaching and managing is that the manager will find there are some people who simply don't belong in the organization, whether selecting for initial job employment or weeding out those whose career pattern and personal talents and skills do not fit the requirements of the organization. In contrast, a teacher is asked to work with all the children, and to bring each along as far as possible, largely without the possibility of actually getting rid of anyone or even unfairly discriminating against those whose potential may be less. I believe this psychological transition required in moving from teaching to managing is one of the most difficult aspects of adjustment for educators.

In light of these considerable similarities between managing and teaching, it might be a little surprising that school management has not developed more fully. I believe that if the similarities were more strongly recognized, the nature of teaching would provide a very sound basis for developing the management requirements and techniques appropriate to education. This is the approach we have followed in developing the techniques set forth in this book.

It is important to view teachers as part of the management team. Their responsibilities and impact on performance clearly justify this. A common definition of a manager is one who is responsible for the performance of others, and surely a teacher falls into this category, if one considers the students and their achievement and development progress as a measure of a teacher's performance. In viewing the teacher as a part of the management team, one necessarily cuts across the assumptions of collective bargaining. Recognizing the need for this and developing the skills required to do it in practice are a great challenge. But a key step in doing so is recognizing the need to view the management team as having three levels — board, administrators, and teachers — all working together to achieve good performance.

The school management policies and practices described in this chapter represent the most effective that we have discovered in a decade of working with more than 100 districts in over 200 management studies. While they depart from traditional school administration thinking in many important respects, every one of them has been tested and proven in practice to actually work to improve school performance in terms of student learning, public confidence, and staff morale. Specific case studies applying these policies and techniques in actual and varied situations are in Part II.

6

THE MANAGEMENT
DEVELOPMENT PAYOFF:
Results of
Good School Management

This chapter assesses the present state of school management against the policies and practices specified in Chapter 5. It also describes the payoff of achieving these school management standards in terms of performance and results.

CURRENT STATE OF MANAGEMENT

Based on my experience with about 100 school districts, Exhibit 6.1 assesses the current state of school management. As you can see, organization and cost control are relative strengths, while the use of performance information and evaluation, development, and compensation for teachers and administrators is a major opportunity for improvement. The comments in this exhibit explain these assessments, and indicate the performance implications. This information is discussed in the following paragraphs.

The highest degree of compliance with the management standards set forth in Chapter 5 occurs in the area of organization (50 percent), and the lowest degree in the area of teacher evaluation and development (5 percent). The other three areas — program planning and evaluation, performance information, and administrative evaluation and compensation — are judged to be at about a 20 percent level of compliance. The opportunities for improvement are substantial.

EXHIBIT 6.1
The Current State of School Management in Practice

STANDARDS	ASSESSMENT		RESULTS	
Key Components of School Management	Degree of Compliance	Comments	Performance	Cost
Organization	50%	Responsibilities are often clearly defined, but sometimes do not adequately emphasize performance. Few districts have developed adequate communication and participation opportunities for the staff.	Clear-cut responsibility for performance, with adequate staff communication and participation.	Some districts may reduce administrative staffing.
Program Planning and Evaluation	20%	Most districts have considerably further to go in developing a process of planning and evaluation that effectively involves the management team, reports to the board, and involves staff participation.	Operational machinery for accepting and implementing responsibility for performance, and for involvement of staff and board. Without this process, information will have limited impact; teamwork is essential to improving performance.	None

Performance Information	20%	Most districts do not have the information, or have failed to analyze and use it.	Limited additional costs of data analysis, particularly for survey and test data analysis (no more than a few dollars per student). Management counsel and training for the district's administrators in how to use the information successfully is essential.
Test Data Analysis	10%	Virtually all districts have test data. Few have analyzed and used these data effectively, to have a basis for applying judgment and interpretation and then to improve performance.	Every district and school should be able to achieve one year's growth for each year in school. Classrooms, grade levels, and/or schools not meeting this standard should be expected to rise. Districts already achieving at this level have also improved performance, but should not expect dramatic changes.
Parent Surveys	5%	Some districts have surveyed parents, but usually with questions so watered down that the results are not actionable.	Parent satisfaction can be achieved by every district. Annual prioritizing against the results of such a survey will ensure continued high levels of satisfaction and public confidence in schools.

Exhibit 6.1, continued

STANDARDS	ASSESSMENT		RESULTS	
Key Components of School Management	Degree of Compliance	Comments	Performance	Cost
Teacher Surveys	5%	Unions have pressed for these, but few districts have yet responded.	The survey, combined with adequate participation, communication and personnel policies, will maintain teacher morale and productivity at a high level.	
Cost	60%	Many school districts are quite frugal, some are not. The complexity of cost control and financial planning today is beyond the capabilities of internal control and projections in many districts.		Demonstrable attention to and results of cost control should generate confidence and support throughout the community, with costs increasing no faster than inflation, and in some cases cost reductions.
Administrative Evaluation and Compensation	20%	Most school districts use a relatively informal approach that is proving inadequate in the face of greater board concern and involvement.	Assures the attention of administrators to their responsibility for performance and a sense of reward and recompense for accomplishing it.	No more than a few thousand dollars for assistance in the preparation and implementation of a plan.

| Teacher Evaluation and Development | 5% | Most districts are using traditional practices rightly objected to by teachers. Consequently, those teachers whose performance is inadequate cannot be dismissed, while teachers performing satisfactorily have little incentive or encouragement to improve. | Enables districts to weed out staff members whose performance is inadequate and to encourage those whose performance is satisfactory. This is the component of school management most important for assuring an effective relationship between board policies and direction, the needs of the community, and the accomplishments of the staff. |

Source: Compiled by author.

95

The relatively high score in organization reflects the successful efforts of most school districts to clearly define responsibilities. Emphasis on responsibility for performance is not always adequate, however. And substantial opportunities exist for improving staff communication and participation. While a few districts may be able to reduce administrative staffing, I have not found any major opportunities to do so.

A simple and operational process of planning and evaluation exists in about 20 percent of school districts today. Sufficient involvement and participation of the management team as well as board and staff in the process of using information and judgment to improve performance are major opportunities for improvement. Because organization and operation of the district are involved, rather than any added staffing, no additional costs would be expected.

Performance information also rates about a 20 percent score, with some variation among the categories. Virtually all districts have test data, but only about 10 percent adequately analyze and use these data to improve performance. Because the data are already available, little if any additional cost is involved. Parent and teacher surveys that are simple, straightforward, and modest in cost are an especially major improvement opportunity. The majority of districts have an adequate grip on costs; for those that don't, of course, the importance of measuring up to this standard is considerable.

Administrative evaluation and compensation is adequate in about 20 percent of school districts. Many, because of their relatively small size, may not need a formal plan; the right principles and policies will be adequate without a formally defined structure. For larger districts, some outside assistance will probably be required in the development of a plan.

Teacher evaluation and development is the most important opportunity for improvement. Only about 5 percent of districts are currently meeting the standards set forth in Chapter 5. Because of the high potential impact on performance, this is an especially important improvement opportunity.

If this assessment of the current state of school management in practice is reasonably accurate, then there would seem to be an extremely significant opportunity to improve school performance by strengthening management. The cost would be quite modest. This is, I believe, a fair representation of the situation today. The payoff from strengthening management in terms of school performance

— student learning, public confidence, parent satisfaction, teacher morale and productivity, and overall cost effectiveness — is substantial.

RESULTS OF GOOD SCHOOL MANAGEMENT

What would happen if these management standards were fully met? And is this feasible? It's too early in the development and documentation of results from good school management to be definitive in answering these questions. But, based on my experience, these are the results in well-managed districts, contrasted to those in poorly managed districts.

Well-managed districts achieve student progress of at least one year annually, i.e., their eighth graders achieving at a level seven years in advance of their first graders. Districts that are poorly managed, on the other hand, tend to fall behind. This rule of thumb holds true whatever the beginning level, so that the impact of socioeconomic differences and other influences on student achievement are substantially eliminated.

Parent satisfaction and public confidence in districts that monitor these factors, using surveys and personal contact, are high in spite of negative national trends. Effective use of staff and local communication channels to promote good performance is essential. Districts that are poorly managed tend to have a public that is well aware of their performance faults. The loss of public confidence brings on a downward spiral of staff morale, support, student learning, and so on.

Teacher morale, satisfaction, and productivity in districts that are well managed can be sustained at a high level. Of course there are always risks and hazards, and no organization can have a perfect record in this regard. But a sustained high level of good and improving performance can be achieved.

Costs in well-managed districts are typically below average, and increasing less rapidly than inflation. Whether or not costs can be reduced depends upon how high they were to begin with. I have seen districts cut as much as 25 percent from their budget without reducing performance, but this is certainly not to be widely recommended. Some districts do have substantial opportunities to reduce costs in administrative and teacher staffing levels, salaries, or the costs of supporting services. Many do not. But all should be able to operate with costs effectively controlled in terms of the programs that are desired by the community and the performance that is actually being achieved.

Obviously if more districts met these management standards, and the correlation with performance that we have drawn is reasonably correct, then the traditional trends of school performance would be reversed. Test scores would increase instead of decline. Public confidence and staff morale would be rising instead of falling. And costs would at least be controlled in proportion to results, if not actually reduced; and they would be increasing less rapidly than inflation. As indicated, no additional cost of management is involved. Indeed reduced costs would be expected to some extent.

Equally important to these substantive improvements in school performance, and essential to their achievement, is the positive contribution of better management to effective and successful teamwork among boards, administrators, and teachers. This would not only help to offset the many pressures toward conflict and fragmentation inherent in the circumstances of schools today, but would contribute positively to improved performance as well. These are the results that should be expected, based on my observations in districts that have moved to strengthen management.

Board confidence in district performance, support for administrators and teachers, and willingness to delegate to the district's staff are all substantially improved. This is in sharp contrast to boards that are fighting among themselves or with administrators and teachers. While some board reaction to evidence of declining performance is only natural, and part of the responsibility of a board, positive steps to improve performance and build confidence are more important. Continued conflict and adversarial relationships will never turn around the declining performance trends. Evidence of good performance and action to improve it where indicated, on the other hand, will support board confidence and willingness to delegate. In turn, the morale and productivity of both administrators and teachers will be raised, and the possibility of sustaining public confidence and parent satisfaction will thus be improved.

Administrative responsibility and success in maintaining good school performance and results will be enhanced. Consequently, the functions of the school management team will be appreciated, and their contribution to good school performance will be maintained and improved. Beyond their own job satisfaction, and a reduction of unnecessary turnover at superintendent level, the contribution of administrators to improved teamwork and performance in schools will benefit materially.

The pride, confidence, and teamwork of both teachers and other personnel will be greatly improved, and as a result performance, productivity, and results will also shift into an upward cycle. Teacher evaluation and development will contribute positively to the skills and achievements of each teacher. While I don't believe that unions should be expected or encouraged to disappear, their functions will be focused somewhat more narrowly on economic issues, where they can be successful in improving the economic position of teachers in our society, a worthwhile and vitally important objective if fair compensation is to be achieved. On the other hand, their function in areas other than compensation may be limited to providing a safety valve that will assure continued attention to communication, participation, and any other concerns that teachers may have. While negotiations can never be expected to be completely without an adversarial character, the ability to limit bargaining in an orderly and constructive process within the context of good management, communication, and participation will reduce the adversarial character. And, I hope, teachers will broaden their bargaining interests to incorporate public, parents, students, and community.

Finally, the historic contribution of education to the political and economic development of our country would be restored, and public confidence rightly given an adequate foundation. Once the corner is turned, the boost in morale and productivity from rising performance and demonstrably good results with adequate documentation and evidence would give a further boost to performance. This is a phenomenon that I have witnessed in many districts that have moved from an unmanaged to a managed state. I believe this can be accomplished not only in every school district, but on a national scale.

Exhibit 6.2 shows in more detail the connection between good performance and good management, and between poor performance and poor management. On the left side at the top are shown the basic indicators of good performance, according to the concepts discussed above, and at the bottom are shown the features of good management that correlate with good performance. On the right side, warning signs of poor school performance, and the management characteristics of districts that fall into this category, are shown.

EXHIBIT 6.2
Indicators of School Performance and Management

GOOD PERFORMANCE AND MANAGEMENT	POOR PERFORMANCE AND MANAGEMENT
Performance	**Performance**
• Student learning high, balanced, appropriate to district objectives.	• Student learning lagging, not monitored.
– On average, 1 year student growth for each year in school.	– Less than 1 year growth annually.
– Departmental standards appropriate and fulfilled.	– No standards, or standards unmet.
– Low achieving students monitored and helped.	• Dissatisfaction among parents, teachers, and/or taxpayers.
• Parents, teachers, and public satisfied with school performance.	– Parents dissatisfied.
– Parents satisfied with progress of their children, in general and all significant details; action to correct deficiencies.	– Taxpayer revolt.
– Public satisfied with school performance and costs.	– Teacher unions, strikes, complaints.
– Teachers satisfied with program quality and working conditions.	– Adversarial relationships.
– Improvement opportunities identified and action taken.	• Costs not controlled, rising more than inflation.
– Relationships of teamwork, trust, and confidence among teachers, administrators, and board members as well as parents, public, and students.	
• Costs controlled, rising no more than inflation; staff ratios monitored, costs scrutinized.	
Management	**Management**
• Board emphasizing teamwork and performance, information and reports from staff, delegating with confidence.	• Board fighting with itself, staff, or public.
Well-defined organization and responsibilities emphasizing performance.	• No performance responsibility.
– Open, active communication with parents, public, and staff.	– No communication.
– Participation of staff and parents.	– No participation.

100

- Availability, analysis, and use of performance information.
  - Student learning, test data.
  - Parent survey.
  - Teacher survey.
  - Cost data.
- Planning and evaluation in schools, departments, district; involving staff, administrators and board.
- Administrative compensation based on performance, with structured decisions.
- Teacher evaluation fair and effective, operational in practice, with positive development and adequate due process; communication, trust, and teamwork; teachers responsible and effective.
- Simple, practical, effective management systems, with emphasis on performance and results, communication and teamwork.

- No performance information, or not analyzed and used.
- No planning and evaluation.
- No basis for administrative compensation, set in a climate of distrust and conflict. Possibly, an administrative union.
- Teacher union needed to force equitable treatment of professional staff. Teachers demoralized, productivity declining.
- Too much administrative overhead and paperwork, without acceptance of responsibility for performance.

Source: Compiled by author.

These indicators are abbreviated, and therefore necessarily superficial. But they reasonably represent our experience in well over 100 school districts and, I believe, are justification for universal application of good school management principles in every school district.

I don't mean to imply, however, that the connection between good management and performance is easy or automatic. Hard work as well as good intentions will be required of school administrators and teachers to bring about the transition described. Schools fulfill such a vitally important and sensitive role in our society that they will never be free from unrealistic expectations or unreasonable complaints. Turning around performance once it has started to decline, and developing management at such a time, is made both more important and more difficult by the decline itself. The results are so important to our society and to our economy, now that public services represent the predominant share of all our activities, that we simply must persevere to turn the situation around.

IMPROVING PERFORMANCE THROUGH BETTER MANAGEMENT

In light of the inadequate management development of education, it's surprising that the decline in performance has not been steeper. The reasons it hasn't deserve to be mentioned — primarily the talent, professional skills, and good intentions of educators. And it is these same reassuring characteristics of educators that make me optimistic that education will succeed in improving performance through better management.

Educators generally have a very high level of dedication to their work. I don't believe this has diminished very much, in spite of the difficulties of the past decade. This basic character of teachers has held up performance in spite of the difficulties faced by education, and is the foundation on which a turnaround of national school performance trends can be based.

A considerable amount of talent is available in education. Both teachers and school administrators reflect a high level of talent and a careful selection process. This has served us well in spite of the inadequacy of management techniques available and the scarcity of sources to develop them.

Education is extremely important to Americans, and, given the small size of most school districts, members of the community, both parents and taxpayers, have often been able to complain and get action where performance deteriorated. Consequently, many school districts of relatively small size, particularly those where community identity is fairly strong, continue to perform well.

The talent available for staffing the teaching positions, relative to the number of positions available, has improved over the past decade. The ability and performance of younger teachers is, I believe, significantly better today than it was 20 years ago.

The technology of teaching has made great strides in the past decade or two. In spite of the criticism of many educational innovations, rightly so in many cases, some have succeeded remarkably well. Although it goes by many names, individualized instruction and the general loosening of the authoritarian structure of teaching seems to me the most impressive. The willingness of education to consider these innovations, adopt and implement them in spite of the dramatic changes they require for teachers, is evidence of an internal vitality that has been a major cause of minimizing the decline that has occurred.

Many of the more serious trends noted earlier in this book may have already reversed themselves in recent years. Students today are more conservative and more interested in traditional school activities and academic work. Obviously this is a trend that will be as beneficial to the schools as the distractions of the 1960s were distressing. Collective bargaining in education is settling down to a much more constructive pattern; strikes are less vicious and difficult, although there is still much to be concerned about in this area, and much to be improved in staff relations.

Many school districts today, in spite of the difficult challenges, are finding ways to develop management policies and practices, and to make them work — to maintain and improve student learning, to develop and sustain the confidence of the public, parents, and taxpayers, to communicate with the staff and develop relationships that lead to confidence and productivity, and to control costs. These accomplishments are the basis on which a turnaround of educational performance will, I am convinced, occur during the next decade or two. But it would be unfortunate if that turnaround came too late to save education from the imposition of such weighty state and federal controls or such an irate public that forces were put into effect that couldn't be countered. Therefore, this book seeks to inform others of practices that are working successfully, to explain them to educators and the public, and thus to foster a better understanding of why the decline has occurred and how to help turn it around.

Education is leading the way in developing and implementing new techniques of public management that are equally needed in other public services. Education benefits from a sound and responsible structure (except in big cities) and is perhaps the best performing public service in this country. This is part of the reason that we are tending to give it more and more responsibility for social services outside the traditional scope of educational responsibilities, rightly or wrongly. Contrasted to social services, whether delivered by governments or through private agencies, education is far more effective and efficient. Education in the United States stands first on a world scale, at least in breadth of coverage, while several other government services in European countries are superior to ours — social services, health care, and city planning, for example.

Education is the most important of our public services in terms of its impact on each of us. It is already the best managed and most productive, standing with industry and agriculture as fields in which the United States has successfully given leadership to the world. Our educational system, even in its slightly deteriorated form today, is still second to none in the world.

Many districts are performing extremely well, especially considering the difficult circumstances in which they operate today. Changing attitudes toward authority on the part of both teachers and students, declining enrollments, public concern, collective bargaining and strikes make it evident that school officials are working in challenging circumstances. In this difficult context, many are performing admirably, judged against the standards set forth in this book, and based on my own management consulting experience with more than 100 districts.

But many districts are not doing so well, the national test score averages are going down, and some districts are in deep trouble. Both federal and state governments are being invited and encouraged to take action — often detrimental to performance — by general public concern and staff frustration. Some districts are caught in a declining spiral of performance that may be irreversible. Some of our children are being educationally handicapped. And public service costs are rising beyond what our economy can afford.

Clearly new management policies and practices are needed to meet these new requirements. Neither the talent nor the techniques of teaching are at fault; both have improved, even while performance has declined. Rather, as with many of our public services, more resources, more talent, and better techniques are not enough — good management is needed to improve productivity to meet needs at a price we can afford.

This book shows educators how they must proceed at all levels. It will also help the consumers of education — parents, students, and taxpayers — understand how well their schools are performing, and what to do if performance is not satisfactory. Most districts will find that boards, administrators, and teachers are able to turn around the situation; some have already done so. Other districts will find that the community at large must take action.

If teachers are to regain the public confidence and respect that they deserve, and the dignity and motivation required, and if our schools are to have public confidence, staff morale, and cost control, then management must be strengthened. This requires defining new management principles and practices and, more difficult, applying them in practice. Some districts have already pioneered in doing so. Thousands of board members, administrators and teachers in the districts with whom I have worked have helped me learn what good management in education is and how it can be applied in practice to make schools more productive and performance better.

Because these policies and practices have only recently been created, tested, and applied, they are not yet documented. This retards their communication, wider application, and use as the basis for further improvement. I hope this book helps to communicate these successful school management policies and practices more widely. Examples of their implementation, and results, are presented in detailed, specific case studies in Part II.

PART II

EXAMPLES OF GOOD SCHOOL MANAGEMENT

This section provides specific practical examples of school management techniques that work to improve performance, using case studies of implementation, results, and follow-up. The background and purpose of the cases and some suggestions on what they mean and how to use them are contained in an introduction to Part II following this page.

7

INTRODUCTION TO PART II:
Background and Purpose of the Case Studies

This introductory section of Part II explains the meaning of the case studies individually and collectively. It provides a road map to give you some idea of where we're going.

Individually, each case study exemplifies the practical, successful application of one of the essential components of good school management today. Collectively, the case studies represent a comprehensive model of school management containing all key components. While each district will need to adapt these techniques to its own circumstances, every district needs each of these components. The cases should help strengthen your understanding of school management and your contribution to its development and thus to the improvement of school performance.

These case studies have been selected from my management consulting experience over the past two decades, and developed into a model of school management primarily through two additional experiences: First, through my work in the *School Performance Research Project*, which I directed for the Illinois Association of School Boards during the past few years with funding from a group of Chicago area corporations and foundations; this developed a

---

These case studies are available in somewhat longer form in the Northwestern School Management Course Case Study Book. This course was developed for and is taught at the Northwestern University School of Education. The book is available from the author c/o: Institute for Public Management, Suite 365, 550 West Jackson Boulevard, Chicago, Illinois 60606.

comprehensive model of school performance information, evaluation, accountability, and management. Second, in the *School Management Course*, where the case studies have been developed into a curriculum with teaching methods and materials through support of the Dean and faculty of the School of Education at Northwestern University, and an Advisory Council of Superintendents.

Of course my clients also deserve a great deal of credit for the management innovation and practical experience that underlie these case studies. To all of these people I am most grateful.

The case studies exemplify in practical, successful application the concepts and techniques of school management described in the first part of this book. These management techniques have been applied in a variety of settings representative of the diversity that exists in school districts and communities: all extend beyond the experience of a single district. While these exact same approaches may not apply precisely in any other specific situation, they have each worked successfully in at least several of the more than 100 districts with which I have been personally involved. Many have been widely emulated in other districts.

Even though the case studies have been shortened for inclusion in this book, you should find that they convey a sense of the original situations for which they were written. While they are each quite specific in relating to an individual district, they have been selected to add up to an overall concept of management as well. This introduction will give you some sense of the purpose and meaning of the case studies. The introductory material to each chapter and case study further describes the situation in which these studies were done and some of the consequences.

Of course I can't fully share with you in this written form the class interaction that accompanies these case studies and the sharing of student experiences that enriches the material here. Typically the case study provides a vehicle for sharing experiences from each student's district. It is then possible to meld this experience into a common perception, with each student leaving with a definite opinion of how this specific technique might apply in his or her situation. I will try to fill in explanatory comments to help give you an appreciation for this. By relating your own experience to what is described, you should find a similar value in the case studies.

Here is a description of each of the chapters and case studies that follow, explaining how they fit into the overall concept of school management and how they're related to each other:

SUMMARY OF CHAPTER 8

This chapter contains the first two case studies. They explain the connection between good school performance and good school management and the contrast between this and the opposite situation of poor performance and management. The differences are emphasized, but well within the limits of my own experience and observation.

Case Study One: Introductory Case Study — District A and B

The purpose of this overview is to create a sharper yet realistic sense of the difference that good management makes in school performance. Teachers, administrators, and board members should — and do — find that they can position their own district on the spectrum of management and performance suggested by the contrast between District A and District B. This positioning occupies the entire range between District A and B.

Case Study Two: Descriptions of Well-Managed School Districts

More complete descriptions of some districts used in the composite of District A are in the second case study, to ensure that one district isn't singled out as a model of good management and performance. These districts include a variety of size and character, to show that good school performance and management are correlated no matter what the circumstances.

A participative class exercise to which we often return (after proceeding through the subsequent case studies) is for all students to try to determine how they would act (as chief executive or in another position) to move from District B with poor performance and management to District A with good performance and management. Or each student can take his or her own school or district at the present time and develop a similar plan of action. You may find it useful to think about this or carry out this exercise, as you read the first two case studies initially or later after you have completed the others.

The management techniques being used by successful school districts to achieve good performance are exemplified in the case studies that follow. One of the most important components is covered in the next chapter: using performance information to build confidence and morale and improve performance, with a participative, communicative process of management that pulls the organization together and builds teamwork.

SUMMARY OF CHAPTER 9

This chapter contains three case studies. They describe a model of information, planning, and evaluation and then give specific examples of its two main components: surveys of parents and teachers and analysis of test data. These case studies are presented here because this kind of performance information is essential to building confidence, morale, and teamwork in school districts today. Without it evaluation, communication, and even fairness and integrity are not enough, at least in today's circumstances of public concern and staff unions.

Case Study Three: Summary Report of the School Performance Research Project

The first case study in this chapter summarizes the results of the School Performance Research Project. Written primarily about information and evaluation, it also touches upon the relationship of these key management functions to communication and participation, and thus provides a good general summary of school management requirements as well. Therefore — and because performance information is essential to effective administrative and teacher evaluation, compensation, and development — this case study appears first. I believe that once you appreciate and understand how information can be used to build morale and confidence, you will see its critical importance to fair and effective evaluation and successful fulfillment of the mutual responsibility of board and staff for good school performance.

Case Study Four: Parent and Teacher Surveys

Parent and teacher surveys, designed to be practical and straightforward, are a key ingredient in the development of effective channels of communication with customers and staff. Other valuable sources include the community, other members of the staff, and students. But parents and teachers tend to provide the most critically important information. These particular surveys were in a special education program. The same format with somewhat different questions has been used in more than a score of other districts.

These surveys differ from most that I have seen in education. They are more hard-hitting and straightforward. Some who have tried surveys have failed to understand that thinking about the action to be taken before the survey is designed is critically important, that surveys must be kept as simple as possible, and that committees often water down the questions so that the answers aren't really very meaningful. About 90 percent of the surveys I've seen done in school districts suffer from these defects. If you follow the formats described here, at least you won't make those mistakes.

I think you'll also see from this case study how easy it is to interpret these data in terms of targeting on certain aspects of school performance as possible improvement opportunities. Because schools have hundreds of different areas in which performance could be improved, and opinions vary as to which are most in need of and deserving of improvement, the need to provide some focus is critically important. Confidence in allocating resources and time can then be much greater. These questionnaires are easy to interpret in this respect.

Extremely complicated, however, is deciding exactly what the underlying problem is and what to do about it. This takes a great deal of time and as much judgment and intuition as analysis and data. You should get some sense of that process too from this report.

Surveys like this are also important in assuring that administrators and teachers understand that communication with parents and staff in a school district is essential. This more anonymous and analyzable channel of such communication should not replace but support and augment more personal and informal channels of communication. In the modern world, communication with customers and participation, trust, and confidence in staff relations are critical ingredients to the good performance of any organization, and schools are no exception.

Case Study Five: Test Data Analysis

The second specific example of information used to improve performance is the analysis of standardized achievement test scores in an urban elementary district. In this district dramatic growth of student learning has occurred over the past several years, starting from a level at about 80 percent of national average growth figures, which is typical of the performance of urban school districts today. This district has found a way to turn around that situation, and to achieve at substantially above national average growth levels, as the data in this analysis indicate.

Part of the key to doing so is using performance information to build confidence and morale while identifying improvement opportunities. You will see in this example that several specific improvement opportunities were identified. A few years later all were realized. Obviously a great deal of hard work was required in this district to achieve these results. I believe that without sound test data analysis the opportunities would not have been identified or realized. The satisfaction of the staff and their motivation to produce the work and achieve the results indicated would not, I believe, have been forthcoming were it not for the sense of accomplishment, confidence, and support developed on the part of board and administrators for the good job that was being done.

Not more than 20 percent of the districts I have seen are doing a good job of analyzing test scores to identify and realize improvement opportunities. Educators are not usually inclined to quantitative analysis, for understandable reasons; the human dimension of their job requirements is obviously much greater. Those inclined to quantitative work might have made better accountants than teachers! Schools are relatively small organizations, and it's not always easy to find someone who combines analytical skill with the organizational position from which to be objective and forthright.

The analysis of standardized achievement test scores is difficult. It is my belief that the scores are completely adequate for group analysis, as indicated in this example. But this takes some analytical sophistication, and has required many decades of development and use of these tests. It does not put aside the very real criticisms of these tests from other viewpoints: whether tests are a proper basis for college admissions, whether they discriminate unfairly, and whether they are always adequate for the purposes they are sometimes used. This example concentrates on their great value in improving school performance and building confidence and morale, for which purpose I believe they are completely adequate.

Naturally the information is only valuable to the extent it is used. Some of the most important uses are exemplified in these two case studies: building confidence and morale and improving parent and teacher satisfaction and student learning. Another important aspect of the use of this performance information is to support constructive, fair, and effective evaluation to employees at both administrative and teacher levels. This involves evaluation, compensation, and development, discussed in the next two chapters.

SUMMARY OF CHAPTER 10

This chapter contains three case studies. They show why so often today school boards are confused about setting administrative salaries, and administrators are becoming frustrated and sometimes angry as a result. Specific examples are given of how to evaluate administrators, including the superintendent, and how to compensate them based on performance to fulfill board responsibility for accountability and to keep administrators satisfied and productive.

Case Study Six: School Management Compensation Survey Report

Obviously a key ingredient of good school management is for administrators to be compensated fairly and equitably in a way that is satisfying, motivating, and encouraging to good performance. This issue has proven a major stumbling block in many districts, as shown by the findings of the School Management Compensation Survey involving more than 40 school districts over the past several years. In this report are described the somewhat chaotic and discouraging situations found in many districts. Boards have become confused about how to make administrative salary decisions in an era of public concern, the taxpayer revolt, and staff unions. They have brought to the board table uncertainties about performance, presumptions about adversarial relationships with the staff arising from collective bargaining, and sometimes their own personal frustrations with salaries in an era of inflation and economic difficulty.

Historically, school administrative salaries have typically been justified without formal policies. Under today's circumstances, this approach has quite often resulted in impasse at board level, or in damaging action such as holding back decisions on administrative salaries until after teacher salaries are negotiated and then rewarding administrators with smaller increases than teachers, or singling out individual administrators for special reward or penalty based upon personal viewpoints of individual board members or specific incidents. One result, rising membership of administrative unions, should not be surprising. To remedy the situation, policies and practices like those described in the rest of this chapter need to be more widely understood, accepted, and implemented.

Case Study Seven: Administrative Compensation and Evaluation Plan

The Administrative Compensation and Evaluation Plan in Case Study Seven is a composite of several that have worked quite successfully over a period of several years. They employ some of the analytical techniques used to support business management compensation plans: organizing the salary plan into categories of positions based on responsibilities; relating these categories to the marketplace of prevailing salaries for similar jobs; keeping salary levels within these categories in specified ranges; and rewarding good performance, both the typical pattern of development during the first few years in a job and the possibility that exceptionally good performance will occur thereafter. All of these factors are encompassed in the plan shown. On the other hand, the pitfalls that have proven damaging in districts that have tried merit pay for administrators without adequate technical counsel or human relations sensitivity are avoided: bonus plans that unduly reward individual performance at the expense of teamwork, plans that offer such a modest performance bonus as to be offensive yet costly, plans that are not founded adequately on performance evaluation and information and thus break down in the face of perceived unfairness, or those that lack relationships of communication, trust, and confidence.

Case Study Eight: Superintendent Evaluation

In this case study the special issue of superintendent evaluation is described in a model that has been used successfully in many districts. It is simple and straightforward. It depends heavily on the planning and reporting process and on the performance information described in Chapter 9. Some approaches to superintendent evaluation require too much time or invite board meddling. This model recognizes the limits on board time and the desirability of a relatively informal approach. Critically important are performance information documenting results coupled with a simple, straightforward planning and reporting process operational at and linking together all levels of the organization from boardroom to classroom.

Administrative evaluation and compensation is extremely important in establishing the responsibility and reward of administrators for the total performance of the district for which they are responsible. Administrative performance typically impacts upon the performance of many teachers. There is always the possibility that any administrative structure will become bureaucratic and remote from the work being supervised. School administrators have not always had a tradition of performance responsibility, sometimes preferring to handle tasks that could not be accomplished in the classroom, without taking responsibility for performance.

Equally important to administrators, and in some respects more difficult, is the evaluation of teachers. This — perhaps the single most critical weakness in school management today, and the most important improvement opportunity — is considered in Chapter 11.

SUMMARY OF CHAPTER 11

This chapter turns to what is probably the most difficult and important aspect of management in education: personnel policies for teachers, particularly evaluation and development.

Case Study Nine: Interview Notes

The first case study provides a composite of scores of discussions I have had with thousands of teachers during the past ten years regarding their dissatisfaction with teacher evaluation. I am convinced that these concerns are founded in fact. The inappropriate and unproductive approach to teacher evaluation still found in most school districts today is unfair and intolerable. Teachers complain that evaluation is negative, unfair, threatening, demoralizing, and unproductive — and they're right. They say that development is practically nonexistent, and they're right again. Because the only logical beginning point for the improvement of this situation is to find out what teachers dislike about the present process, why it isn't working well and what requirements would have to be met for its improvement — and the only place to find this out is by talking to teachers — that is where this chapter begins.

Case Study Ten: Specifications for Teacher Evaluation

The second case study in this chapter shares specifications for teacher evaluation and development in one particular district. It takes the general conclusions of the group interviews a step further into an analysis of the present situation and recommended approach to evaluation relating to one particular district.

Case Study Eleven: Teacher Evaluation and Development Plan

This case study contains a model teacher evaluation and development plan that has been working very successfully for a number of years. It is not the only approach that I have seen work successfully, but in my opinion it is the best. It involves a process of evaluation initiated by the teacher, designed to be positive and beneficial, incorporating multiple views and information, and resulting in individualized development, funded by the board and initiated by each teacher. If every school district were to move toward a positive and effective development and evaluation plan like the one described in this report, the improvement of staff morale and productivity would be dramatic.

Essential to the confidence, support, and teamwork required for evaluation in a field such as education is the performance information described earlier. And without administrators who are geared into performance through responsibility, evaluation, and compensation there is little that teachers can do to improve their own evaluation and development policies. Therefore, successful teacher evaluation is closely related to the other components of good school management discussed earlier, and in some respects it is the most important.

SUMMARY OF CHAPTER 12

In this chapter three case studies cover the most important aspects of school board responsibilities and the subjects of financial planning and cost control.

Case Study Twelve: Financial Planning and Cost Control Model

The Financial Planning and Cost Control Model provides a simplified approach to school finance designed to help school boards focus on the key factors involved and to keep them within their control.

Unfortunately school finance is inappropriately complicated at the present time. It needs to be reorganized by state legislatures to provide a more comprehensible format for school boards, administrators, and the public. We are at such an early stage of development of public management that there still remains to be invented the double entry bookkeeping system and accounting profession provided to business in Venice and London many centuries ago. While these inventions will not be identical for public services, they will be similar in employing a simple concept that builds confidence and simplifies understanding and control of the financial aspects of education. The current taxpayer revolt reflects the inadequacy of our practices at present.

In the meantime, short of this comprehensive reorganization of public finance, those responsible at board and staff levels should focus on the key factors involved. These are revealed in the Financial Planning and Cost Control Model. Particularly emphasized are staffing ratios and salaries, the complexity and uncertainty of financial planning, and the political character of financial decision making in schools.

Case Study Thirteen: Decision-Making Model

A second case study in this chapter shares the analysis and consideration of school closing and integration in one district. It is impossible to cover in detail the many different kinds of decisions school districts are being asked to make today. This case study should serve mainly to provide a flavor of the complexity and factors involved on both the human and financial sides of the question.

Case Study Fourteen: School Board Responsibilities

The last case study on school board responsibility seeks to complete the circle. It presents an overall concept of evaluation for school boards. And it defines the key features of their responsibilities on both the financial and human sides of the organization. This ties together the impact on performance of good management, the Financial Planning and Cost Control Model, and the board's responsibility for monitoring performance and assuring the development of fair and effective policies and practices for administrative evaluation and compensation and for teacher evaluation and development. An overall concept of management in the form of a public management model is also shown.

In total these case studies represent all of the major components of good school management essential to good school performance today. If every district were to accept and implement these practices a considerable improvement in school performance could be achieved. Based on my direct experience this might be on the order of 20 percent. Well-managed districts I have worked with seem to be achieving results that are about 20 percent better than those at the other end of the scale, and generally doing so at lower costs. The confidence and support developed through good management render the staff more satisfied, fairly compensated for a job well done, and more productive.

Good school performance has immediate benefits to the teamwork and satisfaction of school boards, administrators, and teachers. It would obviously benefit students, parents, and taxpayers in our school districts today. The long-run impact on the health of our economy, our capacity as a country in every field of endeavor, and on both the human and financial implications of such problems as unemployment, crime, and welfare would be dramatic.

In the following chapters of Part II of the book, each case study is preceded by an introduction describing background, situation, and results. Where appropriate it is also followed by comments in transition to the next case study. Some of the case studies are excerpts from actual reports prepared in the course of consulting work, with the names of the original client districts changed. Others represent composites of experience in several districts. In some of the case studies, certain sections have been omitted, to permit including the maximum number of case studies and to focus on the most useful material. Omissions are indicated by ***.

8

THE WELL-MANAGED
SCHOOL DISTRICT:
An Overview of
School Management Requirements

In this chapter two case studies are presented. The first provides a summary comparison of two districts, one a high performance, well-managed district, the other a low performance, poorly managed one. The second case study describes the well-managed, high performance district in more detail, including 5 variations based on a composite of 25 districts.

These case studies should sharpen your understanding of the correlation between good school management and good school performance. They show the substantial difference that good management makes both in: (1) internal teamwork, communications, relationships, and morale; and (2) the achievement of students, satisfaction of parents, and overall cost effectiveness and value received for the investment of taxpayers.

Well-managed districts typically exceed those that are poorly managed in terms of performance by a margin of at least 20 percent. And this difference affects both areas of performance — costs may actually be lowered by 20 percent while results such as annual student learning gain are improved by 20 percent.

The human equation that makes this difference is always somewhat mysterious. The management techniques described in later chapters are one key factor. Another, of course, is the human relations skill to implement them successfully in practice. Perceiving and understanding the performance difference that these management techniques can make is critically important.

I have seen districts at both extremes of the spectrum indicated by the contrast between District A and B in the first case study. More districts today fall toward the B end of the spectrum. That is why national indicators of school performance are declining.

Because understanding the connection between school management and performance is so important, these case studies appear first. They are followed by specific, concrete examples of the management techniques that can turn around this performance. While the leadership of superintendents and principals is also critically important, in my experience that alone — even when coupled with the honesty, integrity, and good intentions essential, and typical, of both teachers and administrators — is not enough under today's circumstances. More professional management is also needed.

CASE STUDY ONE
Introductory Case Study: District A and B
Comparing a Well-Managed District with a Poorly Managed One

INTRODUCTION TO CASE STUDY ONE

This introductory case study provides a summary comparison of a high performance, well-managed district with one that is at the low end of the scale.

District A is a composite of the high performance districts further described in the second case study later in this chapter. District B is in the reverse situation, a composite of the worst performance and management practices in schools.

Although the contrasts are drawn fairly sharply in this summary comparison, everything described has been actually observed in a number of situations. School districts today are increasingly differentiating themselves into these two ends of the spectrum. Some are building on strength in spite of the many negative pressures we're all working with today. They have succeeded in achieving an upward spiral of performance in which success in one area tends to reinforce and contribute to success in others. In other districts, a downward spiral has set in; problems are compounded in their negative impact. While the contrasts may be a little extreme, they are realistic, and serve to demonstrate the difference that good management can make in school performance.

I use this case study in my course and seminars to open up initial discussion of the problems occurring in school districts today. It helps to build awareness of the contribution that management techniques can make to solving these problems. The widespread nature of the problems usually comes out in these discussions, and their intensely human character, with the obvious caveat that management techniques by themselves can't make good decisions or maintain good relationships. This human complexity, diversity, and intensity of feelings in school districts on the part of parents, teachers, and students is a critically important factor in determining school management requirements.

CASE STUDY ONE

The following material is organized in three sections: key questions, a description of the local situation at board, administration, and teacher levels, and a brief indication of performance in these two districts.

Key Questions

1. What are the negative pressures on school districts today, and what problems are arising as a result:
    — For board, administrators, teachers?
    — For parents, students, taxpayers?
2. What accounts for the differences between District A and B?
    — What is causing the problems of District B?
    — What management techniques can help District B become more like A? What else is required? What training is needed?
3. Consider these questions from several viewpoints:
    — Superintendent
    — Principal
    — Board member
    — Parent
    — Taxpayer
    — Teacher

Description of the Local Situation

Board

District A. The board is confident of district performance. Information is given through test score analyses, surveys of parents, teachers, students, and graduates as well as reports at each board meeting by administrators and teachers on content and performance of programs. Half of each board meeting is devoted to this purpose. Consequently, the board is comfortable in delegating to the management team; periodic reminders by the board president or superintendent are still needed to ensure that the board does not overlap into administrative responsibilities, and each new board member requires a period of time to become familiar and comfortable with district performance and board operations.

There is a high level of parent satisfaction in the community. Cost comparisons showing effective control are publicized; while not many people in the community understand these data in detail, the general feeling of high performance and effective cost control is widespread.

The board is further reassured by policies and practices that tie salaries to performance, giving the feeling that taxpayers are getting their money's worth, when coupled with other performance indicators. As a result, the board is supportive of administrators and teachers – a conduit for community appreciation.

While problems and incidents arise, and board members have individual concerns and perceptions, these can be handled in a context of general confidence in performance.

District B. Board operation is characterized by conflict, adversarial and combative relations. The board is frequently fighting among its own members, and board meetings are long and argumentative. As a result, it has become increasingly difficult to attract citizens to board positions. Those who are attracted seem abnormally concerned about school performance, in response to national publicity or personal concerns, and interested in conflict.

The board has little or no information on district performance. Every incident or problem causes fear of deep-seated inadequacy and widespread general concern.

Board conflict is distressing and confusing to the staff. Administrators and teachers see their salaries being set in an atmosphere of conflict, confusion and resentment over performance being delivered. Board comments imply that neither teachers nor administrators are worth what they're paid.

Administrators have persuaded the board that firing incompetent teachers is illegal or impossible; therefore, the board has the impression that unsatisfactory performance is tolerated, and that salaries increase annually for each teacher whether or not performance is satisfactory.

Administration

District A. The management team works closely together under the superintendent's leadership. Much of their time is spent planning, evaluating programs and individuals, and in communication. Because of an aggressive, thorough approach to evaluation and information, there is considerable confidence in good performance.

Although there are many incidents and problems with respect to children and programs, there is time to deal with them in the context of a generally supportive and confident setting. Administrators see their salaries and employment being determined in an atmosphere of appreciation and support.

The superintendent has been in his position for about a decade. (As in the case of District B, his long-serving and more authoritarian predecessor was fired after the first lost referendum, school closing, and staff unionization.)

District B. Administrators feel exposed to criticism and uncertain of their treatment. The board has singled out individual principals for criticism, questions, salary actions, in some cases with an apparent desire to dismiss individuals.

Administrators view the protection won by teachers through unions with envy, and would like to achieve the same protection for themselves. The time required for protecting and defending each administrator's position, and the secrecy and tension that results, absorbs a considerable amount of energy for the administrative team.

Evaluation of programs, administrators, and performance is inoperative. Evaluation policies, procedures and formats exist, but no one takes them seriously — because nothing occurs as a result, i.e., no teacher has ever been fired for poor performance, or rewarded for good results. There is no positive development to improve performance.

Administrators are uncertain of their responsibilities, particularly whether the superintendent and board will back them or whether their authority will be undercut by the teachers dealing directly with the board.

The high level of conflict makes it difficult if not impossible for a superintendent to sustain employment for more than two to three years. Following the early retirement of a rather authoritarian and patriarchal superintendent who had served the district for more than a quarter of a century — shortly after the first school closing, teacher strike, and lost referendum — the district has seen a new superintendent every two or three years.

Teachers

District A. Teachers demonstrate high performance, satisfaction, confidence, and morale. In this particular district, teachers are not represented by a union. Unions, if any, function mainly as a safety valve, and bargaining agent for salaries and benefits.

Teachers are participatively involved in every level of decision making and every important issue — 80 percent of district teachers serve actively on various committees in about 30 different subject areas. A considerable amount of time is invested in these activities.

Channels of communication for teachers are available through formal surveys, insistence that administrators deal openly with teacher concerns, and such techniques as the superintendent conducting a needs assessment involving personal interviews with each teacher each year with respect to supplies, facilities, etc.

Performance information is widely available in the district, and serves to support confidence in good performance, even though improvement opportunities are frequently identified. Teachers are perceived as managers in the classroom, with access to all available performance information.

Teacher evaluation is exceptionally thorough, well defined, and accepted and supported by teachers. It leads to substantial efforts to improve teacher performance wherever opportunities or interests are identified.

District B. Teachers carry on in spite of the confusion and conflict at board and administrative levels of the district. The tradition of independent entrepreneurial responsibility sustains about 80 percent of the performance that teachers might be able to achieve under more favorable circumstances. Nevertheless, frustration, tension and the loss of morale directly affects performance.

Teachers are actively interested in the union and seek to use it to improve working conditions to the fullest possible extent, including periodic strikes and frequent grievances. Union leadership is more aggressive and in some respects more successful than district administrators. The balance of power between the union and management favors the former.

Teachers feel blamed by parents for the perceived poor performance of the district. A downward cycle of morale and performance compounds the generally negative effects of more difficult children, parental concern, the taxpayer revolt, and declining enrollment and resources.

Performance

	District A	*District B*
Student Learning	Student growth of one year or more for each year in school in each subject area.	Eight months student growth per year; declining ratio of district scores to national averages.
Parent Satisfaction and Public Confidence	Parents generally satisfied, documented in parent surveys. Contrast to impression that national school results are declining.	Impression of confusion and conflict in teaching and administration, arising from board behavior, lack of evidence of good performance, dissatisfied parents.

	District A	*District B*
Staff Morale, Performance, and Satisfaction	High level of staff participation and communication, relations of trust and confidence, fair and effective evaluation and personnel policies. Consequently, high morale, performance, and satisfaction.	Little opportunity for staff participation and communication; adversarial relationships; evaluation, development and personnel policies considered unfair by the staff. Consequently, low morale, performance, and satisfaction.
Financial Planning and Cost Control	Demonstrated cost control in relation to inflation and enrollment; especially staffing ratios. Financial planning several years into the future. Periodic analysis of each important cost area.	Costs rising in proportion to inflation and enrollment. No forecasting. Public impression of declining cost effectiveness.

CASE STUDY TWO
Descriptions of Well-Managed School Districts

INTRODUCTION TO CASE STUDY TWO

In the second case study, an ideally well-managed school district is described. This is based upon a composite of the 25 school districts with the highest achievement in performance and management that I have actually seen in practice, selected from more than 100 districts with which I have worked during the past decade. These best-managed districts represent a considerable diversity of wealth, community character, socioeconomic levels, instructional methods, and students. Five of them representative of this diversity are described in this chapter — the first one in some detail, and the others more briefly. These five have been selected to represent these categories:

1. Three medium-size elementary school districts in relatively well-to-do suburban areas.

2. Seven elementary school districts in middle to lower class communities. The particular one described is adjacent to a major city, in a working class neighborhood, urban in character, racially balanced (50 percent black, 50 percent white) and successfully integrated.
3. Five high school districts, in a variety of middle-class communities.
4. Five larger urban school districts in medium-size cities, including elementary and secondary levels, and a substantial minority population.
5. Five special education cooperatives and regional programs — providing services for handicapped children, serving large geographic areas and children from several districts.

These districts have been selected because they are the best managed and highest performing ones I have had contact with. They also represent a reasonable cross-section of the kinds of communities, students, and problems with which schools are dealing today. I haven't tried to describe each district in detail individually, but to indicate differences between them.

While the result is intended to be an ideal model of school management and performance, everything described has actually occurred in practice. There's nothing theoretical or utopian about the model. It is simply a collection of the best management methods currently in use, and reasonably represents goals that every district should be able to achieve. There is nothing about the ability of students or the character or wealth of the communities that is essential to the results being achieved.

CASE STUDY TWO

District A-1

This is more detailed background information on the same district described as District A in the Introductory Case Study. It is a medium-size elementary district in a fairly well-to-do area with an enrollment of about 1,500 students. Some decline in enrollment has been experienced during the past 15 years, from a peak about 50 percent higher than at present. To accommodate that decline a school was closed in the early 1970s, with some controversy. Shortly thereafter, a referendum to raise the local tax rate was defeated. Union membership was increasing. The superintendent, who had served for quite a long time, was fired.

The new superintendent was found by the board through the help of a distinguished older faculty member at a nearby university. A relatively young man, he had no prior experience as a superintendent. However, he brought a deep conviction of the importance of management and a willingness to develop and apply the techniques that were needed whether or not they already existed in the field of school administration.

His style of management seemed to have two key features. On the one hand, he was willing to be fairly tough about such matters as cost control, staffing ratios, and taking action where required to dismiss or encourage another career or early retirement – or whatever other approach might make sense under the circumstances – to eliminate from the district's staff teachers who were not performing satisfactorily. On the other hand, his style of management opened up communication and participation in the district to an unusually extensive degree. More than 80 percent of the district's teachers were involved in more than 30 committees, participating in making decisions ranging from curriculum to fringe benefits.

As an example of the extent of this communication, each teacher was personally interviewed by the superintendent each year, as a part of a needs assessment process that developed a list of specific items for subsequent prioritizing by the administrative staff and where feasible board approval for expenditures. The majority of teachers' requests identified in this process could be met immediately from the existing district budget, usually having to do with minor physical facility matters, supplies, equipment, and the like.

Almost immediately upon assuming the superintendency, the first issue faced by the new superintendent was a need to reduce current spending by about 25 percent, in order to accommodate the district to the recently lost referendum that contributed to firing the former superintendent. After extensive consideration and analysis, a reduction in virtually every category of spending of about 25 percent was accomplished. For many years thereafter the district lived in a very frugal financial situation; a relatively flat trend of assessed valuations in spite of obviously rising property values in the early 1970s required careful financial management. Detailed analysis and publication of comparative statistics relative to other nearby districts tended to support the impression of a financially sound and well-managed district in which taxpayers generally need not fear the wasting of their investment in schools.

One feature of this administration has been the extensive use of surveys. The first one involved the entire community, on a sampling basis. Areas of satisfaction and concern were identified, on the part of both parents and taxpayers without children in the public schools. As in most districts the latter group amounted to more than 80 percent of the community. This survey was repeated in subsequent years, providing evidence for improvements in areas targeted.

Three other target audiences for surveys were students, teachers, and parents. Student surveys were conducted annually for several years, as a way of providing feedback to teachers at all grade levels. After a few years, results of these surveys contained so few surprises that it was decided to limit them to new teachers in the first few years of their experience, and to other situations where questions might arise, on the part of the teacher or others, with respect to student attitudes in a particular classroom.

Teachers were also formally surveyed periodically, in addition to the personal communication indicated on the part of the super-intendent. This anonymous reporting channel for teachers assures that all district administrators understand the importance of upward communication on the part of teachers, that they must be responsive to it and that any teacher concerns would always have a way of surfacing. These surveys are repeated periodically.

District parents are also surveyed annually. While these results also have tended to become reasonably predictable, there are always individual classrooms or subjects about which concerns are expressed. Sometimes these are problems which if caught early can be readily resolved. Others prove more difficult, such as changing community desires with respect to the kinds of lunches that are served, concerns about busing that arise from changes in roads or sidewalks in town, or concerns about homework or individual grade levels that change from time to time, sometimes because of changes in programs and faculty and other times inexplicably.

These surveys provide an ongoing source of information on district performance as perceived by its constituents. Because problems are identified early, action can be taken to improve performance wherever the perception indicates this is required, or to change perceptions if this proves to be the problem. As a result of this flow of information, the board, administrators, and teachers as well as parents can be reassured that performance is being maintained at a reasonably high level, in the perception and to the satisfaction of the district's constituents. While this doesn't guarantee perfect results, it does assure that a reasonably high standard is maintained, and that these perceptions are regularly monitored and considered. In effect, these surveys of customer satisfaction give school districts the same kind of performance indicators that a business might obtain by analyzing its sales data or asking its customers. It is information that is fundamental to understanding customer satisfaction and maintaining public confidence, especially in a near monopoly situation where sales statistics are obviously unavailable.

The overall effect of these surveys on communication goes well beyond the surveys themselves. Their existence not only assures a channel of communication and encourages its use, but also prevents issues from becoming too serious and surfacing only at the time of a formal survey. This psychological impact is probably more important than the results of the surveys themselves, although those results have definitely caused action that can be shown to have improved results in subsequent surveys.

Another important feature of management in this district is an extremely aggressive attitude with respect to evaluation. A great deal of time is spent on it, and both the process and forms have been designed to ensure a consistent, fair, and effective approach at all levels of the organization. With respect to teacher evaluation, this district has an elaborate structure involving specified factors and detailed descriptors for each. Principals in the several schools work closely together as a committee to ensure consistency among buildings. Criteria were developed and tested in a highly participative process. (In other districts I have seen equally effective teacher evaluation systems that emphasize the process, and some that involve no forms at all.)

A third characteristic of this district is the analysis of test scores as an indication of student academic progress, and emphasis on the use of these test scores to improve performance. They are reported annually in summary form to the board. They are analyzed in great detail by the district's management team — to identify opportunities for improvement, changing patterns over time, and trends that need to be monitored or require action. For example, a flat spot was discovered in the average annual growth of students at fifth grade, and steps were taken to remedy this over a period of years.

The most important level for analysis and action with respect to student achievement test scores, however, is in the classroom. Each teacher is given an opportunity at the beginning of the year to assess the prior achievement levels of the students in his or her class that year, and to project results at the end of the year, based on both prior achievement and ability. At the end of the year, results are again provided to each teacher. Consequently, teachers have the opportunity to use these data for insight into the relative balance of teaching effectiveness among subjects, and the overall profile of each class in terms of high achieving/low achieving students and those who may have special difficulties. Particularly important is the general satisfaction and confidence that comes from knowing that your own performance is being noticed.

In all of the districts I have seen that provide this kind of fair and effective analysis of test scores, their potentially threatening quality is soon defused. Teachers and administrators working together seem to achieve a consistently high level of student growth in all subject areas. Of course there are variations from year to year and subject to subject that can never be completely removed or fully explained.

A particularly unusual feature of this district is its merit pay plan for teachers. This predated the current superintendent, but was previously an artificial plan without substance. Under his direction, the evaluation, communication, and information procedures described above have been used to undergird this system and to give it substance and meaning for the staff. As a result, the staff has an unusually high level of satisfaction in their jobs, seeing rewards matched to performance for themselves and for others in the district. Relatively young teachers who perform well are rewarded at above average levels. Senior teachers performing at a high level are also well paid. Teachers experiencing difficulty, and those whose performance in the first year or two of employment indicates that tenure should not be given, are encouraged out of the district.

While a merit pay plan is not essential to good school performance and management, it is a powerful plus. However, other districts that I have drawn upon in developing this management model have found that once the evaluation, information, and communication components of good management are met, the additional use of merit pay may not be necessary.

Of course none of these management techniques precludes difficult personnel situations where inadequate performance arises after a long period of satisfactory or superior results. These incidents are always difficult in school districts and require individual handling and extensive remedial and developmental efforts in the context of meeting all due process requirements. No district is immune to these problems. The well-managed ones are distinguished by facing and dealing with these issues, rather than by pretending that they don't exist or can't be managed. In my experience, teaching is such a demanding and challenging field, and so subject to deteriorating results in consequence of personal problems of individuals, that about 1 percent of teachers each year seem to fail in spite of excellent prior records. Some of these can be saved, but some can't. Teacher evaluation must recognize this fact, or the accumulation of inadequate teachers quickly erodes district performance, learning, confidence, morale, and cost effectiveness.

The combination of information, evaluation, and communication described above provides the foundation for an unusually high level of confidence and satisfaction on the part of the community and parents as well as the board. The board is able to function as a channel of community support, appreciation, and gratitude to the teachers of the district for the good job they are doing. This atmosphere of confidence and support sustains the board in the face of the kinds of difficult decisions, issues, and problems that always arise in schools. No district is exempt today from the occasional dissatisfied parent, for whatever reason, whether the fault of the schools or a reflection of a personal problem in the home, the complaint about a bus stop moved to the wrong location, disagreement over the proper placement for a child receiving special education services, or the myriad of other problems with which school administrators and teachers deal on a day-to-day basis from the first separation of kindergarteners from their parents to the growing up of teenagers. However, where these problems can be addressed in the context of a general atmosphere of confidence and support based on evidence, communication, and evaluation, they can almost always be resolved and handled satisfactorily.

Board meetings in this district are relatively short and uneventful. They require about two hours a month. More than half of the time is spent in receiving reports from teachers and administrators on individual programs. Over a period of several years every program in the district and each school is presented in this fashion. Many of the district's teachers have thus had an opportunity to present, explain, and defend their programs and performance personally to the board. All district administrators attend every board meeting. Approximately another two hours per month is spent in meetings of the three board committees, education, planning, and finance, each of which meets on an as-required basis three or four times a year.

Channels of communication from school to community are very open and beneficial because of an unusually active local parent/teacher group. The relationship of board and administration is extremely close and supportive but rooted in sound evidence of good performance, tough evaluation, and the assurance that salaries are tied to performance. The feeling that taxpayers are receiving value for money and the gratitude of the board to the faculty on behalf of the community for the good job that is being done are especially evident. The effect of this feeling on the motivation and morale of the faculty, though no small accomplishment of the administrative team, in turn assures a continuing effort to improve performance and expand programs. That of course is a slow process, but the addition of programs, acceleration of student progress, the closer tracking of low achieving students, and initiatives in math, science, computers, foreign languages and other areas are indicative of this continuing progress.

Because the faculty is provided with satisfactory opportunities for communication and participation, fair and soundly based evaluation, and the satisfaction of having their good performance rewarded, they have lost interest in the benefits to be gained from union membership. The district board and management team have adopted this posture as district policy, noting with some satisfaction the strong sense of teamwork, high morale, and good performance in this district contrasted with the conflict and fragmentation apparent elsewhere. Under these circumstances, only a handful of the members of the faculty have found it worthwhile to continue paying union dues.

However, the option of individual membership and collective representation by a union is always available, and the district is known to be a target for the organizing efforts of local union agents. A few years ago a law suit was filed challenging a personnel action, but the suit was later dropped after some considerable efforts on the part of union organizers to generate controversy within the district. This nonunion position requires an extremely effective and extensive effort on the part of the district's administration to be sure that evaluation is fair and communication open.

The time demands and talent required of administrators are also recognized. The district board has been quite aggressive in seeking to provide fringe benefits and salary increases for the faculty that are in no way behind those prevailing in the area and if anything slightly ahead of other districts. However, because of the district's policy of balanced staff between younger and older faculty members, its average salaries are actually quite a bit below the prevailing levels in other similar districts in the area. As a result, a combination of lower costs for taxpayers and higher school performance to the benefit of parents and students is being achieved. It is recognized that if the district were to slip in meeting the faculty's expectations for participation, communication, and fairness in personnel policies, the ready availability of unions today would provide quick access to making those unmet desires known. In a sense the existence of unions proves an advantage under these circumstances at no cost to the faculty in dues, functioning as an available safety valve.

District A-1 is one example of several districts I have worked with in communities that are generally above average in socioeconomic level. Performance is at a level where dramatic improvements are not really likely. Identification of marginal improvement opportunities, and gradual strengthening and adding of programs in certain areas, provided the focus of progress.

To balance this description, and provide a contrast of greater improvement in a situation where opportunities existed, District A-2 is described below. This district is one of over a dozen medium-size elementary districts that I have worked with in middle to lower class socioeconomic communities. This district, although a suburb of a major city, has many of the characteristics of urban school communities. And it is one of a few districts I have worked with whose beginning performance was such that considerable improvement was possible in student learning as indicated by average annual growth data. Because of the improvement opportunity and what was actually realized, this district also serves as the case study in Chapter 9 on using test data analysis to improve performance.

District A-2

This is an elementary school district bordering a major city with an enrollment of about 1,200 students. The community is similar to many inner city neighborhoods. Its residents are about equally divided between whites and blacks. Highways, railroad tracks, and housing patterns divide the community into three fairly distinct areas, with a pattern of segregation in housing that concentrates the black population mainly in one of these three areas. Another area is predominantly white. The third, separated by railroad tracks, is predominantly comprised of residents who have moved in from the Appalachian area. Each of the three areas thus has a character somewhat distinct from the rest of the community.

Several years ago this district was required by state mandate to integrate its schools. The superintendent, relatively new to the district at that time, developed a plan that involved an unusual combination of grade levels, and elimination of the junior high school. Results have apparently been highly successful. While community housing patterns remain segregated, the schools have been successfully integrated. Most kindergarten, first, second, and third grade students are in one building, feeding into two buildings with fourth through eighth grade, while one school remains a K-8 building with a single classroom at each grade level.

During the ensuing years a considerable emphasis was placed on the analysis of test scores and the provision of support to teachers for the development and improvement of instruction. A team of three master teachers was organized to provide this support. Of the four school principals, two are black women, and two are white men.

The emphasis on support to teachers, improving academic performance, and analyzing test scores — and the reorganization of the district eliminating a junior high school — were all believed to have contributed to a marked improvement in academic performance over a two to three year period. This seemed to be accomplished in spite of the fact that the actual calculation and presentation of test scores to individual schools did not accurately reflect teacher performance, and could have been rather threatening and inaccurate if so interpreted. Nevertheless, a marked improvement in student learning as indicated by test scores was achieved.

At about that time a more comprehensive test score analysis was completed and considered at length by the management team and in summary by the board. While highly reassuring as to the progress made over this period of time, further opportunities for improvement were also revealed.

A second analysis two years later showed that virtually all of these improvement opportunities had been realized. The explanation for this marked improvement seems to lie in the efforts of administrators and teachers to fill in these gaps once they were identified. Obviously this speaks well for the intentions and talents of those involved. I believe this is typical of the motivation and dedication of educators, if adequate performance information and analysis are available.

This two-year period was also one in which this district found itself in some financial difficulty, and had to reduce spending levels fairly sharply. Thus the improvement in results was achieved in the face of declining resources. The district's support team for teacher development continued to operate during this period. There seems little question that they contributed positively to these results. The test data analysis involved is shown as Case Study Five in Chapter 9.

Both of the first two districts described are at elementary level. To provide balance, District A-3 is a high school district. At this level, the importance of department heads in the planning evaluation process should be noted. This district also reflects the typical pattern of more adversarial staff relations at secondary level. The particular district described here has been selected from about a dozen districts like this that I have worked with.

District A-3

District A-3 is a high school district in a suburban area close to a major city, in a community of about average socioeconomic characteristics. This district has a superintendent who has served for about a decade, following an earlier career in nearby elementary districts, and thus has a long-standing association with this community. Enrollment has declined sharply during this period of time, resulting in the closing of one of the three high schools in the district. This was accomplished in a carefully planned process over a period of several years.

The district's management style might be characterized as streamlined. Some years ago department head positions were eliminated in favor of a smaller and full-time management team comprised of seven directors reporting to a principal in each building. For instructional management purposes several departments are grouped together under each of these directors, while one oversees pupil personnel services and another building operations.

Like many districts in similar geographic areas, this district has experienced a somewhat complicated and difficult period of labor relations during the past 20 years. Initially one of the first school districts in which teacher unions successfully organized, it developed a complicated and lengthy contract during the 1960s. In the 1970s, labor relations within the district would appropriately be categorized as adversarial with frequent conflicts. Several strikes occurred. This situation limited the participation and communication of teachers in the management process and inhibited some communication channels. Certainly it made the job of management team more difficult. A very sound approach to teacher evaluation and well-defined administrative responsibilities, evaluation, and a compensation plan were developed in spite of these challenging circumstances. Recently, labor relations have turned to a more positive and settled format. It appears that teachers have now elected union leadership more oriented toward a positive working relationship with the district's administrative team. Bargaining is concentrated more narrowly on economic issues. The possibility of improving channels of communication, staff development, and relationships is recognized, and being taken advantage of.

Board operations in this district are notably more volatile than in either of the two previous examples. Certain issues such as the school closing and related issues of building utilization sparked considerable local controversy and publicity. Nevertheless, in spite of board controversy and a difficult labor relations situation, a long-serving superintendent who is relatively aggressive about management development has successfully held the situation together. Obviously continuing to maintain staff and board relations successfully in this district presents a greater challenge than in the first two examples. The administrative compensation plan developed by this district and used successfully for the past several years serves as the basis for Case Study Seven in Chapter 10.

District A-4

For the fourth example I have chosen a unit district in a medium-size city. This district is typical of about a dozen I have worked with in this category. Two particular features seem to distinguish districts in small to medium-size cities, making them more similar in many ways to large urban school districts than to the relatively smaller suburban ones described in the three previous examples. First, at a board level, these districts are subject to public attention in a way that most suburban districts are not. Typically cities of this size have both television and radio coverage of school board meetings as well as widely read local newspapers. Consequently the political role played by school board members is a fairly heavy one. The handling of this situation required on the part of the superintendent is a good deal more complicated.

In some of these districts, I have seen an extraordinary diversity of background and position in the community represented on the board. One, for example, included on its board the owner of a local company, the president of a local bank, a former teacher in the district now employed by another district, a carpenter, and a foreman in the local steel mill. Such diversity would be uncommon in a suburb. Beyond presenting the superintendent with a more challenging job of handling these people and positioning himself successfully in this setting, such boards often seem to succumb to pressures that exist in the suburbs but are perhaps not quite so strong. These tendencies are to allow personal concerns to dominate behavior in a board meeting or to develop into a pattern of internal board conflict that overtakes almost every issue that the board faces.

The second feature that seems more challenging in these districts is staff relations. In this respect scale is not an advantage. Relatively small districts have been able to succeed without well-developed formal channels of communication because personal respect for the individuals involved and frequent contact between teachers and administrators is relatively easy in a small community with a few schools. These tasks become extremely difficult and sometimes impossible in a large district, especially if board and staff relations are strained.

Another complicating factor in districts of this size as in many major cities is the insulation and protection that key administrators in the district have been able to achieve for themselves. Because of the stresses and strains at the board level and in staff relations in such districts, and partly to protect themselves against unfair board actions, principals have often developed a highly protective posture verging on if not actually formally acknowledged as collective bargaining. In districts where principals have moved in this direction it can be extremely difficult for a new superintendent to take over sufficient authority to survive for very long. Or if a superintendent is successful in asserting his authority, very often it is at the expense of other more positive programs.

District A-5

It seems worth briefly describing a special education agency as an example for two reasons. One, these programs represent a great accomplishment of education in the last decade or two, and are now a very important part of most school districts. Second, they represent a major point of contact between the school system and other social service agencies.

A number of features of these agencies stand out in my experience as distinguishing and especially challenging management requirements. One is that, like most social service agencies, they require very careful definition of the job to be done and the business they're in, if staff energies are to be focused on practical and appropriate objectives. Second is the organizational complexity of these agencies; they typically span several school districts and must maintain successful relationships with teachers and administrators in spite of this cross-cutting organizational pattern. Under these circumstances the need for communication and evaluation to build confidence and support is perhaps even greater than in a regular school district. For this reason I believe the communication and evaluation reflected in the case study shown in the second part of Chapter 9, drawn from a special education setting, is particularly useful. Of course another characteristic of these agencies is that the services they're delivering and the problems of children with which they're dealing tend to be extremely complicated, in many cases on the forefront of what is known about human nature and development.

In the particular regional special education program from which the case study of parent and teacher surveys in Chapter 9 is drawn, the history of its development was quite volatile. In its early years some resentment developed at the federal funding being channeled in this direction, and at the somewhat removed level of organization at which these services were being provided, relative to local school districts. As a result of some dissatisfaction with this structure and the feeling that an expansionary definition of the role of this agency was being planned, a restructuring occurred involving a change of name and a more narrow definition of the mission of the agency as well as a considerably revised organizational structure. The new organization included a sunset clause that provided for reaffirmation of its mission and structure after three years, or termination and revision. Consequently the evaluation study shown as Case Study Four in Chapter 9 was partly designed to provide information for this required decision.

Management Implications

Unfortunately it isn't feasible to describe in detail the other districts on which I have drawn in developing the management concepts and practices set forth in this book. Many of them are also performing successfully and managed soundly, and I have drawn freely on their experience as well as the five districts described above. A few of them are in trouble, and conflict and fragmentation in those districts are also reflected in the thinking and writing here. All of this experience — the five districts described above, another twenty considered as examples of good management and performance and also used in developing these case studies, and more than 100 other districts with whom I have worked and had personal firsthand contact during this period — has provided the basis for the management concepts set forth in the first part of the book and the case studies that follow. Unfortunately these case studies cannot fully reflect the human dimension of feelings, attitudes, concerns, and relationships in the districts involved. Nevertheless, I hope these examples will provide you with reassurance that these techniques can work in any setting.

Perhaps it is worth summarizing here the key general management principles reflected in the descriptions of this chapter, and then the specific techniques exemplified in the case studies of the next four chapters:

1. Organization needs to be well defined in terms of responsibilities and relationships, with communication and participation of teachers in management.
2. Performance information and reporting of program progress, content, and evaluation to boards must be well developed, and on

this basis board confidence in district performance, delegation to the staff and support of the district sustained.

3. The availability, analysis, and use of information to improve performance is perhaps the single most important ingredient and improvement opportunity, for management in education. In my experience with organizations in education, government, and industry, one of the most important management practices is the use of information to indicate where performance is good and where improvement opportunities exist.

CONCLUSION OF CHAPTER 8

If one aspect of management had to be singled out as most important it would have to be the overall acceptance of responsibility for performance and the maintenance of an internal process of communication and evaluation adequate to sustain good performance. This human equation of school management is of central and critical importance.

One of the best ways to encourage the climate of trust and confidence, communication and support that is essential is to begin with performance information. The information required is relatively straightforward, and either already available or relatively inexpensive to produce. The process is difficult to initiate without some information, and it is unlikely to be successful in building confidence and support without documentation of good performance and identification of improvement opportunities.

For all of these reasons the logical first element of management to be considered in the following case studies is performance information, and the concept of school performance that underlies it, with specific concrete examples of this performance information in actual use. These are the subjects of Chapter 9.

9

PERFORMANCE INFORMATION:
Planning and Evaluation to Improve Performance

This chapter contains three case studies providing a comprehensive introduction to the collection, analysis, and use of school performance information in a fair, effective process of program planning and evaluation.

Case Study Three is the summary report of the School Performance Research Project. This project was sponsored by the Illinois Association of School Boards and funded by a group of corporations and foundations. The purpose was to identify information and evaluation policies and practices to improve school management and performance. The research also consolidated my experience in consulting with more than 100 school districts into a model of school performance and management.

Case Study Four provides specific examples of parent and teacher surveys, a key component of performance information. And Case Study Five presents a detailed and comprehensive analysis of standardized achievement test scores.

The use of performance information to support confidence and morale and to identify and achieve improvement opportunities is one of the most important components of school management. Without it neither administrators nor teachers can hold together the communication and participation, confidence and support, and positive, constructive approach to evaluation and compensation that are essential to good school performance. With performance information, not only can improvement opportunities be identified and addressed, but the good performance that most schools are already achieving in most areas can be fairly recognized and rewarded and used to build confidence and support of the board and staff as well as of parents and community.

The techniques used to develop this performance information are simple, straightforward, and inexpensive. They do require willingness of administrators to accept responsibility for performance, an attitude that is growing but by no means yet universal. Some school administrators still feel they should be judged only on a political basis without documented information and evidence. Where school boards find they are being served by administrators who have not yet adopted a more modern presumption of managerial responsibility for performance, either training, firm demands, or new administrators may be required, preferably to be considered in that sequence. I have seen all three work effectively. Most effective, however, is for administrators to take the initiative in helping their boards to understand the purpose of information and then to develop the information that is required, recognizing the hazards and pitfalls involved and the need to assure adequate communication and participation of teachers in this process.

Of course the human relations of convincing the staff that positive and constructive consequences will result from having information is a great challenge, especially in a field as hard to measure as education. But, once they recognize its importance, most administrators are able to accomplish this successfully. The information needs to be used in a process that is fair and effective, participative and humane, with adequate communication and participation of the staff. But the process cannot be started without the information. And the information is relatively easy to develop. Therefore in most districts it makes sense to start with this aspect of management development and then proceed to the more challenging tasks of administrative evaluation and compensation and teacher evaluation and development.

CASE STUDY THREE
Summary Report of the School Performance Research Project

INTRODUCTION TO CASE STUDY THREE

This report summarizes results of the School Performance Research Project. The study was conducted over four years, to identify information and evaluation policies and practices that can improve school management and performance. Improving school performance and management, one of our largest and most important public services, is obviously of crucial importance to all of us, not least those of us involved directly in education. I am grateful to the districts participating, to the Illinois Association of School Boards who sponsored the research project, and to the corporations and foundations who funded it. In addition to this summary, the complete text of the report, as presented to the Illinois Association of School Boards, is also available separately.

CASE STUDY THREE

The purpose of the research is to help school administrators provide the leadership to improve school performance — by success- fully meeting the new management requirements of schools today — and thus to raise student learning, public confidence, staff morale, and cost effectiveness.

The management requirements of schools today are much tougher than ten or twenty years ago, for two main reasons: (1) Changes in the circumstances of education have rendered traditional school administrative practices obsolete; and (2) the human and qualitative character of education makes it challenging to manage.

The management requirements are, specifically: (1) increased emphasis on performance and results, including evaluation, informa- tion, and compensation; and (2) continued emphasis on teamwork, in spite of pressures toward conflict and fragmentation.

This case study appeared in a somewhat shorter form as an article in the January 1982 issue of *The School Administrator* published by the American Association of School Administrators. Appreciation for their permission to reproduce it here is gratefully expressed.

School administrators who understand and can meet these new management requirements are successfully maintaining and improving school performance. But not all administrators have yet succeeded in this, and school district problems, because these requirements are not being met, affect both teachers and administrators.

Teacher perceptions that evaluation has traditionally been unfair and inaccurate in education are correct, based on our experience. With the help of unions, teachers are now able to subvert these practices. Consequently, evaluation has broken down in most school districts today. Yet teachers feel unfairly criticized and underappreciated. The result: declining morale and performance. Without evaluation, teachers not performing satisfactorily cannot be dismissed, and the job satisfaction of good performers is diminished. A downward spiral of performance and morale is encouraged, evident in many big cities today.

The impact on administrators is more often in strained relationships with the board. Board members are prone to conflict, overinvolved, unwilling to delegate, and resist administrative compensation decisions. The board may leave salaries until after negotiations with teachers, then hesitate because of uncertainty as to what administrators do, or uneasiness about district performance. The result: reduced morale, strained relations, high superintendent turnover, and even some administrative unions.

These problems of teachers and administrators are contributing to the school performance decline. There is nothing wrong with the talent or technology of teaching. Both have improved over the past decade or two. The human equation of organization and management is breaking down, because of the changes outlined earlier, and the management requirements they have created. The following paragraphs will discuss the techniques necessary to meet these requirements.

Base Program Evaluation on Performance Information

A comprehensive, participative process of reporting within the district and to the board is needed in order to build confidence, support, and teamwork. This must include evidence of performance.

Use of Performance Information

While actual use of information to improve performance is the purpose, analysis is essential, and the information must be available.

Standardized achievement test data should be analyzed to indicate student learning, and used to improve it. These data are available in virtually every district, but rarely used effectively. They must be reported to the board and analyzed by administrators and teachers. Annual student growth for each grade, school, and classroom should be compared to district history and national norms.

Parent satisfaction should be surveyed regularly, with clear-cut and straightforward questions emphasizing customer satisfaction, and with results analyzed and action taken. Teacher opinions should also be obtained through surveys, adding professional judgment to complement parent opinions, and assessing working conditions and evaluating practices as well. Financial information should be used, for planning, analysis, and cost control — especially staffing ratios.

Planning, Evaluating, and Reporting on Program Performance

A process of planning, evaluating, and reporting on program performance should be developed in detail for staff and summary for the board. This should include regular presentations to the school board by administrators and teachers, describing and evaluating programs.

Inside the district, analyzing and applying judgment to performance information should be a major part of the job of every administrator, and to some extent each teacher.

A formal planning process should be established whereby principals and department heads assess the status and situation in their respective areas, set forth conclusions (needs, problems, strengths, weaknesses, and priorities), and recommend action. Paperwork should be minimized, e.g., a one-page plan summary for each school or department. Staff should also take advantage of multiple views, e.g., a committee of principals or department heads.

Assure Fair Evaluation

It is essential to relate program evaluation to the performance of each administrator and teacher, and then to compensation —

definitely for administrators and if possible also for teachers. The "if possible" is required because only a handful of districts today have sufficiently well-developed programs of staff communication, participation, and evaluation to consider performance-based compensation for teachers. Where these prerequisites are met, paying teachers for performance results in higher productivity and job satisfaction. Most employees prefer to feel that their salaries are earned, and the public naturally views such a basis for compensation more favorably.

In summary, every district should have a formal administrative compensation plan that links salaries to performance. Program evaluation with performance information should provide the basis. Traditional teacher evaluation practices are woefully inaccurate and unfair, and rightly criticized by teachers. Needed is a more constructive, participative, communicative process, geared to individualized staff development, with dismissal proceedings separate from the primary purpose of staff development.

Build Teamwork through Management Responsibilities

Equally important to the evaluation and information techniques described above is the need for continued emphasis on teamwork in school management, in spite of pressures toward conflict and fragmentation. The need for good working relationships and defined responsibilities among board, administrators, and teachers is as great today as it was 20 years ago — it's just more difficult.

The board must support and build teamwork with administrators and teachers in the district, in spite of collective bargaining. Board overinvolvement usually grows out of genuine concern with school performance. Performance information and evaluation is essential to building the board confidence that is a prerequisite to delegation. Administrative leadership in an era of board concern with performance and staff unions is obviously challenging — and impossible without the evaluation and information techniques described above. And teachers must be viewed as part of the management team, the first line of responsibility for performance and results. Their participation and communication in the management process are critically important to good school performance.

The assumption of management responsibility for performance and results at all levels of the organization is essential. School districts cannot function successfully with parts of the organization permanently in an adversarial relationship, or operating without responsibility for performance and results.

How do districts measure up to these school management standards? Not very well, at least not yet. The standards have grown out of changes in the circumstances of education. Administrative practices and skills have not yet caught up. Fewer than 10 percent of school districts today are using information and evaluation fairly and effectively. Perhaps 20 percent have gotten administrative compensation and evaluation onto a reasonably sound basis. Fewer than 5 percent have teacher evaluation and development soundly established. Obviously this leaves much room for improvement. When that improvement is accomplished, the national trends of school performance will turn up.

Administrative leadership is the key to moving forward with these essential management improvements in school districts. The support and understanding of boards and teachers are also needed. And I would hope that those of us helping to define and teach school management also have something to contribute.

CASE STUDY FOUR
Parent and Teacher Surveys

INTRODUCTION TO CASE STUDY FOUR

This case study presents the results of parent and teacher surveys conducted in a regional hearing impaired program (RHIP). Also included is an analysis of student learning.

Although these surveys relate to a special education program, they are quite similar except for a few specialized questions to those used in regular education. Their emphasis on hardhitting, straightforward questions readily comprehensible to parents and encompassing all of the major features of school performance is essential to effective surveys. In a regular school district, internal analysis would include more extensive treatment of school by school and grade by grade performance, and provision would be made for feedback of the information to individual teachers on a confidential basis.

These surveys were provided to all parents and teachers (not a sample). There is value in asking all, whether or not a response is received. And the results of a comprehensive survey tend to be more convincing in terms of action to school administrators. The additional cost is modest.

The surveys and student learning analysis were completed during the same year, because of a need to reconsider the status of the agency involved at the end of that year. Normally these are sequenced during a two- to three-year period, so as not to overwhelm administrators with more information than they can learn to analyze and use successfully at one time.

Results in this report generally reflect the highest level of parent satisfaction encountered in such surveys. This reflects a very high level of program performance in the parents' view. It is probably also affected by the fact that this particular group of parents complained strongly about a fragmented program in this region a few years earlier, a situation subsequently corrected by this agency.

Teacher opinions provide more basis for action. Subsequent internal, more detailed interviewing of teachers with regard to concerns identified in this survey revealed two particularly interesting points.

First, while paperwork is a matter of concern and complaint, teachers did not really expect action to be taken, nor did they feel that any improvement could be accomplished. It seemed that paperwork was accepted as a necessary evil in spite of its time-consuming and somewhat burdensome character.

Second, the indications in this report for a closer and more effective working relationship between professional diagnosticians at the central office and practicing teachers in the classroom in six remote sites were found upon further investigation to be a highly significant opportunity for performance improvement. This has become a major focus of attention within the program since this report was made. Progress is being made, and the resulting opportunity to improve the level of student progress is very substantial. While this may suggest a general improvement opportunity in hearing impaired programs, it is perhaps particularly relevant in this agency because program sites are physically distant from the central office. An unusually sophisticated diagnostic staff is available there for analysis and recommendations regarding each student placed in a program.

It is expected that both the parent and teacher surveys will be repeated in substantially this form in future years, probably not every year but at least as often as every three years. The accumulation of data will improve the indication of areas of strength and opportunity for improvement, and the accumulation of historical background will improve the interpretation of data.

The impact of this report when presented to the board appeared to be one of considerable satisfaction in the good performance indicated and in the aggressive identification of improvement opportunities, as well as appreciation for the staff's courage in pioneering with such an application in a program perhaps even less measurable and more subject to political controversy than regular education.

Heavily involved in the design, development, and execution of the evaluation approach in the report were the agency director, the program director, the entire central diagnostic staff of the agency, its field supervisory team of approximately six individuals each supervising one of the programs, and teachers at each program site who were interviewed during the course of the work. This extensive participation, a leadership style strongly oriented to performance on the part of the program director, and the necessity of reconsideration of the agency's status at the end of the year in which the study was made all probably combined to make it feasible to undertake such an ambitious and pioneering evaluation effort within a single year.

This hearing impaired program serves several dozen school districts generally located in relatively affluent suburbs. As is the case in most well-developed hearing impaired programs, parents seem to take a highly active interest in program structure and quality. In this case, many have probably moved to this region because of the special education programs available here. This agency has had a somewhat difficult history in terms of its political setting and organization, as is the case with many special education cooperatives.

CASE STUDY FOUR

This report is organized in five sections: summary, parents, teachers, students, and parent and teacher surveys and results.

Summary

The project — a pioneering effort to develop performance information for a regional hearing impaired program — has had two objectives: (1) To provide an initial base of information and evaluation plan for ongoing use within the program; and (2) To contribute to the board's consideration in reviewing the Regional Hearing Impaired Program's first three years of operation.

In spite of its pioneering nature, the study is believed successful with regard to both objectives, and has developed a sound data base in theee areas: (1) Parent opinions; (2) Teacher opinions; and (3) Student learning and progress. Staff commitment to quality and willingness to pioneer in evaluation have made this possible.

The key observations based on these data are that: Parents are extremely satisfied with the programs in which their children are enrolled. Teachers also reflect a high level of satisfaction, and have identified a number of possible improvement opportunities deserving consideration by RHIP management and staff. Student progress is also encouraging, and the information developed provides a base line against which future performance can be compared. Further highlights and summary observations are shown in Exhibit 1.1.

Overall, it appears that an extremely effective job has been done in establishing and operating the RSEP Regional Hearing Impaired Program.

The commitment of RSEP's Regional Hearing Impaired Program to the highest possible quality of performance, with documentation of performance and identification of further improvement opportunities, is commendable and should be recognized and encouraged by those responsible — administrators, board, and the underlying constituent districts and joint agreements. Emphasis on performance in terms of parent and teacher satisfaction and student learning is particularly commendable in an obviously hard-to-measure, crisis-prone, and challenging program.

The emphasis on performance documented with information — to identify improvement opportunities and prove that a good job is being done — should help to provide the foundation for continuing public confidence, staff morale, student learning, and cost control. The RSEP Regional Hearing Impaired Program management team should use the performance information and preliminary analytical observations in this report as the stepping off point for more detailed analysis of performance, and ultimately action to maintain and further improve performance in the future.

Data should be gathered by the hearing impaired program in a similar format during coming years. Analysis will be more meaningful as historical comparisons are developed.

Parents

Virtually all parents are satisfied with the RHIP program. Of 92 parents responding, 84 report they are definitely satisfied with their child's educational program. The other eight indicate they are partially satisfied. None said they are not satisfied.

A similar level of satisfaction is indicated with respect to child progress, teacher qualifications, and effectiveness. This level of satisfaction applies across all subject areas and specialized services. However, there is some indicated dissatisfaction with extracurricular activities and athletic programs, particularly transportation arrangements.

These data reflect the highest level of parent satisfaction with an educational program that we have observed to date. They seem especially commendable in light of an obviously challenging program, and the reputation for consumer activism and high standards of parents of hearing impaired children. This is an unusually high level of parent satisfaction for the program to seek to maintain in the future. More detailed analysis by those involved in the program should yield further insights into possible opportunities for improvement.

Teachers

Teacher responses (to virtually the same questions addressed to parents) suggest a larger number of possible opportunities for improvement, no doubt reflecting the higher professional standards and more intensive program knowledge of teachers. However, the general level of satisfaction with programs is equally high. Of 43 teachers, 39 reported that they are definitely satisfied with the program in which they are teaching. The other four indicated they are partially satisfied. None indicate that they are dissatisfied.

Several opportunities for improvement, subject to further interpretation and judgment on the part of RHIP staff personnel, are worth further consideration: (1) The relationship of diagnostic services to classrooms; (2) Student learning in communication skills, art, and physical education; (3) Psychological and social work services; (4) Extracurricular activities and athletic programs; (5) Availability and maintenance of auditory training equipment; and (6) Reduction of paperwork and record keeping required of teachers.

As with the Parent Survey, further detailed analysis by staff personnel should produce further indications of opportunities for improvement.

Students

In addition to surveys of parents and teachers, analysis of test scores and teacher judgment were used to assess student progress and the nature of the population being served.

Whereas the Parent and Teacher Surveys drew upon survey techniques and formats tested and proven in practice, the analysis of student progress was necessarily more tentative and experimental. The following observations should therefore also be considered tentative and preliminary.

The Population Being Served

Some observations on the nature of the population being served can be made from the student progress analysis:

1. A surprisingly high proportion of students have a native language other than English — 27 out of 222 or about 12 percent.
2. Children on average were identified at age two, and began a program at age four. These averages were lower for the younger children, as might be expected, suggesting progress in early identification.
3. The average child has been in the RHIP program for seven years.
4. No substantial trends appear in the degree of impairment or use of amplification.
5. Future analyses can be compared to the base line data collected this year, and individual sites and classes can be compared.

Student Progress

A relatively high level of mainstreaming has been achieved, 38 percent of their school day on average for all students.

As indicated by curriculum levels, test scores, and the comparison of verbal to nonverbal I.Q., student progress is good, but further analysis is required.

The average child is performing on the third level of the RHIP curriculum; the information gathered permits comparing sites and classrooms on this basis. The average child is performing at a fifth grade level in reading, and sixth grade in math, social studies, and science. It appears that an increase in these scores of about one grade level occurred last year. Given an average age for the total student population of 11, these scores seem quite high. However, considerable further analytical work is needed.

Average I.Q. scores are relatively high in the nonverbal testing at 107, and as expected lower in verbal testing at 88. Moving toward closing this gap seems a desirable although obviously extremely challenging objective. Continued monitoring of progress in doing so seems worthwhile.

Teacher judgments have also been obtained with regard to student progress in communication skills and in behavior and family involvement. These data also seem useful for monitoring general program performance over time and for comparing sites and classrooms.

In general, these data are considered useful as an indication and monitor of performance. The data should have increasing value in future years as a historical base of comparison is gradually developed. The emphasis given to student progress in judging performance, even though these data reflect only a small portion of the total impact of the program on its students, is believed important to sustaining and building public confidence, staff morale, and future performance.

Parent and Teacher Surveys and Results

On the following pages (in Exhibits 9.1 and 9.2) are the actual questionnaires used in the parent and teacher survey with the answers received. This format of presentation should give you a good opportunity to understand the kinds of questions appropriate to such surveys — and indeed the specific questions asked. And I think seeing actual responses will help to see how the results might be used.

The questions are hard-hitting and straightforward and provide a ready opportunity for those with concerns about performance in the schools to express their opinion. While these questions include

EXHIBIT 9.1
Regional Hearing Impaired Program Evaluation Project – Parent Survey Results

	Definitely	Partially	No	Don't Know	Total
DIAGNOSIS AND PLACEMENT					
1. Diagnostic services through RHIP have been satisfactory.	75	12	0	2	89
2. My child's educational needs are being met in the present program.	75	17	0	0	92
3. Communication of diagnostic findings and relationships with diagnostic personnel have been satisfactory.	76	13	1	1	91
4. The proportion of time my child is mainstreamed is about right relative to abilities.	72	11	0	5	88
EDUCATIONAL PROGRAM					
1. In general, I am satisfied with the program my child is attending.	84	8	0	0	92
2. My child is making satisfactory progress in school this year.	86	6	0	0	92
3. My child likes school this year.	77	14	1	0	92
4. My child has qualified and effective teachers.	82	8	0	1	91
5. The curriculum is appropriate.	74	15	0	0	89
6. My child is making satisfactory progress in:					
— Language skills	69	20	1	0	90
— Communication skills	69	20	1	0	90
— Mathematics	67	19	1	2	89
— Social studies	59	21	2	3	85
— Science	57	20	0	7	84
— Art	66	10	2	7	85
— Physical education	68	13	1	5	87

7. Specialized school services are meeting my child's needs satisfactorily in the following areas:

– Audiological services	75	2	3	6	86
– Psychological services	55	6	1	12	74
– Social work services	55	11	0	12	78
– Case management (teacher consultant)	58	9	0	9	76
8. Extracurricular activities are available and satisfactory.	45	20	16	4	85
9. Athletic programs are available and satisfactory.	44	17	15	10	86
10. I am satisfied with the amount of homework my child has.	61	10	4	1	76
– Or: Too much					5
Too little					10
11. Auditory training equipment is available where needed and satisfactorily maintained.	56	7	3	19	85

RELATIONSHIPS AND COMMUNICATION

1. Communication and cooperation are satisfactory between parents and:					
– Teachers	83	9	0	0	92
– School administrative personnel, e.g., principals and assistant principals	66	12	3	9	90
– RHIP program personnel	66	9	1	11	87
2. Teachers and other supporting school personnel know each child as well as they should.	77	11	0	2	90
3. Children are treated fairly in school.	76	8	3	3	90
4. Parents are treated well when they visit the school.	88	3	0	0	91
5. Student behavior in school is satisfactory.	69	14	1	7	91
6. Student disciplinary policies and practices are appropriate.	71	11	2	7	91
7. Parent conferences and written reports are helpful in communicating my child's progress.	89	3	0	0	92

continued

EXHIBIT 9.1, continued

	Definitely	Partially	No	Don't Know	Total
8. Parents have an adequate opportunity to be informed about school programs:					
— In general with regard to the school my child is attending.	76	11	2	0	89
— Specifically with regard to the hearing impaired program.	87	3	1	0	91
OTHER SERVICES AND FACILITIES					
1. The school building and classrooms are appropriate.	85	3	2	1	91
2. Building and classrooms are clean and adequately maintained.	88	1	0	2	91
3. Schools are adequately supplied with equipment for educational and other purposes.	75	8	0	8	91
4. Student bus services are satisfactory.	62	20	5	1	88

Source: Compiled by author.

160

EXHIBIT 9.2
Regional Hearing Impaired Program Evaluation Project – Teacher Survey Results

	Definitely	Partially	No	Don't Know	Total
DIAGNOSIS AND PLACEMENT					
1. Diagnostic services through RHIP are satisfactory.	20	18	1	4	43
2. Placements of children are appropriate.	28	11	2	2	43
3. Communication of diagnostic findings and relationships with diagnostic personnel are satisfactory.	21	15	4	3	43
4. The amount of time children are mainstreamed is appropriate.	34	5	0	4	43
EDUCATIONAL PROGRAM					
1. In general, the program in which I teach is satisfactory.	39	4	0	0	43
2. The students are making satisfactory progress in school this year.	38	5	0	0	43
3. The students like school.	31	11	0	0	42
4. The professional staff is qualified and effective.	35	7	0	1	43
5. The curriculum is appropriate.	24	17	0	1	42
6. The students are learning satisfactorily in:					
– Language skills	35	5	0	3	43
– Communication skills	26	13	2	2	43
– Mathematics	36	7	0	0	43
– Social studies	31	7	1	4	43
– Science	28	12	1	1	42
– Art	19	9	3	12	43
– Physical education	20	10	5	8	43

continued

EXHIBIT 9.2, continued

	Definitely	Partially	No	Don't Know	Total
7. Specialized school services are meeting the children's needs satisfactorily in the following areas:					
— Audiological services	32	5	1	5	43
— Psychological services	14	20	5	4	43
— Social work services	18	19	2	4	43
— Supervisory services, case work, teacher consultant	28	9	1	4	42
8. Extracurricular activities are appropriate and satisfactory.	14	15	7	5	41
9. Athletic programs are appropriate and satisfactory.	17	16	3	6	42
10. The amounts of homework assigned are appropriate.	24	9	0	10	43
11. Auditory training equipment is adequately available and maintained.	8	13	13	7	41
RELATIONSHIPS AND COMMUNICATION					
1. Communication and cooperation are satisfactory between teachers and:					
— Parents	30	9	1	3	43
— Principals	21	14	6	2	43
— Support service staff	35	8	0	0	43
— Regular classroom teachers	24	16	0	2	42
— Central diagnostic staff	16	18	5	4	43
— Teacher consultants	29	9	2	3	43
— RHIP administrators	11	22	4	6	43
— Media services	26	10	0	7	43
2. Teachers and other supporting school personnel know each child as well as they should.	25	13	4	1	43

162

Item					
3. Children are treated fairly in school.	34	7	0	1	42
4. Parents are treated well when they visit the school.	40	1	0	1	42
5. Student behavior in school is satisfactory.	19	19	5	0	43
6. Student disciplinary policies and practices are appropriate.	21	18	4	0	43
7. Parent conferences and written reports are adequate for communicating children's progress.	37	4	0	2	43
8. Teachers have an adequate opportunity to be informed about school programs, policies, and practices:					
– With respect to the hearing impaired program.	28	12	0	2	42
– With respect to the school and district in which the hearing impaired program is sited.	27	10	1	4	42
9. Parents and community are supportive of the hearing impaired program and appreciative of its work.	22	16	0	5	43
10. Mainstreamed children are well received in the school.	20	17	0	6	43
OTHER SERVICES AND FACILITIES					
1. The school buildings and classrooms are appropriate:					
– For the hearing impaired program.	23	17	3	0	43
– For the regular school in which the hearing impaired program is situated.	35	6	1	1	43
2. Buildings and classrooms are clean and adequately maintained:					
– For the hearing impaired program classrooms.	29	10	3	0	42
– For the school in which these classrooms are located.	33	7	1	2	43
3. The schools are adequately supplied with equipment for educational and other purposes.	30	10	2	1	43
4. Student transportation services are adequate.	21	15	5	2	43

continued

EXHIBIT 9.2, continued

	Definitely	Partially	No	Don't Know	Total
WORKING CONDITIONS					
1. In general, I am satisfied with my teaching position in the hearing impaired program.	36	7	0	0	43
2. Working conditions are generally satisfactory.	37	6	0	0	43
3. Communication, trust, and confidence between administrators and teachers are satisfactory:					
– Within the hearing impaired program.	31	10	2	0	43
– Within the school at which the hearing impaired program is situated.	20	19	3	1	43
4. The paperwork and record keeping required of teachers is appropriate.	4	21	16	1	42
5. Personnel policies and decisions are fair to teachers.	25	16	1	1	43
6. Teacher evaluation policies and practices are reasonably fair and effective.	23	17	1	2	43

Source: Compiled by author.

some that would be unique to a special education program, most are quite similar to those that would appear in a similar questionnaire for a regular school program.

I think you will also see from the answers that it is not very difficult to interpret results. The weaknesses tend to stand out (although in this parent survey there are very few weaknesses). A much more complicated process of considering what these weaknesses mean is required. This takes a good deal of time on the part of both administrators and teachers. It is, however, very much worthwhile.

The focus on improving the effectiveness of the relationship and communication between the central diagnostic staff and the classroom teachers in this program is believed to be a very major improvement opportunity, one that is being addressed very aggressively in this program now, with positive results.

While the satisfaction of parents and teachers is one critically important ingredient in measuring school performance, there are also other constituents of school districts whose opinions are important too. Students are one. At higher grade levels their opinions tend to be more valuable than those of parents. The student's own perceptions are more valid, and the parents tend to know less about current trends and problems when their children reach secondary school level. Community members also have useful and important opinions. Their views tend to be secondhand in nature and a reflection of what parents and teachers think about school performance. And they tend to be somewhat more predictable in the sense that taxpayers without children in schools are generally more concerned with cost control and less with program quality and performance, although the differences are not as dramatic as you might think and most taxpayers are quite willing to see funds spent on schools if results are proportionate.

The other most important information about school performance is the indication of student learning available from the analysis of standardized achievement test scores, and that is the subject of the next case study.

CASE STUDY FIVE
Test Data Analysis

INTRODUCTION TO CASE STUDY FIVE

This case study consists of a comprehensive achievement test score analysis for an elementary school district.

The most important indicator of student performance area is the analysis of standardized achievement tests. By and large everyone would agree that student learning is the single most critical ingredient in school performance. Most would also agree that regardless of the importance one attaches to the arts and the more subtle intellectual and physical skills of life, learning in the basic academic subject areas is the first and most important requirement. It is in precisely these areas that the standardized achievement tests have been developed and refined over decades with extensive national comparative references that make them uniquely valuable as indicators of school performance.

Used effectively, the analysis of standardized achievement test scores can virtually guarantee every district that its children will advance on average at least one year for every year in school. I have yet to find a community or a school that cannot achieve this fundamental goal. Yet a majority of urban schools today fall far below this simple, common sense standard.

Admittedly, once the results are available, some fairly tough administrative action may be required. Some teachers may simply not be able to achieve these results, and appropriate action will have to be taken — counseling, guidance, remediation, or, if all else fails, termination. Districts wanting good performance and sound evaluation will require remedial and training programs in order to help some teachers to be able to produce satisfactorily. However, in my experience, well over 90 percent of the teachers now in the classroom can achieve these results. The vast majority already are, and indeed are exceeding this simple standard by a considerable margin.

In this case study you will see an urban district, with students of average intelligence and relatively low income, that has moved its average annual growth from eight months to more than twelve months (national average growth is ten months). This was achieved through aggressive administrative leadership, dedicated and talented teachers, and hard work by both. A key ingredient was the analysis of test scores to reveal where opportunities for improvement existed. This was less important in the early years but more important as greater achievement growth was sought.

If every school district analyzed test scores effectively, used them administratively to build confidence and morale and to identify improvement opportunities, provided them to teachers so that they could understand strengths and weaknesses of performance and act out their generally good intentions to be as productive as possible in this regard, and presented them to school boards so that they could understand the present performance of the districts for which they are responsible and the action being taken to improve it, then public confidence, staff morale, and student performance would all increase dramatically. The impact on our national capacity and achievement could be dramatic.

These test scores are available in practically every district in the country. But in my experience no more than 10 percent are using them effectively and successfully. Another 75 percent to 80 percent are probably performing satisfactorily in spite of not using these data effectively. Sometimes they are impeded by a fear on the part of teachers and administrators, by unawareness of the importance and positive use to which these data can be put, by simple technical inadequacy in analytical abilities to cope with the rather challenging nature and required simplification of the data that are often returned by the test companies, or by any number of other reasons. Nevertheless, the effective analysis and fair use of standardized achievement test scores is something that every teacher, administrator, and board member should insist upon. Many will find that their districts are not performing satisfactorily in terms of the analysis that is being done and the use that is being made of these data. Therefore, this may be the single most important case study in the book.

Standardized achievement test data are particularly useful at elementary grade levels. Some district-wide indicators are also available at a high school level such as college admission tests (but please note that these are designed to be predictors of future performance and not measures of past achievement) as well as some of the achievement and advanced placement tests that are helpful. And certain subject areas have tests of their own (i.e., chemistry). In other high school departments, indicators need to be developed on a department by department basis and may vary a good deal from place to place depending on the nature of the program and its objectives.

Background on the District and Report

The report took data already available in the district and organized it in a way that indicated progress over the past few years, given the limitations of data available and change in district structure noted in the report.

A covering letter and the summary exhibit (9.3) were presented to the board. The indication of considerable progress in student learning in the district was received quite favorably.

The entire report was reviewed in detail by the management team of the district, with the revelation of considerable positive district progress coming as something of a surprise, and the indications of differential performance among schools and grades were also new information. A third level of analysis by individual teachers in classrooms is planned in the future in this district, thus completing the three levels at which test data analysis is appropriate.

The emphasis on growth from year to year and these three levels of analysis are generally required, although the format of presentation is often more elaborate or sophisticated than in this case, for example using charts and graphs.

The district is in a racially mixed suburban area adjacent to the inner city. The superintendent is an energetic leader who has held his present position for about five years and seems securely in charge of the district.

In the first year or two of his tenure the district was successfully integrated, including elimination of the junior high school and creation of the structure indicated in the material attached. It appears that this integration was accomplished with considerable success by the time of this report, resulting in a settled situation in the district, including the academic progress indicated in the test score analysis.

The district has put a considerable emphasis on improving academic progress at all grade levels over the past several years, and has supported teachers and principals with trained consultants who have worked diligently and with some success to gain teacher acceptance and development. The indications of academic success at junior high school levels since the reorganization, and the general academic progress of the district, were generally felt by the management team before this report, but not documented in evidence available to them. Test scores had been analyzed internally, but without correct calculations on a growth basis. Consequently, they were potentially misleading regarding individual teacher performance, although they were reviewed with the teachers as a group in each school. Comparisons among schools were generally avoided, largely out of fear that the implications for individual principals would be awkward for the analyst. The analyst was a competent school psychologist and special education director, with somewhat limited practical analytical background and experience, and in a small district awkwardly placed.

The district is generally stable in demographic character and size, and would be characterized by most observers as a lower to lower middle class neighborhood. Physical features of the community, both railroad lines and streets, tend to create several somewhat different neighborhoods. Below is a table updating progress since the time of the original report. As may be seen, continued progress is evident with all of the performance gaps identified in the original report substantially filled in: (1) improved annual growth in the lower grade levels; (2) improved annual growth in the fourth grade; and (3) reading scores raised to approximately the level of math scores.

Progress report updating average annual growth in standardized achievement test scores in Brookdale School District:

	Avg.	*Average Annual Growth by Grade*						
		2nd	*3rd*	*4th*	*5th*	*6th*	*7th*	*8th*
Total Reading								
1980-81	1.4	1.2	1.3	1.1	2.0	1.5	1.4	1.8
1979-80	1.0	0.9	1.0	0.9	1.2	1.2	0.9	NA
1978-79	1.0	0.8	1.0	0.5	1.5	0.8	1.4	NA
1975-76	0.8	0.6	0.9	0.3	1.4	0.6	0.8	NA
Total Math								
1980-81	1.5	1.2	1.4	1.4	1.8	1.9	1.4	1.5
1979-80	1.0	1.0	0.6	0.9	1.2	0.8	1.3	NA
1978-79	1.2	1.2	1.2	0.7	1.4	0.9	1.7	NA
1975-76	0.8	1.0	1.1	0.4	0.9	0.6	0.5	NA

The covering letter and report follow:

February 29, 1980

Superintendent
Brookdale School District
760 Bradford Street
Brookdale, Illinois

Subject: Report of Achievement
Test Score Analysis

Dear

Attached is our report of achievement test score analysis for the Brookdale District.

As you know, this analysis has extended the district level data, presented and discussed with the Council three weeks ago, to a second level of analysis according to subjects, schools, and grades. The purpose has been to provide a better understanding of district performance, both strengths and weaknesses, as a basis for identifying realistic improvement opportunities and for recognizing good performance at all levels of the organization. Such analysis can help build staff satisfaction, recognition, and reward, provide a foundation for board and public confidence in the performance of their schools, and foster an orientation to improving student learning throughout the organization. However, the report also notes the inherent limitations of such data, and the need for caution in reaching conclusions and recommendations.

By far the most important observations contained in this report relate to the significant gains in student learning during the past few years.

- The district has improved from below national averages in annual growth for reading and math to a level at or above these national averages last year. It improved from 0.8 to 1.0 years of growth annually for reading (1974-75 to 1978-79), and from 0.8 to 1.2 years of growth annually for math (1974-75 to 1978-79).

- During the past five years, average annual growth has improved at every grade and at every school for both reading and math. Improvement of student learning has been particularly strong at: (1) Lincoln School; (2) Upper grade levels, especially the seventh grade; and (3) Several individual grade levels at various schools, as indicated in the report.

This performance improvement would appear to reflect the success of the district's restructuring and initiation of instructional coordinator positions, as well as reflecting favorably on the general performance of district teachers, supporting staff, and administrators.

Further opportunities for improvement are also suggested in the report attached.

- District average annual gains for both social studies and science are below national norms, averaging 0.7 years of growth annually.
- For the district as a whole, the fourth and sixth grades for both math and reading and the second grade for reading are below average annual growth of one year.
- Nine grade levels, including at least two grades in each school, had average annual growth last year of less than one full year, and thus represent particular opportunities for further improvement.

Further review and discussion of the more detailed data attached by you and your staff will, we hope, provide a better analytical basis for insight, judgment, understanding, and action within the district, and help to focus attention on those areas of past success as well as future opportunity.

The gains in student learning during the past few years appear to be a significant accomplishment. They provide an important step as well as momentum toward the district's goal of improving educational performance. The satisfaction of your staff in this accomplishment, and their motivation to continue the upward progress in student learning, should, we hope, be enhanced by knowing these results.

It is important to note, as an element of caution in interpreting these data, that the district's adoption of a new test last year and reorganization of grades and schools two years ago provide a temporary impediment in the interpretation of test data, and warrant additional caution even beyond what would normally be required. As these data are updated annually in future years, this limitation will diminish.

We would welcome the opportunity to present and discuss this report with you and the Council and any other groups that you might consider appropriate.

Sincerely yours,
Fredric H. Genck

CASE STUDY FIVE

The following excerpts from the report of achievement test score analysis (Brookdale School District) are organized in five sections covering: purpose, cautions and limitations, testing suggestions, summary of comments and observations, and excerpts from detailed comments and data.

Purpose

Analysis of standardized achievement test scores should help teachers, administrators, and board to: build support and confidence in district performance and cost effectiveness, based on documented evidence of student progress; identify improvement opportunities, to maintain and improve performance; encourage teamwork and morale through recognition of performance and the cooperation, effort, and talent that is required to achieve it; and foster responsibility for and orientation to performance throughout the organization.

The analysis in this report builds upon the understanding gained through organization and evaluation work earlier this year. This analysis of test data should be supplemented with other information — we have particularly recommended teacher and parent surveys — and of course with the judgment and understanding available to district staff. Our outside perspective, analytical skill, and experience with other districts are, we hope, a useful supplement.

Cautions and Limitations

These cautions were also noted in the first report of test data analysis, at district level, and are repeated here.

Standardized achievement test data cannot stand alone as evidence for the evaluation of educational performance. They are subject to wide and inexplicable variations, at best providing only a clue and indication of actual learning results. But their long history and proven value make them useful in any situation where the ambition to maintain and improve educational performance exists.

Some local circumstances in Brookdale further limit the interpretation and analysis of test data. The reorganization in 1977-78 complicates comparisons among schools before and after the change, and the adoption of a new test last year temporarily makes comparisons with earlier years subject to possible errors. Both of these limitations will lessen over time, and should be only temporary impediments.

Testing Suggestions

Testing at the eighth grade level and in science and social studies should be considered. Not testing in these areas limits the analysis of performance, and may imply diminished emphasis.

We have also recommended that the district proceed to the third level of test data analysis, which involves teachers and permits refinement of analysis according to classrooms, ability levels, and individual children. The data are also more useful to teachers as part of their management information to fulfill responsibility for educational performance.

Summary of Comments and Observations

As summarized in the covering letter, these scores reflect favorably on the district's improvement of student learning during the past few years, and this in turn suggests successful board policies, administrative leadership, and teaching effectiveness as well as a probable favorable impact of such major changes as the district's reorganization to achieve integration and initiation of instructional coordinator positions. The data should also provide a better basis for focusing attention on further improvement opportunities.

One highlight of the district's performance is that its average annual growth has increased markedly during the past five years. Reading has improved from 0.8 to 1.0 in average annual student growth, and math has improved from 0.8 to 1.2 in average annual student growth. This improvement is accounted for mainly by higher reading and math gains in the upper grades, and at Lincoln School. However, improvement in average annual growth has occurred in each school and at every grade level over the past five years.

Annual gains continue to be below normal in the second, fourth, and sixth grades for reading and in the fourth and sixth grades for math, while gains for social studies and science are below normal, averaging 0.7 average annual student growth.

I.Q. scores have remained stable at district level over the past five years, averaging 97. However, there is some advantage for the Lincoln School, where the five year average is 100, and the sharp increase last year in second grade scores at Wilson might reflect favorably on the intensive efforts at early grade levels there during the past few years.

Five years ago the district was experiencing an accumulating deficit in annual growth over the grades. This has been reversed in the Lincoln School and upper grades. There has also been a widening gap between verbal and nonverbal I.Q. scores, reflecting a lag in language development, with advancing grades.

Highlights of annual growth by school and grade are:

- Strengths:
    - Lincoln School has made remarkable gains in average annual growth, last year in math and in both of the last two years in reading.
    - The seventh grade increased sharply last year, and slightly the year before, in both reading and math.
    - The sixth grade has also shown improvement, last year in math and in both of the last two years in reading.
    - The fifth grade has remained at a high level in reading and has improved substantially in math.

- Opportunities for improvement:
  - The fourth grade is achieving a low level of annual gain, and has improved only slightly over the past five years in reading and in math (except for the Lincoln School).
  - The second and third grades are also at a low level for reading, although they are above normal gains for math. Reading growth in these grades has not improved over the last four years (again except for Lincoln). While no deterioration in performance in second, third, and fourth grade has occurred since reorganization, no significant improvement has been accomplished yet either.

Exhibit 9.3 summarizes the district's average annual growth for reading and math by school and grade, as well as indicating the improvement in these scores that has been achieved over the past five years.

As may be seen in Exhibit 9.3, some grades and schools are achieving considerably more than one year's growth annually, while others have not achieved this standard. Those below one year's growth should logically be the most realistic opportunities for improvement. Also, during the past five years, a considerable improvement has taken place in average annual growth, as indicated by these data. Every grade level and every subject have shown improvement in both reading and math scores. The greatest improvement has occurred in these areas:

1. By grades: seventh grade math, seventh grade reading, fifth grade math.
2. By schools: Garfield math, Lincoln reading, Lincoln math.
3. By schools and grades: Lincoln fifth grade math, Lincoln fifth grade reading, Garfield fifth grade math, Garfield seventh grade math, Lincoln third grade reading, Adams seventh grade math.

These summary data in Exhibit 9.3 should be subject to more detailed analysis and consideration within the district to identify both strengths and opportunities for improvement.

Excerpts

These are excerpts from more detailed comments in subsequent data sections of the report, based on data in Exhibits 9.4, 9.5, and 9.6.

EXHIBIT 9.3
Summary of Annual Growth and Improvement in Annual Growth
(Brookdale School District)

| School | Grades | | | | | | Total |
	2	3	4	5	6	7	
Annual Growth: 1978-79							
Lincoln							
Reading	1.3	1.9	0.9	3.0	0.9	1.4	1.6
Math	1.1	1.5	0.5	3.0	0.5	1.5	1.4
Wilson							
Reading	0.6	0.8	NA	NA	NA	NA	0.7
Math	1.0	1.1	NA	NA	NA	NA	1.1
Adams							
Reading	NA	NA	0.5	1.1	0.7	1.2	0.9
Math	NA	NA	1.0	0.7	0.6	1.5	1.0
Garfield							
Reading	NA	NA	0.5	1.3	0.8	1.4	1.0
Math	NA	NA	0.4	1.8	1.1	1.9	1.3
District							
Reading	0.8	1.0	0.5	1.5	0.8	1.4	1.0
Math	1.2	1.2	0.7	1.4	0.9	1.7	1.2
Improvement in Annual Growth: 1974-75 to 1978-79							
Lincoln							
Reading	+0.6	+1.0	+0.5	+1.4	+0.2	+0.6*	+0.7
Math	+0.4	+0.3	+0.1	+1.6	−0.5	+0.6*	+0.4
Wilson							
Reading	0**	+0.1**	NA	NA	NA	NA	+0.1
Math	+0.1**	+0.2**	NA	NA	NA	NA	+0.2
Adams							
Reading	NA	NA	+0.1**	0**	0**	+0.3*	+0.1
Math	NA	NA	+0.6**	−0.1**	+0.1**	+1.0*	+0.4
Garfield							
Reading	NA	NA	+0.1**	+0.1**	+0.1**	+0.5*	+0.2
Math	NA	NA	0**	+1.0**	+0.6**	+1.0*	+0.9
District							
Reading	+0.2	+0.1	+0.2	+0.1	+0.2	+0.6	+0.2
Math	+0.2	+0.1	+0.3	+0.5	+0.3	+1.2	+0.4

*1978-79 school compared to 1975-76 District total
**1978-79 school compared to 1975-76 total for Bunche, Palm, and Woodland
NA = These grades not at these schools

Source: Compiled by author.

EXHIBIT 9.4
Summary of Average District Scores and Average Annual Growth by Subject

Subjects	Average District Score*	All Grades	Grade					
			2	3	4	5	6	7
			Average Annual Growth by Grade					
Reading								
1978-79	4.3	1.0	0.8	1.0	0.5	1.5	0.8	1.4
Change from 1974-75	+0.2	+0.2	+0.2	+0.1	+0.2	+0.1	+0.2	+0.6
Math								
1978-79	4.7	1.2	1.2	1.2	0.7	1.4	0.9	1.7
Change from 1974-75	+0.5	+0.4	+0.2	+0.1	+0.3	+0.5	+0.3	+1.2
Social Studies								
1977-78	5.8*	0.7	NA	NA	NA	NA	0.5	0.8
Change from 1974-75	0	0	NA	NA	NA	NA	0	0
Science								
1977-78	5.9*	0.7	NA	NA	NA	NA	0.4	1.0
Change from 1974-75	+0.1	0	NA	NA	NA	NA	-0.1	+0.2
Subtests								
Word Knowledge (vocabulary)								
1978-79	4.3	0.8	0.7	1.0	0.3	1.2	0.8	0.9
Change from 1974-75	+0.1	0	-0.1	+0.2	-0.1	+0.1	+0.2	-0.2

continued

EXHIBIT 9.4, continued

Subjects		Average District Score*	All Grades	Grade					
				2	3	4	5	6	7
				Average Annual Growth by Grade					
Reading Comprehension	1978-79	4.3	1.0	0.6	0.7	0.7	1.6	0.6	1.6
	Change from 1974-75	+0.2	+0.3	−0.1	−0.2	+0.5	+0.2	0	+1.4
Language	1978-79	5.4*	0.7	NA	NA	0.1	1.5	0	1.3
	Change from 1974-75	+0.2	+0.1	NA	NA	−0.2	+0.2	−0.3	+0.8
Spelling	1978-79	5.6	1.4	NA	1.4	0.7	1.5	1.3	2.0
	Change from 1974-75	+0.8	+0.3	NA	+0.4	0	+0.2	0	+1.0
Math Concepts	1978-79	4.9	1.0	NA	0.8	0.5	1.6	0.9	1.4
	Change from 1974-75	+0.4	+0.4	NA	−0.1	+0.2	+0.6	+0.2	+1.4
Math Computation	1978-79	5.3	1.0	NA	1.1	0.6	1.1	0.6	1.5
	Change from 1974-75	+0.4	+0.2	NA	0	0	+0.2	0	+0.9
Math Problem Solving	1977-78	4.6	0.8	NA	0.7	0.5	1.3	0.6	1.0
	Change from 1974-75	+0.1	+0.2	NA	+0.1	+0.1	+0.4	0	+0.3

*For grades shown on right side of page.   NA = Not applicable.
Source: Compiled by author.

178

EXHIBIT 9.5
District Reading Scores and Annual Growth

Year				Grades				Average (For All Grades)
	1	2	3	4	5	6	7	
Total Scores								
1978-79	1.7	2.7	3.5	4.0	5.4	6.1	7.0	4.3
1977-78	1.9	2.5	3.5	3.9	5.3	5.6	6.4	4.2
1976-77	2.0	2.5	3.4	3.7	5.0	5.6	6.2	4.1
1975-76	1.9	2.6	3.4	3.6	5.2	5.6	6.4	4.1
1974-75	2.0	2.5	3.3	3.8	5.0	5.6	6.4	4.1
Average for all years	1.9	2.6	3.4	3.8	5.2	5.7	6.5	4.2
Change from 1974-75 to 1978-79	−0.3	+0.2	+0.2	+0.2	+0.4	+0.5	+0.6	+0.2
Annual Growth								
1978-79		0.8	1.0	0.5	1.5	0.8	1.4	1.0
1977-78		0.5	1.0	0.5	1.6	0.6	0.8	0.8
1976-77		0.6	0.8	0.3	1.4	0.4	0.6	0.7
1975-76		0.6	0.9	0.3	1.4	0.6	0.8	0.8
Average for all years		0.6	0.9	0.4	1.5	0.6	0.9	0.8
Change from 1975-76 to 1978-79		+0.2	+0.1	+0.2	+0.1	+0.2	+0.6	+0.2

Source: Compiled by author.

EXHIBIT 9.6
District Math Scores and Annual Growth

Year				Grades				Average (For All Grades)
	1	2	3	4	5	6	7	
				Total Scores				
1978-79	1.9	3.2	3.9	4.4	5.9	6.2	7.4	4.7
1977-78	2.0	2.7	3.7	4.5	5.3	5.7	6.6	4.4
1976-77	1.8	2.6	3.7	3.9	5.2	5.7	6.0	4.1
1975-76	1.7	2.7	3.6	4.0	5.2	5.7	6.4	4.2
1974-75	1.7	2.5	3.6	4.3	5.1	5.9	6.4	4.2
Average for all years	1.8	2.7	3.7	4.2	5.3	5.8	6.6	4.3
Change from 1974-75 to 1978-79	+0.2	+0.7	+0.3	+0.1	+0.8	+0.3	+1.0	+0.5
				Annual Growth				
1978-79		1.2	1.2	0.7	1.4	0.9	1.7	1.2
1977-78		0.9	1.1	0.8	1.4	0.5	0.9	0.9
1976-77		0.9	1.0	0.3	1.2	0.5	0.3	0.7
1975-76		1.0	1.1	0.4	0.9	0.6	0.5	0.8
Average for all years		1.0	1.1	0.6	1.2	0.6	0.9	0.9
Change from 1975-76 to 1978-79		+0.2	+0.1	+0.3	+0.5	+0.3	+1.2	+0.4

Source: Compiled by author.

Subjects

District average annual growth is strongest for math and weakest for science and social studies, as shown in the following table:

Subject	Average Gain in 1978-79
Math	1.2 years
Reading	1.0 years
Social Studies	0.7 years
Science	0.7 years

Average annual growth in math is presently above national norms and in reading is equal to national norms. However, if weak grades in both subject areas should be improved, to effect further overall improvement in annual growth. Also, the average annual growth in science and social studies of only seven months would seem to leave considerable opportunity for further growth. Both math and reading scores show a similar wave pattern, with weakness at fourth and sixth grade levels.

I.Q. Scores

In general, total district average I.Q. scores have been level over the past five years at approximately 97. Within this overall pattern, there has been a fairly sharp increase in average I.Q. at the second grade level, now concentrated at Wilson School, and rising from 92 in 1974 to 100 last year. This may be a temporary and inexplicable fluctuation, or it could reflect an improvement in the early educational program of the schools or in the population being served. In either of these latter two cases, the opportunity to capitalize on this gain in future years for the district could be substantial, and may require some adjustment of objectives and teaching techniques at the higher grade levels.

The Lincoln School has enjoyed a three point advantage over district averages in the past five years, but lower scores in the second grade last year may suggest a change in this advantage in the future.

The district has experienced a gap between verbal and nonverbal I.Q. scores expanding with advancing grade levels, e.g., a one point difference between 98 and 97 at fourth grade level and a three point difference between 99 and 96 at sixth grade level. However, the gap has been closed during the past two years at a fourth grade level, and this may indicate the beginning of a long-term improvement.

CONCLUSION OF CHAPTER 9

The three case studies in this chapter have described an overall concept of school performance accountability, evaluation, and management and then given specific, concrete examples of parent and teacher surveys and test data analysis.

The next two chapters turn away from this performance information side of school management to the people side. But remember that the information is essential to a process of communication and evaluation that is fair and effective and to placing individual evaluation of both teachers and administrators in the context of confidence and support as well as documented evidence of good performance. It is only in this context that individual evaluation in education can be made tolerable and operable in practice. Without the information the people side of school management isn't possible. Once the information is available and used, however, it is then necessary to strengthen administrative evaluation and compensation and teacher evaluation and development in order to fully realize the benefits of good school management.

10

ADMINISTRATIVE EVALUATION AND COMPENSATION:
To Improve Fairness and Performance

We turn now from performance information to the evaluation, compensation, and development of the two basic levels of professional staffing in school districts: administrators and teachers. Without performance information — to provide a foundation of confidence and support, to encourage board willingness to delegate, to build morale and satisfaction internally, and to identify improvement opportunities so that action can be decided and taken — neither administrative or teacher evaluation have much chance of being successful. However, given the availability and use of information, these two further steps of school management then become of critical importance.

Both teacher and administrative evaluation are serious problems today. Traditionally administrators have had their salaries decided on a basis that is simplistic and often somewhat unprofessional. Those practices are no longer adequate. The symptoms of the problem are confusion at a board level and dissatisfaction at administrative staff levels. These symptoms are evident in many school districts today, as described in Case Study Six, a survey of administrative compensation in a group of districts.

A sound, practical solution to this problem is exemplified in Case Study Seven, a structured administrative compensation plan geared to performance and evaluation and working successfully in more than a score of school districts that I have worked with over the past ten years. The same principles are being applied in smaller districts where a formal plan is not really necessary. Their more widespread application would contribute considerably to improved school performance.

Finally we share a model of superintendent evaluation that is practical and workable, without requiring too much time or paperwork on the part of the board, and appropriately encouraging their delegation and building their confidence. This represents the application at superintendent level of the comprehensive model for evaluation shown in Case Study Eight, reflected in both administrative and teacher evaluation plans. What follows is a more specific description of each of these three case studies:

Case Study Six is the report of a management compensation survey in several districts, describing the general situation with problems, recommendations, and comparative data. It explains the problems surrounding administrative compensation and evaluation today – why boards are getting confused and making damaging decisions or none at all; why administrators are becoming frustrated and angry with their treatment and sometimes forming administrative unions as a result; why the lack of board confidence in district performance as well as public concern and the taxpayer revolt underlie these compensation difficulties. The need for a sounder basis for board decisions and a more positive approach from the point of view of administrators will, I think, be evident from this description.

Case Study Seven is an example of a recommended administrative compensation and evaluation plan. This is the kind of solution to the problems described in Case Study Six that is working most successfully today. Salary plans like the one described in Case Study Seven are working in many districts, and have been for a number of years. Common pitfalls into which most merit pay plans in education have fallen are avoided, e.g., failing to recognize the need for performance information and a fair and effective evaluation process coupled with communication and participation, or tying salaries to performance in ways that are technically inadequate in a field so hard to measure and where teamwork is so important.

Case Study Eight is a brief description and format for board evaluation of the superintendent. This special issue of administrative evaluation is critically important to the relationship between board, faculty, and administrators as well as the superintendent. The approach described in this case study is simple and straightforward. It will help tie the district together, and is an example of evaluation that can be replicated at administrative and teaching levels as well.

CASE STUDY SIX
School Management Compensation Survey Report

GENERAL REPORT: ADMINISTRATIVE COMPENSATION SURVEY

This is the general report of the 1979/80 Administrative Compensation Survey, conducted by the Institute for Public Management for seven years for Chicago area school districts. It provides the basis for better compensation decisions by school boards: contributing to the improvement of school performance, administrative morale and productivity; strengthening board/administrator relationships; and helping to ensure fairness to administrators. The report, organized in three sections, is based on personal interviews with board members, administrators, and teachers in more than 30 districts.

Administrative Compensation Policies and Practices

Management compensation is a divisive issue in many school districts today, often creating tension and conflict between the board and the management team, damaging morale and productivity in the district, and reducing the attractiveness of administrative positions compared to the relative security and nearly comparable rewards enjoyed by teachers. Many school board members are uncomfortable in setting administrative salaries. They recognize that there is a risk of overpaying administrators in response to rising teacher salaries, and that there is inevitably a certain amount of self-interest involved in administrative salary recommendations. They fear board exposure to public criticism, resulting from the feeling that salaries are high compared to average citizens, or themselves. Finally, there is a problem with possible frustrations over the general difficulties of managing a school district in an age of concerned parents, organized teachers, declining enrollments, and resistant taxpayers.

Superintendents typically understand the board's uneasiness, but are also rightly concerned with the morale and motivation of the management team. They realize that inadequate salaries will diminish the supply of management talent, and that compensation set in an atmosphere of suspicion and distrust damages administrative morale and effectiveness regardless of actual salary levels. The superintendents also must deal with the possibility of their authority being eroded by boards unable to deal effectively with the difficult issues involved in setting compensation.

The lack of a positive approach and adequate structure for board compensation decisions is frustrating to administrators. They see their compensation established in a process that is secret, sometimes without any apparent basis, often in an atmosphere of board/super-intendent conflict. They may consider pay for teachers only slightly below their own, without the responsibility and requirements of their own positions, and with greater security and practically guaranteed annual increases unrelated to performance. In this situation, the risk of low morale and less than maximum administrative effectiveness is high, and the possibility of administrative unions not out of the question.

Practical but structured compensation plans can provide for board decision making that is a positive contribution to administrative morale, demonstrably fair to administrators and so perceived by them. These plans usually have certain features in common. First, administrative compensation decisions are separated from the teacher salary schedule so as to preclude conflict of interest in the negotiating process. Second, administrative salary decisions are made at an appropriate time of the year that does not give administrators the feeling that their compensation is less important than teachers', subject to remaining funds that may not already have been bargained away to other groups of employees. And finally, board policies with respect to how administrative compensation is determined are clearly specified, available to all concerned, and demonstrably fair to the management team. As a result, the board each year has a means for knowing its own policies, what decisions it should make, what information it should take into account, and how to go about the process. A smoother process, better decisions, and constructive contribution to the board/superintendent relationship are possible.

While compensation plans can take a variety of forms depending on the size and nature of the management team in the district, they typically contain these elements:

- Objective comparative salary information, thoroughly analyzed and presented in an understandable format.
- Well-documented organization and responsibilities.

- Internal equity among management positions based on the relative responsibilities and requirements.
- Recognition of staff perceptions of the difficulty of various positions.
- Quantifiable factors such as number of people supervised, budgets, and work year.
- Differential for added responsibilities and work loads beyond teachers.
- Sufficient information on the educational performance so that the board can feel confident that compensation decisions are a fair return for good performance.

The administrative performance appraisal process should provide for more than just the judgment of the superintendent in determining relative administrative performance among members of the management team. But at the very least the board should be assured that total administrative compensation costs are justified by the overall administrative and educational performance of the district, rather than just keeping up with prevailing salary levels elsewhere.

Related Management Issues

Evaluation of district performance is one of the most important opportunities available to school districts today. It should be a positive and constructive experience for both board and staff, enabling all to take pride in the district's performance as reflected in the learning of the students and satisfaction of their parents. And it should enable the board to have a basis on which to feel confident in deciding the compensation of administrators.

Yet, in contrast to these requirements, and even though the data and reports that boards receive are typically voluminous, most school board members have little understandable and usable information on the performance of the district for which they are responsible. Not always recognized is the direct connection betweeen the absence of this information and the difficulties school boards have in communicating with their constituents as well as staff, defending performance to the former and encouraging its improvement to the latter. Most school boards can and should improve their own performance in this respect.

Performance appraisal should enable the board to inform and convince the public that a good job is being done (among other reasons so that they will be prepared to fund the district adequately) and develop a sense of responsibility for and orientation to performance on the part of the staff, in order to contribute to improved performance as well as to the satisfaction and morale of the staff itself.

Information on the performance of the district provides the only fundamental justification and rationale for administrative compensation. But individual administrative salaries need not be tied directly to some measurable performance, a goal not only unnecessary but impossible in a field as subjective and difficult to measure as education. Every board and superintendent does, however, need to understand as well as possible the overall educational performance of their district. Having accomplished this purpose, most districts will also find it advantageous to develop an individualized performance appraisal process that can apply to each administrator, always of course subject to the judgment and interpretation of the superintendent and other supervisors.

Districts will find that certain information is essential to appraising performance. A knowledge of student learning is necessary for this process. A substantial indication of this can be gained from analysis of standardized achievement test scores. However, the analytical requirements, especially for simplification of data, and recognition of markedly different uses at teacher, school, district, and board levels, are not often satisfactorily met. Considerable caution is needed to avoid an academic and research orientation and to preserve an educational and managerial point of view instead. Where this is accomplished, analysis of standardized achievement test data is an extremely useful supplement to teacher, administrative, and board judgment. Consumer satisfaction and staff feedback can usually be inexpensively monitored through simple surveys, carefully structured to focus on the most important aspects of performance as viewed by these customer groups. Cost control, particularly key staff ratios, should also be a part of the information used in this process, as should other indicators, which may include attendance and dropout rates or other local measures that may be relevant and available.

Performance information, appropriately analyzed and interpreted, taking into account district circumstances and objectives as well as the performance of other similar districts, can be extremely valuable to boards in identifying opportunities for improvement and priorities for the future, in fulfilling their own responsibility for performance, and in convincing the public that a good job is being done. The knowledge of strengths and weaknesses gained through such information can help target district administrative and teacher efforts on those areas most subject to improvement.

In moving toward the strengthening of performance appraisal to meet the new requirements of managing education effectively today, boards should understand that neither the skills nor the attitudes to effectively bring about the strengthening of performance appraisal may be available within their district. Schools are a very emotional business, as are any businesses that involve people. Educators are typically more oriented to human relations than to analysis. The tools and techniques of performance appraisal are neither well known nor well developed as they apply to school districts. Many of the traditions of education, developed in an earlier era when circumstances were different, run against the requirements of performance appraisal.

In spite of these difficulties, the advantages of appraising performance seem compelling. It enables the board to effectively represent the public, improves district performance, and raises public confidence. It can also improve board/staff relations and orient board, administrators, and teachers to educational performance. Finally, it provides the board with adequate confidence in district performance to permit constructive compensation, a necessary part of good school management.

Comparative Administrative Compensation Data

Comparative salary data are shown in Exhibit 10.1, which summarizes school district administrative compensation data in the Chicago suburban area compared to business, university, city manager, federal government, and hospital administrators. School administrative salaries are substantially below those for comparable positions in industry, somewhat lower than comparable positions in universities, the federal government, and hospitals, and somewhat above those of city managers.

EXHIBIT 10.1
Summary of Comparative Compensation Information*

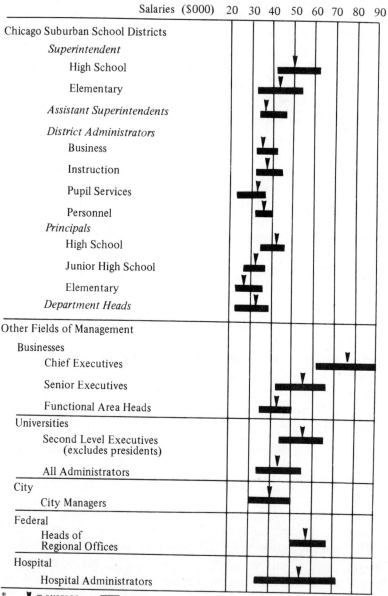

Salaries ($000) 20 30 40 50 60 70 80 90

Chicago Suburban School Districts
Superintendent
   High School
   Elementary
Assistant Superintendents
District Administrators
   Business
   Instruction
   Pupil Services
   Personnel
Principals
   High School
   Junior High School
   Elementary
Department Heads

Other Fields of Management
  Businesses
    Chief Executives
    Senior Executives
    Functional Area Heads
  Universities
    Second Level Executives
    (excludes presidents)
    All Administrators
  City
    City Managers
  Federal
    Heads of
    Regional Offices
  Hospital
    Hospital Administrators

* ▼ = average ▬ = range
Source: Compiled by author.

190

CASE STUDY SEVEN
Administrative Compensation and Evaluation Plan

INTRODUCTION TO CASE STUDY SEVEN

The solution to the problems described in Case Study Six is presented in the following case study, which shows an administrative compensation and evaluation plan that is working successfully in a number of districts. This case study consists of excerpts from an actual recommended administrative compensation and evaluation plan, which is typical of the analysis as well as compensation and evaluation recommendations that are working effectively in a number of school districts now. These include unit, elementary, and high school districts, with both division head and department head patterns of organization.

Techniques draw heavily on established policies and practices of management compensation in industry, such as relying on marketplace indicators as a key basis for salaries, and emphasizing a plan structure with positions grouped in categories based on relative responsibility, with a range of salaries established for each category.

The plan departs from many applications of industrial management practices to schools, however, in two key respects. First, salaries are not tied directly to any indicators of performance. This is impossible in a field so hard to measure, with shared responsibility for performance. And it discourages the teamwork that is essential to good performance in schools. Instead, multiple indicators of performance are used to justify salaries and tie them to results, encouraging management responsibility and justifying public expenditures. Second, performance information is used to support board confidence, and encourage positive compensation decisions and delegation of responsibility to the management team. Performance information — defined in the evaluation recommendations of this report — is also a key factor in building public confidence. These two features of the plan are believed crucially important to practical implementation and positive impact on school performance in practice.

Prior to this plan, these districts had no documented administrative compensation and evaluation plans, a typical situation in school districts today. Historically, administrative salaries had been recommended by the superintendent to the board, and these recommendations were accepted and adopted. More recently, administrators saw their salaries being set in an atmosphere of conflict at board level, without any documented basis. This seemed to them to contrast with the job security being won by teachers through collective bargaining. Since administrative salaries were decided after negotiated settlements with teachers, the feeling was that whether or not any funds were left over would be a factor. And administrators felt that their increases were generally somewhat smaller than those won by teachers. Naturally, some administrators thought that perhaps they too would be better off with a union.

District administrators were heavily involved in the preparation of the plan, including modifications after this report was presented. They assembled additional information on salaries in other districts that resulted in some adjustments in the ranges and salaries proposed in this report.

Board reactions to the report were generally quite favorable. Some board members felt it was important to tie performance to salaries. Others felt that district administrators deserved more security in their working conditions and salaries. Implementation of the report, with decisions by the board including some funding of the discrepancy between this district's salaries and those indicated by the marketplace, was accomplished almost immediately.

Three particular features of the evaluation plan are believed to be critically important to the feasibility of implementation and positive impact on school performance. First, evaluation is supported with performance information, used to analyze and improve performance internally and to build board confidence, discourage meddling, and encourage delegation. Second, a general process of planning, monitoring, and reporting on progress within the district focuses on a dialogue between administrators and the superintendent regarding the situation, progress, and plans of their school or department, initially orally, later with limited documentation. Insightful, practical analysis and understanding of current trends are emphasized, with teacher participation. Third, provision is made for the application of superintendent judgment and encouragement of teamwork, in addition to the planning/monitoring process and performance information. This softening of quantitative information and analytical planning is considered essential, especially in the early stages of launching the planning and evaluation process.

This plan is a composite of several plans working successfully in a variety of districts. They include several high school, elementary, and special education districts and a unit district in a medium-size town. Exhibit 10.2 gives a summary of the key features and steps in the development of an administrative compensation and evaluation plan.

EXHIBIT 10.2
Development of an Administrative Evaluation and Compensation Plan

---

Key Features and Objectives
- A more formal, structured, and documented plan.
- A sound basis for board decision making.
- Administrators treated fairly.
- Emphasis given to performance: student learning, public confidence, staff morale.
- Recognition and reward for administrative contribution to performance and cost effectiveness of the district.

Requirements
- Participation of administrators in preparing the plan.
- Objective analysis of present compensation.
- Documentation of responsibilities according to scope, level, importance, and impact as a basis for compensation categories.
- Comparison of district salaries to the marketplace in education and elsewhere.
- The design of a structured plan with categories, ranges, and policy and procedural guidelines for salaries and for the annual decision-making process.
- Presentation and review of the plan with administrators and board.
- Preparation of final report to guide implementation.
- Superintendent recommends specific salaries annually within the context of the plan.
- Evaluation implementation during a period of one to two years, including performance information, in a simple, workable, participative process that builds confidence, morale, and support, and improves performance.

Source: Compiled by author.

CASE STUDY SEVEN

This report recommends an administrative compensation plan and evaluation plan for District #1. It is based on interviews with administrators and board members, analysis of internal and external salary information, and the experience and research of this organization in school management, performance, and evaluation.

There is an important difference in implementation requirements between the two plans: The compensation plan is ready for implementation this spring — and will continue to provide a framework for board decision making in the future. The evaluation plan requires more extensive implementation, including development of performance information as well as a planning and evaluation process. One to two years will be required. However, implementation should be initiated this year.

The overall purpose of both plans is to assure fairness to administrators, sound decisions by the board on behalf of the public, and maximum contribution to the education and cost effectiveness of the district.

The report is organized in three parts:

1. Analysis of the Present Situation
   - Background
   - Present Salaries
   - Outside Comparisons
2. Recommended Administrative Compensation Plan
   - Objectives
   - Policies
   - Plan
   - Procedures
   - Control
3. Recommended Evaluation Plan
   - Concept
   - Planning and Reporting Process
   - Information
   - Administrative Evaluation
   - Teacher Evaluation and Development
   - Implementation

Analysis of the Present Situation

This section discusses the background of administrative compensation and evaluation in District #1, analyzes present salaries, and shows comparisons with salaries in other districts.

Background

Both the board and superintendent recognize that administrative compensation and evaluation in District #1 need to be strengthened to provide fairness to administrators and board confidence in compensation decisions and district performance. Administrative compensation decisions have proven difficult during the past two years. Cost of living increases have substituted for performance-based raises and the preparation of a formal plan has been deferred.

Principals have become uncomfortable with the uncertainty and conflict involved in setting their salaries, particularly during the interim when the district was without a superintendent, and in light of other controversial situations during the past few years. It is only natural for administrators to be aware of the turnover of board members and superintendents, and to desire a more structured, predictable, and demonstrably fair process through which salaries are determined.

As discussed in the report of application of the School Performance Research Project to District #1, the district's use of evaluation and performance information to defend and improve performance can be strengthened in several important respects. Administrative evaluation is one of the most important. For the past two years during the district's transition to a new superintendency, administrative evaluation has been relatively limited.

Recognizing the importance of this situation and the need for action, the superintendent and board have taken the initiative to obtain the technical experience and outside perspective needed to develop a new administrative compensation plan and evaluation plan for District #1. This report is the result.

Present Salaries

As a first step in the development of a compensation plan, the district's present administrative responsibilities and salaries have been analyzed. Administrative salaries are shown with positions grouped according to categories that as fairly as possible reflect the scope and levels of responsibility involved. Also shown are the number of months worked and enrollment of each school as well as present salaries. Where certain portions of salaries are specified to be for extra duties this has been noted, as is the portion of compensation paid by the vocational center for the Director of Business Affairs.

Outside Comparisons

District #1 salaries appear to be generally in line with those prevailing in other school districts in Illinois for similar responsibilities; principals' salaries may be slightly low. Four different comparisons have been made:

- State-wide averages. These data include both small downstate districts with lower salary levels and those in the Chicago area with higher salary levels.
- State-wide averages adjusted downward in an approximation that attempts to allow for the higher levels of salaries in the Chicago area. As may be seen in Exhibit II, salaries are particularly higher in the Chicago area for secondary principals.
- Chicago area salaries adjusted downward by approximately 10 percent to 15 percent. While this comparison is not directly relevant to District #1, it is useful background information.
- Salaries in some nearby districts. It should be noted that there are only a few districts and positions in each of these categories. Consequently, data are hard to be confident of since they reflect very few districts and lack the greater validity that comes with larger numbers of positions included in all of the other data.

From these data, it appears that District #1 salaries are generally in line with prevailing levels, although elementary and secondary principals may be slightly low.

Recommended Administrative Compensation Plan

This section presents and describes the recommended administrative compensation plan for District #1.

Objectives

The plan is designed to provide fairness to administrators, a sound and appropriate structure for board decision making and control of administrative salaries on behalf of the public, and maximum contribution of administrative compensation expenditures to the overall educational quality, performance, and cost effectiveness of the district as well as the motivation, morale, performance, productivity, and job satisfaction of administrators and staff.

The plan is specifically designed to contribute to the quality of District #1 educational performance and management, including student progress, staff relations, public confidence, and cost control. It will compensate administrators equitably, relative to the scope and level of their responsibilities, salaries paid for similar responsibilities in other organizations, and the quality of performance of each administrator's assigned job responsibilities. The plan will also allow for recognition and reward of good performance, and provide an incentive for maintaining and improving performance, thus attracting and helping to retain needed administrative talent.

Individual development will be encouraged, and a career structure that helps meet needs for administrative talent locally and nationally. Finally, the plan will control costs, so that salaries are reasonable from a public viewpoint, and the board has a sound basis for its decision making.

Policies

What follows is a discussion of compensation policies that were designed to achieve the objectives specified above.

The board should have a clear and understandable basis for making compensation decisions, one that is demonstrably fair to administrators and the public, and administrators should be able to understand the basis on which their salaries are to be set, to offset superintendent and board member turnover or particular events.

Compensation should be fair and equitable to the administrators concerned, particularly in terms of internal equity, external comparisons, and relationship to the individual administrator's stage of development and quality of performance. Decisions for compensation should be made prior to reemployment commitments, while recognizing that other factors may affect timing or announcement of these decisions, and that adjustment during the following year may sometimes be required. Administrative salaries should be separated from the teacher salary schedule and related to performance.

District #1 administrative salaries should have a reasonable relationship to prevailing salary levels for similar positions in central and northern Illinois (recognizing that higher and lower salaries are found in the Chicago area and in smaller downstate districts respectively). Internal salary structure should reasonably reflect the importance and difficulty of positions in terms of the capabilities required to carry them out, the scope of responsibilities involved, and the overall impact on educational performance.

Maximum opportunity for recognition and reward to good performance and encouragement for individual administrators to grow and develop in their capabilities, responsibilities, and personal skills should be provided. The compensation plan should permit District #1 to recruit effectively for the administrative personnel it needs to accomplish its objectives, attracting and retaining the talent required, and maintaining satisfaction, morale, and motivation over time. Annual salary increases should be used to adjust salaries within the guidelines of these policies and to reward performance.

Costs should be controlled to assure that all expenditures are fully justified from a public viewpoint and to result in a reasonable cost of administration.

Compensation policies should permit and encourage recognition of particular circumstances and situations and the handling of individual employees on an individual basis. Responsibility for recommending administrative salaries should be delegated by the board to the superintendent, within general guidelines established annually for funds to be made available for this purpose, and subject to final review and approval by the board, within the policies and procedures established in this report.

Plan

The recommended compensation plan, shown in Exhibits 10.3 and 10.4, is a performance-based plan incorporating categories and ranges. Key features of the plan are described in the following paragraphs. District #1 administrative positions are organized into six categories for compensation purposes:

- Administrative directors.
- Secondary principals.

EXHIBIT 10.3
Recommended Administrative Compensation Plan: Structure

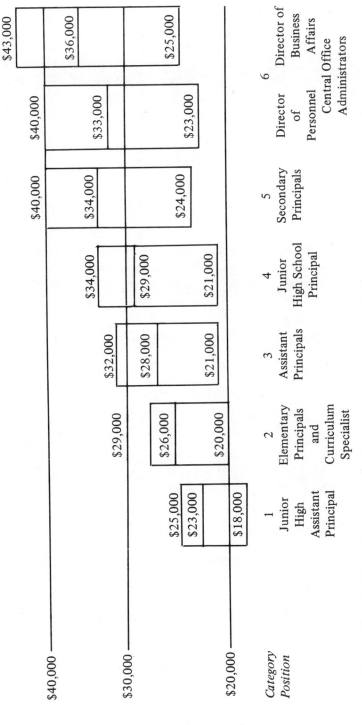

Source: Compiled by author.

199

EXHIBIT 10.4
Recommended Administrative Compensation Plan: Data

Category and Position	Number	Present Compensation		Target Salary	% Range		$ Range	
		Average	Range		Lower Level	Upper Level	Lower Level	Upper Level
6 Director of Business Affairs	1	$39,000		$36,000	30%	20%	$25,000	$43,000
Director of Personnel	1	$35,534		$33,000	30%	20%	$23,000	$40,000
5 High School Principal	2	$32,965	$32,550-$33,380	$34,000	28%	18%	$24,000	$40,000
WAVC Director								
4 Junior High School Principal	1	$31,465		$29,000	26%	16%	$21,000	$34,000
3 Assistant Principals:	4	$28,710	$28,210-$29,210	$28,000	24%	14%	$21,000	$32,000
High School Assistant								
High School Dean								
WAVC Assistant								
H.S. Athletic Director								
2 Elementary Principals (6)	7	$24,755	$22,785-$28,210	$26,000	22%	12%	$20,000	$29,000
Curriculum Specialist								
1 Junior High Assistant Principal	1	$22,785		$23,000	20%	10%	$18,000	$25,000

Source: Compiled by author.

— Junior high school principals.
— Secondary assistant principals.
— Elementary principals.
— Junior high school assistant principals.

In the recommended plan administrative compensation is based primarily on performance, but within the context of a decision-making structure that assures reasonable fairness and equity to administrators and a process of board decision making both justifiable to the public and understandable to board members and administrators. The six salary categories in the plan have been based on analysis of the relative importance of each position to the overall educational performance of the district. The resulting categories appropriately reflect these responsibilities and provide a sound basis for internal equity, since salaries are related to the scope and importance of each position.

A key board decision required by the plan is the relationship that District #1 administrative salaries should have to prevailing market levels in other Illinois school districts. The target midpoint of each salary category provides for relating District #1 compensation to that of other school districts in Illinois. The recommended relationship is one that approximates parity with state-wide averages adjusted to account for the lower salaries paid in smaller downstate districts and the higher salaries paid in the Chicago area. This feature of the compensation plan provides for fairness in terms of external salary comparisons.

The ranges for each position, which expand from lower to higher categories, provide the opportunity to recognize performance and competence as it develops over time in each position. This performance factor is believed to be of critical importance to the positive use of administrative compensation in rewarding good performance and contributing to the overall quality of education in District #1.

The bottom and top of each range provide an established minimum and maximum salary for any position in that category, and therefore serve as a check to ensure at least minimum compensation for every individual member of the management team and to put a reasonable ceiling on compensation expectations short of the expansion of responsibility or promotion. The fact that these ranges overlap substantially is intentionally indicative of the greater importance placed on performance in a job rather than the size of the job itself. The ranges extend twice as far below the target level as above, to provide adequate opportunity for growth during the early years that an administrator holds a position without raising inappropriately high expectations beyond the target level while providing opportunities to reward outstanding performance. The ranges become larger in percentage as well as dollar terms for higher positions to recognize the greater scope of opportunity for outstanding performance and a superior contribution to overall district educational performance.

Recommending administrative salaries within the plan should be delegated by the board to the superintendent subject to specific required approvals and controls specified later in this report. Senior administrators performing well in their positions for a substantial number of years would be expected to be at or above the target level of compensation for their category. Annual increases, however, would be expected to be lower for them than for their less experienced colleagues. Overall, the district's average compensation should be expected to approximate the target level, assuming continuation of a policy of parity.

Annually, perhaps approximately at the middle of the school year, the board should consider superintendent recommendations for the total budget to be allocated for administrative salary increases. Factors to be considered should include the district's financial situation as well as expectations for prevailing patterns of increase in school districts in Illinois, since this is essential to maintaining the policy of parity with salaries elsewhere. While estimates will necessarily be involved, discrepancies between actual salaries and those predicted can be adjusted in future years or if necessary on an interim basis. The result should be a total budget allocation for guidance of the superintendent in preparing individual recommendations.

Within this framework, the board should delegate to the superintendent responsibility for specific salary recommendations. These should be based upon the framework of the compensation plan and on performance evaluation as discussed in the third part of this report. Superintendent recommendations for administrative salaries should be presented to the board with sufficient and appropriate analysis regarding both compensation and evaluation.

Control

Two features of the recommended plan are sufficiently important to deserve separate summary attention at the end of this chapter.

They are the balancing of fairness to administrators with a soundly structured board decision-making process, as highlighted in the following paragraphs.

Fairness to administrators is provided through the structure of the plan and the annual decision-making process. Categories of positions with targets and ranges of compensation provide assurance that salaries will bear a reasonable relationship to prevailing compensation in other school districts and to the scope of internal responsibilities. Delegation of compensation recommendations to the superintendent with a sound performance evaluation process provides compensation based on performance and resultant public and board justification.

Board control of administrative salaries through a soundly structured decision-making process is also provided. Annually the board can determine the total allocation of resources for administrative salaries, in light of the relationships with prevailing salary levels elsewhere implicit in the plan and in terms of local financial circumstances and budget availabilities. Although detailed administrative analysis and recommendations should be expected, this decision is uniquely the responsibility of the board each year.

Because comparisons to prevailing salary levels elsewhere and internal responsibilities are built into the plan, the board should have a readily available and understandable basis for interpreting administrative recommendations. The need for administrators to defend recommendations on the basis of internal equity and external fairness is an important feature of the plan in terms of board decision making as well as administrative confidence that the basis for fairness is built into the plan. If salaries become out of line with the policy, this should be apparent to administrators and board, and corrective action can be taken. The intention to provide internal and external equity in the context of performance-based compensation is made clear by the plan.

Tying of administrative salaries to district performance provides the board with the single most valuable use of the authority for setting salaries delegated to it by the public. This is the most important way in which a school board fulfills its responsibility for accountability to the public while maintaining fairness to the staff.

The administrative compensation plan recommended in this chapter provides the board with the structure needed to assure sound decision making, delegate with confidence to the superintendent, maintain adequate control over administrative compensation, ensure fairness to administrators, and fulfill the board's responsibility for district performance to the public.

Recommended Evaluation Plan

Presented and described in this section is a blueprint for a comprehensive and systematic accountability plan for District #1. Although the compensation and evaluation plans are designed to be complementary, they differ in two important respects: First, evaluation is a much more complicated and difficult aspect of school management in which the available techniques are less well developed. And second, implementation of the evaluation recommendations will necessarily require a period of years, including the development of performance information as well as a process of planning, analysis, and evaluation. In contrast, the administrative compensation plan can be used immediately as a framework for decisions this spring.

Recognizing the inherent complexity and difficulty of evaluation is important, especially in education. Nevertheless, as the proper basis for administrative compensation and justification to the public for expenditures being authorized by the board, evaluation is probably the most important single issue to be addressed by the district's administrative team and board. These recommendations reflect the best available practical experience and research on evaluation as well as our firsthand involvement in implementation over a period of more than eight years.

Concept

As a general framework for evaluation in District #1, Exhibit 10.5 shows a concept of school performance and the four major components of evaluation that will be discussed in the remainder of this chapter. As may be seen from the exhibit, four concepts of school performance should be used to organize the evaluation process:

- Student progress, including academic learning, student behavior, and personal development.
- Parent satisfaction and public confidence in schools, including involvement and support.

EXHIBIT 10.5
School Performance Concepts and Evaluation Components

School Performance Concepts	Evaluation Components			
	Performance Information	*Program Planning, Monitoring, Reporting Process*	*Administrative Evaluation*	*Teacher Evaluation and Development*
Student Progress: Student learning and academic progress. Student discipline and behavior. Personal/social growth and development.	*Test data analysis;* and other indicators.	Board/superintendent.	Program.	Fair and effective. Constructive impact on staff morale as well as district performance.
Parent Satisfaction: General satisfaction with schools; progress of children. Specific satisfaction and concerns, each aspect of school performance. Public confidence, support, and involvement.	*Parent survey,* and other communication channels.	Administrators.	Information.	
Staff Morale: Teacher satisfaction with schools, programs, working conditions. Other staff. Communication, teamwork.	*Teacher survey,* and other communication channels.	Staff.	Individual.	
Financial Control: Cost control. Financial planning.	*Cost data* and financial plans.			

Source: Compiled by author.

205

- Teacher morale and satisfaction, including trust, confidence, communication, and teamwork.
- Cost control and financial planning.

While these concepts are not a perfect representation of school performance or complete in every detail, they provide a general framework to help focus planning and evaluation on subjects of major importance.

Exhibit 10.5 also shows the four components of evaluation essential to effective operation in practice: (1) A general institution-wide performance planning, monitoring, and reporting process should involve the board and superintendent as well as administrators; (2) Performance information roughly paralleling the performance concepts should be utilized; (3) Administrative evaluation should incorporate both the planning process and performance information, as well as an individualized reporting and evaluation process; and (4) Teacher evaluation and development should also be an important component of the overall evaluation process. While the overall plan would be incomplete without acknowledging this component, it is treated only to a limited extent in this report since it has not been directly a part of the study.

Exhibits 10.6 and 10.7 are examples of formats and criteria for evaluation.

CASE STUDY EIGHT
Superintendent Evaluation

A particularly important aspect of administrative evaluation concerns the relationship between the board and superintendent. Traditionally, strong, authoritarian superintendents permitted little actual evaluation of their performance by the board. More recently many boards have become overly aggressive in this regard and have dismissed superintendents with or without adequate justification in part because the evaluation process did not exist or had broken down at board/superintendent level.

The approach shown in Exhibit 10.8 is simple and straightforward. It does not require extensive paperwork or very much time on the part of the board, both of which are seen to be essential prerequisites to a practical approach. It encourages board support,

EXHIBIT 10.6
The School Performance Accountability System: A Suggested Preliminary Format

School Performance Concepts*	School Report**		
	Findings	*Conclusions*	*Recommendations*
Student Progress	A description of the present situation in the school.	Needs, problems, strengths, weaknesses, priorities.	Plan of action, steps to be taken, responsibilities, timing.
• Student learning.			
• Behavior.			
• Development.			
Parent Satisfaction			
• General.			
• Specific.			
• Involvement.			
Staff Morale			
• Teacher.			
• Other.			
• Communication, teamwork.			

*This conceptual framework for considering school performance needs to be developed in a more specific and detailed form; a more detailed draft is attached.

**Each of these three sections might require a page or two of text, supplemented by discussion.

Source: Compiled by author.

EXHIBIT 10.7
Examples of Detailed Performance Criteria

STUDENT PROGRESS
- Student learning and academic progress.
    - One year's growth on average in each classroom each year.
    - Adjustment for students, circumstances, in each classroom.
    - Particular attention to students achieving below expectation.
- Student behavior and discipline.
    - Satisfactory student behavior, appropriate to age level.
    - Discipline by teachers and principal appropriate, fair, accepted.
    - Acceptable attendance, dropout, suspension, and expulsion rates.
- Personal/social growth and development.
    - Judgment of school staff.
    - Special events.

PARENT SATISFACTION
- General satisfaction: schools; progress of children.
    - Academic programs.
    - Progress of their children.
    - Relationships and communication with school.
    - Supporting services.
- Specific satisfaction and concerns, each aspect of school performance.
    - Staff perceptions.
    - Parent survey results.
- Public confidence, support, involvement.
    - Communication – school to parents.
    - Parent participation; conferences, other.
    - Other evidence of parent support.

STAFF MORALE
- Teacher satisfaction: schools, programs, working conditions.
    - Academic programs.
    - Progress of children.
    - Supporting services.
    - Working conditions: evaluation, communication, supervision.
- Other staff members: secretaries, aides, support staff.
- Communication, teamwork.
    - Staff meetings.
    - Participation by teachers in extra responsibilities.
    - Support for district policies and programs.
    - Principal's classroom presence and staff contact.

ADDENDUM INDIVIDUALIZED TO EACH PRINCIPAL:
- Personal growth and development plans.
- Personal contribution, leadership, and management style.

Source: Compiled by author.

EXHIBIT 10.8
Recommended Approach for Board Evaluation of Superintendent

District Objectives and Accomplishments	Performance Information	Personal Factors
A simple process with minimum paperwork and practical, straightforward objectives and reports is best.	Use performance information to build confidence and morale, and identify opportunities for improvement.	The first two components of evaluation should reduce this one to minor considerations.
• Reported to the board (at least annually); discussed.	• Student learning – test results, especially average annual growth. District data summarized, compared to history. Used internally to identify improvement opportunities and take action.	Some boards prefer formal checklists, filled in by each member, compiled by the president. A short, informal discussion can be equally effective. Or the board president can survey each member by phone.
• Resulting from participative process involving management team and teachers.	• Parent surveys – general satisfaction, and specific improvement opportunities.	Subjects can be as simple as:
• Other presentations to the board on programs, from administrators and teachers.	• Teacher surveys – internal communication channel, complements parent survey.	• Board support, materials, operations, and relationships.
Key components of school management essential to good performance should be included:	• Financial planning and cost control.	• Personal leadership, behavior, and style.
• Administrative organization, evaluation, and compensation.	Such information should be presented to the board periodically during the year.	Findings and suggestions might then be discussed with the superintendent by the board president.
• Teacher evaluation and development.	*Result*: board confidence and support for district performance, delegation to the superintendent and management team.	*Result*: early awareness of relationship problems.
• Planning and evaluation process – development, analysis and use of performance information.		
Result: board comfortable that the district is moving in a thoughtful direction with priorities that the board understands and approves.		

Source: Compiled by author.

209

confidence, and delegation to the administrative and teaching staff of the district. It is designed to build teamwork, trust, and confidence at all levels of the organization. It does require performance information and a process of planning and reporting, previously discussed.

The need to evaluate the performance of the superintendent is one of the most important and difficult challenges facing school boards today. It is best to avoid complicated time-consuming approaches in favor of the model described in Exhibit 10.8. The model is organized in three sections: district objectives and accomplishments, performance information, and personal factors. Each section is described briefly below.

The first and most important part of the model is a simple process of setting objectives and reporting accomplishments. This should involve minimum paperwork with short, straightforward reports. At most these should be a few pages long. The result should be board comfort that the district is moving in an appropriate direction with thoughtful priorities, with a common understanding of this direction on the part of the board and the superintendent. Because these objectives should be developed with participation of the management team and teachers, this summary for the board reflects a process that should be operational throughout the district.

The second and equally important part of board evaluation of the superintendent should involve regularly reported information in all of the important categories of performance — student learning, parent surveys, teacher surveys, and financial planning and cost control. As a result of this information, the board should have confidence in and support for district performance and be willing to delegate to the superintendent and management team.

Finally, boards will find it necessary to consider the personal behavior of the superintendent, if only to avoid problems arising suddenly in this regard. This should be a very simple process that ideally might be handled quite informally by the board president in discussion with other board members and then the superintendent. This category should be of minimal importance unless there is some particular problem.

This model of evaluation is replicated for other administrators, except that personal factors become a more important process of evaluating personal impact on the organization and considering personal and career development opportunities and needs.

CONCLUSION OF CHAPTER 10

Administrators are critically important to successful schools because they take responsibility for performance and affect the achievements of many teachers. Yet there is another sense in which teachers are even more important. Obviously they represent the delivery level of educational services. There are many more of them than administrators. And their evaluation is both difficult and extremely important both to good performance, high morale, and the job satisfaction and productivity of teachers themselves.

Because of the greater challenge involved in strengthening teacher evaluation and development, most districts will find it advantageous to move first in the area of administrative evaluation. Smaller districts are often able to move more quickly to the teacher level of organization in strengthening management and in the communication and relationships that permit this. In any case, you must get to this level if you are going to obtain the improved performance that good management promises. Chapter 11 addresses this issue.

11

TEACHER EVALUATION AND DEVELOPMENT:
To Improve Confidence, Performance, and Morale

Teacher evaluation and development is the most important and most difficult aspect of school management. The power of teachers to subvert unfair practices through union organization today is obvious and real. Demands for public accountability have often generated legislative and administrative responses that are awkward, clumsy, and offensive, and sometimes also very expensive in direct cost, time lost, or negative performance impact. A climate of general concern about school performance, and some evidence of decline, naturally makes educators nervous about evaluation. A history of unfair practices, authoritarian leadership, and ineffective, unfunded development doesn't provide a sound base to build on. Yet, teacher evaluation and development is the single most important factor to improved school performance, since the effectiveness of teachers is the essence of school performance.

This chapter consists of three case studies describing problems perceived by teachers with evaluation and development and recommendations to correct them. They proceed from more general problem-oriented descriptions to quite specific recommendations.

Case Study Nine presents interview notes and conclusions from discussion of evaluation and development with teachers at the Kohl Teacher Center. These teachers were highly competent professionals who discussed teacher evaluation and development in a very open way.

212

Case Study Ten contains specifications for teacher evaluation and development. Parallels will be seen to the more general discussion, but issues peculiar to this district will also be noted.

Case Study Eleven presents a recommended teacher evaluation and development plan — a complete set of recommendations for staff development and a comprehensive new evaluation system in this district. These recommendations have been completely implemented during the past six years, and are working to make teacher development more practical and effective.

CASE STUDY NINE
Interview Notes

INTRODUCTION TO CASE STUDY NINE

The place to begin in strengthening teacher evaluation and development, whether speaking of the entire institution of education, a single district, or an individual teacher, is with the teacher. I have done this in many districts by speaking directly with teachers individually and in groups, in the classroom and elsewhere. These discussions are always interesting and revealing as to why teacher evaluation is not operational in most districts today and why teachers object so strenuously to what they perceive to be unfairness and inadequacy.

Most of these discussions in individual districts retain a strong flavor of the particular circumstances and features of evaluation and even individuals involved in that particular district. But I have had one occasion to discuss teacher evaluation and development with a particularly insightful and talented group of teachers, thanks to a relationship I have enjoyed for several years with the Kohl Teacher Center. This private foundation-sponsored facility offers a friendly and inviting atmosphere in which teachers find their own curriculum planning, instructional methods, ideas, and materials greatly stimulated. The staff seems to me to have an exceptional ability to provide teachers with a setting in which they can fulfill their desires to invest more of their time in the improvement of their own performance and development of their own capabilities as teachers. While you may find this a little surprising in an age of tough bargaining and aggressive teacher unions, I believe it reflects the underlying character of most teachers today, as I think has probably always been the case. Teaching is a profession that involves a great deal of giving and interest in the development of other people. There are few limits on what can be accomplished. Perhaps for these reasons, or perhaps just because of the character of the people who have chosen a teaching career in this country, this quality seems to flourish in a setting like the Kohl Teacher Center.

For purposes of the school management model described in this book these interviews have served a critically important role. They provide a more generic assessment by teachers of evaluation and development practices and requirements, in a setting conducive to their professional responsibility and creativity, comfortable for open and honest discussion, and not specifically related to the practices of any one district. I hope these notes are an adequate reflection of the intensely positive and responsible discussion that they report.

If we are able to respond to the concerns and requirements for successful evaluation specified by these teachers, the performance of our schools would be greatly improved. This is perhaps the most challenging of the management requirements of schools, one that we must address with a sensitive appreciation of its difficulty and the early state of its development at the present time. Since our economy will probably soon be comprised predominantly of services, these views on teacher evaluation may also have broader relevance. I have used them in other public services, nonprofit agencies, and service aspects of business such as research and management.

CASE STUDY NINE

At the heart of school performance is the need for teacher evaluation and development that work positively to improve performance, morale, confidence, and learning — rather than threatening, frightening, and demoralizing teachers, or not really evaluating performance at all.

This section outlines a case study of teacher evaluation to constructively improve teacher performance and development, contribute to better school performance, and add to the job satisfaction and productivity of teachers.

This approach to teacher evaluation is based mainly on discussions with teachers and staff members at the Kohl Teacher Center.

It also reflects our management consulting work with more than 100 school districts during the past eight years, and our research on fair and effective evaluation. This research included performance information, administrative and program evaluation, and the most important and difficult aspect, teacher evaluation, which is the subject of this section.

Present Practices

Perhaps the easiest way to summarize teacher evaluation at present is to highlight frequent comments of teachers during our discussions of this subject with them. In general, teachers seem to feel that most present evaluation policies and practices of school districts are unfair and ineffective. Consequently, with the power acquired by teachers through unions, evaluation is inoperative in many school districts today. There are many reasons why evaluating educational performance is extremely difficult, challenging, and complicated.

Defining the academic, social, emotional, and community dimensions of performance, deciding who is accountable for what, and defining what business a school is in, as a basis for determining how it can be evaluated, are part of the problem, compounded by the fact that schools can't be measured in the same ways a product can.

Added to this is the fact that evaluation is often threatening and frustrating rather than constructive and positive, because some policies and practices seem designed to be adversarial rather than to build teamwork, morale, and productivity. Rigid checklists of teaching style and personality traits are still common, and reducing the effect of personality and providing for consistency among buildings are rare. In conjunction with this, or perhaps because of it, recognition and reward for good performance are limited, and little worthwhile development is provided for teachers. Yet teachers want to be evaluated, and recognize that this can contribute to good performance.

Supervisory requirements expressed by teachers are very demanding and, they report, not often met. Educators will comment that principals must be competent, professional educators — good teachers themselves. It is also felt that skills at coaching, counseling, guiding, and developing people are essential to competent supervision.

However, fewer than one-quarter of principals are seen by teachers to adequately measure up to these criteria.

Obviously these brief comments can only superficially describe the complexities and intricacies of teacher evaluation today. We hope they convey a sense of the frustration and inadequacy that surrounds such an important element of school management.

There is considerable variation among districts we have viewed. Some are successful in evaluating teacher performance fairly and effectively. Others have given up even attempting to evaluate teachers, leaving principals to fend as best they can for themselves, or developing elaborate policy manuals without actually evaluating in practice. The results are deteriorating teacher morale, and student learning, and ultimately the human, economic, and social cost of poor school performance. Obviously the consequences of getting teacher evaluation right are tremendously important not only to educators but to our nation.

Key Features of Fair and Effective Teacher Evaluation

These features of teacher evaluation are characteristic of approaches that are working successfully. How they can be applied in any one district requires a deep and sensitive understanding of how that district's present policies are working in practice and how they are viewed by teachers, administrators, and board members.

A Well-Documented Plan, Designed To Be Fair and Constructive

Teachers can't understand, accept, and implement a plan that isn't fully defined; therefore, documentation is the first prerequisite to an efficient plan. The design should offset the naturally threatening qualities of evaluation in any field, especially one as difficult to measure and emotionally sensitive as education. Performance evaluation can be a positive, constructive experience if thoughtfully developed and effectively implemented.

Separating Evaluation for Dismissal from Development

Only a few teachers are likely to fall in the dismissal category, and legal due process requirements demand considerably different procedures, including documentation. Distinguishing development-oriented evaluation from dismissal helps defuse and diminish its threatening and negative qualities, and encourages the participation and involvement of teachers essential to good evaluation.

Separating Program from Teacher and Administrator Evaluation

Rarely can school performance be traced to a single individual. Usually parents, teachers, administrators, and even the board and community, have inseparably contributed. Program evaluation should be used positively, to defend district performance and quality to public and board, demonstrate aggressive identification of improvement opportunities, action, and results, and build teamwork, satisfaction, and responsibility.

Teacher Participation in Defining and Operating Evaluation

Constructive dialogue and a spirit of teamwork and cooperation rather than threatening, adversarial relationships, are absolutely essential to an effective teacher evaluation plan. Communication, and attention to small problems where important (e.g., materials), will help to establish the proper atmosphere for this. Provisions should be made for teachers to explain and defend what they are doing, as well as for teachers to evaluate the evaluators. More dialogue, interaction, exploration, communication, conversation, and reflection on performance between teachers and administrators, are the cornerstone of constructive evaluation.

Information To Help Offset Subjectivity

Dropout rates, test scores, surveys of parents, teachers, students, community, and graduates will form the basis of a file of objective information, which can be referred to when necessary. However, the limits of such data in understanding performance should be recognized.

More Effective Teacher Development

Staff development should be individualized by evaluation, diagnosis, and prescription. More practical teacher development rather than inservice days, and college courses, which are often inadequate, should be made available. Also, the valuable practical knowledge of experienced teachers should be used to train others.

Multiple Views To Offset the Risks of Personality, Style, Opinion

Principals should review evaluations as a group, and team leader and central office perspectives should be included in final evaluation reports. A panel of master teachers, who will be close to the process of teaching and familiar with its exigencies, should also be a part of the evaluation team. Self-evaluation letting the teachers review and evaluate their own performance will increase the sense of participation and thus make it a less threatening experience for teachers.

Abilities of Administrators To Evaluate Performance

Before any kind of performance report is decided upon, evaluators must be given enough time to observe classroom and other factors, developing understanding of circumstances, styles, strengths, and weaknesses of each teacher. Also, enough administrators must be available to provide time for dialogue, communication, and reflection on performance. Finally, it is important to monitor results for consistency, among schools and over time. Practical evaluation training for principals and others involved and selection criteria for principals appropriate to these requirements will give evaluators a structured system to work within.

Recognition and Reward for Good Performance

Teacher salary schedules encourage going back to graduate school for easy courses, and so are a disincentive to quality, perpetuating incompetence, dissatisfaction, and frustration. Because merit pay has been soundly designed and effectively implemented, teachers are more satisfied and performance is better. However, although merit pay is a valuable system for increasing a sense of job satisfaction, it is usually not well designed or implemented, and so hasn't worked well in practice.

Obviously these criteria add up to a very demanding set of requirements. No wonder teacher evaluation isn't working very well in school districts today. Yet, if the good performance of schools is to be recognized, and performance is to be improved where it can and should be, teacher evaluation that works and that teachers find acceptable is essential.

Exhibit 11.1 is a summary of ten key management techniques for teacher evaluation and development. These ideas are reflected in the discussion notes in this case study and in the specifications and recommendations contained in the next two case studies.

CASE STUDY TEN
Specifications for Teacher Evaluation

INTRODUCTION TO CASE STUDY TEN

Following the description of the problems teachers see in their evaluation and development described in Case Study Nine, we turn now to specifications for evaluation and development from one district. These encompass the same principles listed at the end of the previous case study, but relate them to the circumstances of a particular district. The plan is not spelled out in detail, but instead is a transition between the problem described in the first case study in this chapter and the much more detailed solution in the third case study. You will of course see many common themes.

In these materials you might want to note the tendency of educators to desire the equivalent of a report card in judging teacher performance. There is a high level of interest in what form or instrument is to be used for evaluation purposes. My experience, on the contrary, is that the process, purpose, policies, and procedures of evaluation are vastly more important than the form. In most of our work, we have found ourselves by the end of the analysis to be fairly indifferent to what form is used, as long as it is a simple representation of performance and not a checklist of personality characteristics or some rigid formula of teaching style. I know one district that functions extremely effectively with a form that consists of nothing but three words: observations, conclusions, and recommendations. Others use more elaborate descriptions of teacher results and behavior successfully as well.

Remember too that none of these approaches to evaluation can work effectively without a framework of communication and participation and without the confidence and support that comes from performance information.

EXHIBIT 11.1
Ten Management Techniques for Teacher Evaluation and Development

Technique	Purpose
Prepare a well-documented plan, designed to be fair and effective.	To permit staff understanding of purpose and procedures, and to contribute positively to performance, development, and morale.
Build staff communication, teamwork, trust, and confidence.	To encourage good working relationships and job satisfaction, and to offset trends of fragmentation and adversarial relations.
Separate evaluation for development from dismissal and discipline.	To distinguish positive teacher growth and development from the quite different requirements of dismissal due process procedures.
Provide for teacher participation, dialogue, and involvement.	To make evaluation and development a two-way street, with teachers and administrators sharing views on performance and improvement.
Develop a program planning and reporting process.	To communicate, monitor, and report in order to build responsibility, participation, communication, confidence, and teamwork.
Use performance information.	Test data analysis and parent/teacher surveys: to build board/public/staff confidence; and to identify improvement opportunities.
Use multiple views to offset personality, style, and opinion.	To make evaluation tolerable and effective for teachers.
Individualize staff development.	To make it practical, get it funded, and relate it to evaluation.
Train principals and monitor results.	To ensure consistency among schools and grades, and needed skills in evaluation, communication, and staff relations.
Recognize and reward good performance.	To emphasize positive aspects of evaluation, build morale.

Source: Compiled by author.

CASE STUDY TEN

This report reflects interviews with more than 100 teachers, administrators, and board members, including visits to every school – the first diagnostic step in reviewing teacher evaluation. Following discussion of a preliminary draft with board, administrators, and the Instructional Council, some changes have been made and a third section has been added. This summary report, highlighting more detailed interview notes, is organized in three sections: (1) findings and observations based on interviews; (2) suggested specifications for Shelley teacher evaluation; and (3) recommended next steps.

Findings and Observations Based on Interviews

These observations reflect major themes and common concerns, principally with regard to tenured teachers.

Evaluation Is One of the Most Important and Difficult Issues Confronting Education Today

Shelley is in the forefront of recognizing and addressing this need, and evaluation is actually operational in Shelley Public Schools. Healthy staff relations and strong academic programs provide an excellent starting point for addressing this issue. Thoughtful, responsible, and insightful staff contributions reflect communication and trust in the district, without which it would be impossible to discuss such a difficult subject. Community identity and character are also significant assets. For these reasons, the Shelley Public Schools seem well positioned to strengthen teacher evaluation.

Teachers Would Like Evaluation To Be More Positive and Constructive

The threat of dismissal and feeling of an adversarial process is diminishing the extent to which evaluation can be used for constructive staff development and performance improvement purposes. Teachers believe that a more communicative, participative, process would be beneficial. However, the need to take action (in those few cases where teachers are not performing adequately to meet district standards is recognized. If this could be separated more clearly from the developmental purposes of evaluation, more effective development might result.

Evaluation should help to build pride, confidence, and teamwork, rather than only revealing shortcomings. It should build on strengths to improve performance, foster growth, and add to job satisfaction, morale, and productivity. In light of this, it should be noted that discussion is more effective than a score card, as a parent conference is more effective than a report card, in understanding, communication, and development.

In short, the present evaluation process seems negative and adversarial rather than motivating and satisfying. It tends to be demoralizing, threatening, frustrating, and stressful rather than helpful, encouraging, and positive in terms of teacher growth and development. In reacting to these observations, the Instructional Council seemed to feel that lack of consistency, the desire for more communication, and a vaguely threatening quality about evaluation were more important than the actual threat of dismissal.

In spite of the problems, a high level of satisfaction with evaluation was evident in several schools, along with recognition that evaluation is difficult and that the present process can be improved. Teachers want more help on how to develop and improve, more immediate feedback, and a process that is less mysterious and negative. Clarification of purposes and standards would help; for example, does the scoring key refer to an ideal teacher, the best teacher in the district, or the average teacher?

When considering the various aspects of evaluation, you should keep in mind that concerns are not necessarily clearly distinguished from broader concerns about communication and relationships among organizational levels and uneasiness over the evident accountability pressures in education today.

Teachers Want Evaluation To Be Fair

The importance of the individual evaluator in fair and effective evaluation is recognized; yet, ways to reduce the effect of personality on evaluation are desired. Unfortunately, there doesn't appear to be any machinery to assure consistency between schools; it is apparent to teachers that some principals are harder graders than others. One way of solving this is to incorporate the views of more than one individual, which could reduce the effect of personality on evaluation.

Teachers are well aware of the extreme difficulty of measuring education. Just a few of the difficulties involved are:

1. Little tradition of analysis, few tested and proven techniques and skills.
2. Importance of the ability of children.
3. Circumstances beyond the control of teachers.
4. Possibility that the most challenging children are given to the best teachers.
6. Children may learn better in later years because of something a teacher did earlier.
7. Problems that children bring with them to school today may be more challenging than they were in earlier years.
8. Testing procedures are not always adequately controlled to ensure sufficient accuracy to support comparisons.

However, emphasis on results that can be measured could reduce attention to more important factors that cannot be measured, dehumanizing education and diminishing benefits to children. Teachers are sensitive to the need to preserve human as well as academic standards, and not become overly quantitative.

Staff Development Is Not Seen To Be Effective

Faculty talent is not being adequately utilized in staff development, and analysis of teaching performance needs to be complemented with follow-up capability for useful developmental activities.

Recent formation of the Shelley Professional Staff Development Policy Board is encouraging and might provide a basis for further strengthening of staff development in the future. Many other questions were raised by teachers. Those questions were stimulating but not necessarily immediately answerable. The following is a summary of the most important issues.

- How is responsibility for school performance shared among board, administrators, and teachers?
- Why do teachers perceive rewards going to administrators and blame to teachers?

- Can information be used to indicate performance without overly quantifying the process, unfairly reflecting on teachers or misdirecting efforts away from the imponderables of human development?
- What is the function of administrators: to monitor performance, foster development, or dismiss when required?
- Is the teacher responsible for input or output?
- Different styles of teaching can be equally effective; would creativity and productivity be stimulated by assessing results, rather than style?
- Is there a need to preserve the creative tension that results from evaluating performance, and administrative authority to act when needed?
- How can outside observation and perspective be made more valuable to teacher development, as a means of reflecting upon performance and development opportunities and offsetting the natural isolation of the classroom and individual character of teaching?
- There seems to be a feeling on the part of teachers that evaluation is a tool designed to be used against teachers. For example, is the need to make written justification of "1" scores intended to discourage high scores?
- How can evaluation be improved for teachers without eroding the authority of principals, in those situations where action is needed, and where evaluation may be essential and constructive to needed improvement?

Suggested Specifications for Shelley Teacher Evaluation

These are general guidelines against which a new Teacher Evaluation Plan might be developed.

Separate Dismissal from Development

Without this distinction, the risk of dismissal for a few teachers diminishes positive and constructive evaluation and development for the vast majority of teachers. It is vital to clarify the purposes of evaluation, and distinguish between development and discipline and possibly dismissal, following necessary and appropriate due process procedures. It would also be wise to consider a possible third category in the evaluation process for nontenured teachers since their probationary status is inherently different from tenured staff.

Separate Program Evaluation from Personnel Evaluation

Unless program evaluation is distinguished from personnel evaluation, evident pressure for performance analysis impedes a fully constructive and positive teacher evaluation process.

It should be recognized that multiple factors and responsibilities are involved in total program performance, e.g., students, teachers, parents, materials, curriculum, board policy, administrators, and various other circumstances. All these factors should be included in the total evaluation process and in final evaluation reports.

There are many reasons for having an effective program evaluation process in a school district, not the least of which is to defend the district's good performance and quality to the public, board, and state. Information gathered in evaluation can be used to prove that a good job is being done, and to identify improvement opportunities. Finally, because teachers are most closely involved in administering programs, they should be involved in appraising and reporting program progress and performance. Other suggestions are shown in Exhibit 11.2.

From these specifications, we turn to a specific recommended teacher evaluation and development plan that has been working successfully for several years.

CASE STUDY ELEVEN
Teacher Evaluation and Development Plan

INTRODUCTION TO CASE STUDY ELEVEN

This is a teacher evaluation and development plan that has been working successfully for many years. Evaluation is positive and constructive and contributes materially to the performance of the district and the teachers. An active process of communication is maintained and problems are identified and corrected during the year where appropriate. Often as many as 10 percent to 20 percent of the teaching staff is found to be having specific difficulties early in the year — e.g., with a new teacher, new grade level assignment,

EXHIBIT 11.2
Other Teacher Evaluation Suggestions

Redefine, clarify, and strengthen the teacher evaluation process.
- Develop written guidelines.
- Incorporate multiple views (e.g., central office administrators, department heads, other principals, team leaders for grade or subject).
- Consider teacher self-evaluation, to initiate the process.
- Provide for more informal observations and feedback (and probably more frequently).
- Provide for expanded dialogue, interaction, exploration, communication, and reflection on performance.
- Informalize the process, and reduce its threatening quality, to encourage openness and sharing of concerns and improvement opportunities.
- Link evaluation more closely with development.
- Consider more recognition and reward for good performance.
- Reconsider evaluation filing and record keeping requirements; some material might be destroyed after use.
- Train evaluators and monitor results to gain more consistency among schools and over time.

Retain the present evaluation form, with some modifications.
- Convert personal characteristics to pass/fail, yes/no.
- Simplify scoring.
- Reconsider language.
- Consider written comments.
- Continue the supplementary letter, but with prior discussion.

Strengthen staff development.
- Diagnose opportunities for improvement, as part of evaluation.
- Individualize development prescriptions.
- Inventory development techniques effective for specific situations.
- Use experienced teachers for staff development.
- Adequately fund staff development.

Improve teacher communication and feedback.
- Continue policy of teamwork, communication, and participation.
- Survey teacher opinions and concerns regarding school performance, working conditions, evaluation, and administration — objectively and anonymously.
- Consider strengthening the involvement of teachers in policy development.

Source: Compiled by author.

226

new program, new textbook, new curriculum, etc. Quick action is believed to have a material impact on overall performance. Every teacher has a development plan individually prepared and district funded. Evaluation is initiated by the teacher and reviewed with a panel of three administrators at classroom, school, and district level. A positive and effective teacher evaluation and development plan like the one described in this report can substantially improve the productivity, satisfaction, and morale of teachers. Its cost is negligible. The participative and communicative style of management required to develop and operate it in practice is demanding but well within the capabilities of most school administrators.

Background on the District

This is a small suburban elementary district which has experienced a sharp decline in enrollment during the past several years. Expectations of parents are high, and over the years the district is believed to have performed well against these standards. In recent years, an aggressive effort to individualize the instructional program has been made. This involved a high level of staff participation, and some controversy. The staff is represented by a union. For a time, bargaining was fairly heated, with some effort to form a consortium of bargaining units among several nearby districts. Since the present plan has been adopted, staff relations and union activities have been rather quiet. Teachers were highly involved in the preparation of this plan, participating heavily on a group and individual basis throughout the year. The covering letter and report follow.

April 8, 1976

Superintendent
Marie School District #73
7316 Morton Street
Walden, Illinois

Dear

It has been a great pleasure for us to be associated with you and your staff during the past several months of our work together on the staff development and teacher information study.

As noted in the original proposal, the work has been of a "creative and exploratory character . . . a pilot study, working closely with teachers." The focus was broadly on the general concerns of the Staff Development Committee — teacher effectiveness, staff development, and management information — although two issues stood out as being of greatest concern:

- How to develop needed management skills for the teaching/learning process; and
- How to support this teacher management and decision-making process with appropriate and useful management information.

The expected end result was to be both a better understanding of the underlying problems of staff development and what might be done to meet them, and a conceptual scheme of management information to meet the needs of your teaching staff. These objectives implied that a pioneering effort was required, and the risk of failure was openly recognized by all concerned. In fact, these objectives have been met and, we believe, exceeded, with practical recommendations that go beyond teacher information and staff development with direct implications for the improvement of teacher effectiveness and performance.

Staff Development

The results of the first phase of the work led to a focus in the second phase on efforts to identify a practical approach to strengthening both the staff development process and the preparation and utilization of information on teacher performance. The purpose was to improve staff development for teachers having difficulty in using information or in other aspects of teaching, and to improve the availability and use of information on educational performance. It was recognized that to move in this direction would require innovative approaches, and would demand implementation in the face of what many educators see as intractable obstacles — the insistence by teachers on fairness and openness in evaluation systems, and the general fear surrounding evaluation.

The solution that evolved in this second phase of the study was simple, but dramatically different from practices in common use. It focused on individualizing the staff development process. The basic outline of this approach, along with a number of alternatives, was reviewed with the teaching staff of the district, and their participation obtained in evaluating this idea, whether it would be helpful assuming it could be successfully developed, and how best, as a practical matter, to organize the process and support it with defined responsibilities and required information.

The primary resulting recommendation is that Marie School District should implement a staff development process, outlined in detail in this report, that focuses on: (1) diagnosis of individual teacher development needs, based on appraisal of performance initiated by the teacher; (2) review and discussion of performance with each teacher by a team representing grade level, school, and district viewpoints, resulting in recommendation of an individualized staff development program; and (3) support for the process with information regarding teacher performance, which will need to be developed.

Sincerely yours,
Fredric H. Genck

REPORT OF THE STAFF DEVELOPMENT AND TEACHER INFORMATION STUDY: MARIE DISTRICT #73

This report is organized in three sections presenting findings, conclusions, and recommendations. Several sections of this report have been omitted and where this has been done, as in other case studies, omissions are indicated by ***.

Findings

Staff Development and Teacher Concerns

The concerns of teachers focus heavily on the ineffectiveness of present staff development practices and policies, not just in Marie but generally in education. To understand the nature of teacher concerns was the main task of the first phase of this study. These observations have not heretofore been expressed in a way that could provide a basis for action. Some of these concerns go beyond the recommendations and scope of this study.

Teachers are demanding an open, fair, explicit management process which supports and improves teaching in the classroom. Especially, teacher personnel policies must be spelled out and found acceptable by the teachers themselves if they are to prove workable in practice.

Because of the threat of evaluation and possible resulting termination of employment where reduction in staff is required, teachers are fearful of expressing their concerns with their own performance at the present time. Protestations that evaluation is not being conducted are unbelievable in the face of actual staff reductions.

Teachers require outside support, guidance, and observation in the course of appraising their own performance and diagnosing ways in which their development can be furthered. At the present time there is no satisfactory process for accomplishing this; attempts to do so will require that the threat of evaluation be diminished at least to the point of making it tolerable.

In terms of their development, teachers are as different from one another as are children. Any staff development program that is to be effective must recognize this individual character and the need for differentiation. There is also a differentiation among levels of teacher development that can be vitally important in staff development. Some teachers are not only fully developed and competent in their own teaching practices but are also able to pass on these skills to other teachers. In fact, in the view of other teachers, the best and perhaps the only way to learn teaching is from another teacher in a practical situation. A large group of teachers, probably by far the majority in a district like Marie, have developed to a fully professional level of competence as teachers. The main problem with respect to their further development is not remedial in nature but rather analogous to the kind of sophisticated coaching and counseling and observing that might be done with a fine athlete, actor, musician, or artist, to help understand where and how skills might best be further developed.

A few teachers in any district, including Marie, are experiencing difficulties in accomplishing the expected educational performance and results. They require assistance in identifying the nature of their problem and developing a course of action that can correct it. The need for action is pressing, and it is with respect to these teachers that the present absence of any positive diagnostic program is of greatest importance. Some of these teachers are relatively new to the profession, and others are not.

The present staff development programs are viewed by teachers as of limited effectiveness. College courses, in spite of the fact that they are a major factor in teacher compensation, are generally regarded as being of modest value. Inservice days are considered at best to be relevant only to the needs of a few teachers, and usually not to the kinds of needs that are critical.

Teachers are widely dissatisfied with the flat career and compensation structure under which they work. The fact that better teachers are not given commensurate rewards by their employers is seen as fundamentally unfair (apart from the obvious advantages in educational performance that might accrue from rewarding better performance). The fact that there are no promotional opportunities for teachers and no opportunities to increase their compensation through better performance has not gone unnoticed by the teachers themselves, and accounts for dissatisfaction and frustration on the part of the better teachers. They believe changes are needed in teacher personnel policies to overcome these evident deficiencies.

The implications of these observations are significant. They go beyond the initial focus of this phase of the work on teacher information and staff development, and suggest that the underlying problem is in fact much broader. In the first instance, the nature of the problem is that the staff development process must be considerably strengthened, as well as individualized, if the problems about which teachers complain are to be rectified. To do so requires dealing with the management process of the district, as well as with staff development and teacher information.

Other possible implications of these observations were recognized to be beyond the scope of the present study, and were simply noted and deferred for consideration later. These include implications for teacher compensation and promotional opportunities. The inference might well be drawn that present teacher compensation practices are of little value in either motivating good performance or encouraging sound development, being at best neutral and perhaps an impediment.

***

Development and Teacher Variation

The teaching process itself, perhaps especially under a philosophy of individualization, is subject to extreme variations in implementation and style from teacher to teacher. This observation, while perhaps obvious to practicing teachers, appears to be a vitally important requirement in any staff development and teacher information efforts. Variations in teaching style from one classroom to another are pronounced. Opportunities and requirements for teacher development correspondingly differ in striking ways. Any effort to standardize teaching style seems likely to prove dysfunctional.

Diagnosing staff development needs and appraising teacher performance must accommodate a sufficient breadth of viewpoint, which probably can only be accomplished through using more than one individual to do it, so that variations in style and personality are at least mitigated if not totally overcome.

***

A Third Category — Information on the Performance of the Teacher — Is Least Developed

Of the three categories of information analyzed during this study, that regarding the performance of the teachers is by far the least developed at the present time, and affords the greatest opportunity for strengthening the overall information system. This aspect of information concerns the combination of observations, judgments, and opinions with regard to the educational results and performance that each teacher is achieving in the classroom. This should of course be recognized to be a subject of considerable difficulty in education. In fact, the ultimate end results are obviously unmeasurable if one views them as the impact on a child's future lifetime.

Nevertheless, it is possible to obtain data that is useful in judging teaching performance, even if only in a context of considerable judgment, experience, and even intuition. The obstacle to doing so is partly the absence of the data in a usable form, and the relatively underdeveloped state of skills and techniques in analysis and interpretation of such information in school districts. But most important is the threatening quality of such information if practices and procedures for its utilization and incorporation in performance appraisal are not demonstrably fair to teachers. Unfortunately, this is rarely the case. If Marie is to move forward in this area, it will be necessary to move in advance of current practice, as the district has been prepared to do in its educational programs.

Although this section deals primarily with information, one of the most important conclusions of this study is that information with regard to teacher performance is less important than judgment and the process in which diagnosis occurs.

Providing Performance Information

Little information regarding their own performance is presently made available to teachers. Information itself is recognized to be capable of providing only a small portion of the total basis for understanding teacher performance. Nevertheless, some kinds of information have been found useful to teachers, and to the extent information can be utilized in understanding performance it tends to provide a more objective basis for the appraisal process. The most useful information falls into the following three categories:

- *Analysis of test data results* that show the performance of the children in a classroom relative to levels of achievement that can reasonably be expected for them, on a change-during-the-year basis, and with comparisons to results achieved in other district classrooms and by each teacher in previous years. While such information is recognized to be highly sensitive, and to require safeguards in handling, not to use such information in understanding teacher performance runs the risk of observations contrary to factual evidence.
- *Feedback of opinions from students* as to how well they liked their experience in the classroom and how they viewed their teacher. While such opinions are not a direct measure of teacher performance, or more than an indication of what is going on in the classroom, they provide an extremely useful source of information to teachers, and they are a valuable aid in judging performance.
- *Feedback from parents* as to how they view the experience of their children and the performance of their children's teachers.

Team Evaluation of Performance

Much more important than the information itself is the opportunity for discussion, and application of judgment, by the teacher with a small group of highly experienced professionals. The kinds of data indicated above should not be expected to provide more than 5 percent or 10 percent of the understanding required of teacher performance. By far the more important part must necessarily depend upon subjective observations and human judgment. This form of information necessarily provides the core of understanding with respect to teacher performance. The sources of this judgment are perhaps more important than the character of the information itself, which might be allowed to take almost any form that seemed relevant and useful. At least four participants are seen to have essential contributions to make to this process – the teacher, the team leader, the principal, and a district administrator.

The teacher should be the starting place for analysis of performance, for two reasons. One is that only the teacher is exposed to the children and classroom on a virtually full-time basis, and therefore is in the best position to observe what is happening. This is important even though a teacher's objectivity suffers the same disadvantage we all have in viewing our own performance. The second reason is that if performance appraisal is to be meaningful and understood it is essential that the teacher be the initiator of the process. Typically, teachers have a reasonably good perception of whether or not they are having difficulties, and if so what the general nature of the problem is, often including what might be done to correct it. The missing link is not the teacher's inability to understand what was going on but the fact that under present arrangements there is no opportunity to express this.

The second key participant in providing judgmental information on teacher performance is the team leader. The interaction among grade level teams is extensive, whether through sharing individual classrooms, informal contacts, discussions surrounding individual children, or merely day to day contacts because of classroom proximity. Although the intimacy of contact with each teacher's children and classroom is not as great as for the teacher, the perspective provided by the team leader's proximity to the situation is a major advantage. To fulfill this role it is essential that the team leader be selected for teaching competence and for skill in observing and aiding the performance of other teachers, a requirement not currently operational in the Marie District.

The third key participant in the development of judgmental information on teacher performance is the principal. Having responsibility for overall school performance, and for the fitting of individual teacher activities into a total program, makes it essential that the principal be involved in the collection of judgments on teacher performance. Balancing the principal's judgment with that of a team leader is also important, so that at least two sources of observations are available within the school itself.

Finally, it seems essential that there be some participation in the development of observations on teacher performance from a district level. This provides a source of perspective outside the school, and helps to ensure some consistency across the district and over time. Although the constraints of a small central office staff are obvious in a district like Marie, still it seems desirable if possible that this role be fulfilled at a level short of the superintendent, in order to preserve a perspective and objectivity at that level for monitoring the overall process.

These four sources of professional observations and judgment on teacher performance are considered essential to developing a proper basis of judgmental information for understanding teacher performance. Because these judgments necessarily represent at least 80 percent to 90 percent of the total performance appraisal for teachers, they are collectively much more important than the data discussed above. To bring them together is a time-consuming and challenging process.

Establishing Evaluation Processes

The process through which this information and judgment are assembled is more important than the information itself, and at the present time does not exist. As is common in education, the process of human responsibilities and relationships is more important than the information. At the present time, there is no such process, except at a most informal level. Therefore, it is impossible to have an explicit diagnosis of teacher performance, or for the information that is available to be utilized in any constructive way.

The most critical element in the development process is the diagnosis of needs, which is in practice inseparable from appraisal of teacher performance. The obstacle seems primarily to be the fear that surrounds the evaluation process in teachers' minds.

The district's announced policy of not evaluating teachers and of not structuring its test data so as to be useful for this purpose has not succeeded in alleviating the fear and concern in teachers' minds over evaluation. It seems that the evident need to reduce staff suggests to teachers that some evaluation must be occurring. In any event, the absence of an evaluation process is precluding the diagnosis of staff development needs, which is the requisite first step in developing and utilizing information with respect to teacher performance.

Because no process is specified, teachers, even if they understand their development needs, have no one to tell about it. The sharing of observations is discouraged by the threat of evaluation, particularly under circumstances where procedures and responsibilities are not specified, since the process is said not to exist. This step of diagnosis with the involvement of more than one individual outside the classroom is believed to be the most important aspect in any staff development process and the one most essential ingredient in improving teacher effectiveness.

The second aspect of the utilization of information with respect to teacher performance is the prescription of an action program to improve teacher performance once diagnosis has been accomplished.

Compared to the individualized model, which seems highly appropriate, the prescription step of staff development is at the present time poorly utilized in most school districts. Extra pay is given to teachers for taking college courses, which are widely seen to be of little value in improving teacher effectiveness. Inservice days are held that seem to assume that all teachers can benefit from the same development activities at the same time.

This study did not include evaluating the feasibility or desirability of modifying extra pay for course credits or changing inservice days. The clear implication for improving teacher performance information, however, lies in the direction of individualized staff development activities. While these are discussed in more detail in the next section, they focus heavily on the utilization of experienced teachers in the development of other teachers.

***

Conclusions

This section sets forth the conclusions of the study with respect to requirements for staff development policies and practices.

Strengthening Staff Development

Strengthening staff development represents the most practical and significant opportunity for increasing teacher effectiveness. Within the broad objective of this study to increase teacher effectiveness, staff development clearly represents the most significant and the most practical opportunity available for doing so. At the present time the process in Marie, as in education generally, is neither well targeted on specific teacher development needs or characterized by action programs that are having a positive effect on teacher competence, in spite of the obvious central importance of staff development to the overall educational competence and performance of the district.

The Importance of Teacher Effectiveness

Teacher effectiveness is obviously at the heart of educational performance for the district, and a positive staff development program is essential both to good performance and to fairness to the teaching staff. It seems almost unnecessary to point out the vitally important role that staff development should play in contributing to the overall teaching effectiveness of any school district. The teaching staff is any school district's most important resource, asset, and expenditure, a characteristic common not only to education but to most professional service organizations. Obviously in such enterprise no function of management is more important than the process of selection, development, and compensation of the professional staff, including the broad subjects of their relationship to their employer, working conditions, and general morale. Viewed in this way, it seems only common sense that staff development should represent a major focus of attention in any school district. Important are the quality and effectiveness of programs and, where warranted, the investment of funds to capitalize on opportunities for improving teacher effectiveness through staff development.

Changing Present Programs

Compared to the importance of staff development, the weakness and inadequacy of present programs in education is striking, and Marie is no exception. The primary programs for staff development in Marie as in education generally are additional compensation provided to teachers for taking college courses and accumulating credits, and inservice days during which various presentations are scheduled. In the view of teachers, as reflected in their opinions expressed during the course of this study, neither of these programs is very helpful.

College courses tend to be theoretical and of little practical value to the practicing teachers, in their view. This observation is not only a direct and specific finding of this study, but is generally recognized to be a view widely held by teachers, and one that is common in professional fields. As with doctors, actors, lawyers, consultants, and indeed managers, development beyond certain basic skills is inherently a do-it-yourself task. The most productive learning seems to come from watching other professionals, borrowing elements of their style, and adapting and incorporating them in one's personal practice of the trade or craft involved. This essential character of development in any professional field is neither recognized nor provided for by present staff development programs in Marie or in education generally.

Professional development generally must be predicated on an understanding of the teacher's present level of performance and the areas in which further improvement is both possible and desirable. Making these judgments is greatly aided by the perspective provided from viewpoints other than the individual practitioner. For example, conductors, directors, coaches, and supervisors in their respective fields provide a diagnosis of their respective practitioners whether they be musicians, actors, athletes, or craftsmen, both in diagnosing weaknesses and opportunities for improvement and in suggesting action to realize them in practice. Similarly in fields such as law, consulting, and science, small teams provide a setting in which more senior practitioners can pass on skills and techniques to younger or less talented individuals in a practical setting. This principle is also reflected in the organization of medical education.

Two particular obstacles to this approach to the staff development process are believed to exist in Marie and in education more generally. First, the classroom situation inherently limits the opportunities for teachers to observe other teachers in action, both because of obvious physical constraints as well as limitations of time. Developing a process that can overcome these problems seems feasible but will require thoughtful and creative attention. The interaction already taking place through the team organization of the district is functional and beneficial in this respect.

Second, fear of evaluation has caused the teaching staff to resist strongly any efforts to develop the performance appraisal process, without which diagnosis of teacher development needs has no adequate basis. While moving toward a more open, explicit, and demonstrably fair process of performance appraisal can help to overcome this problem, fundamentally the teaching staff of the district must accept the vital need for performance appraisal if their development is to be adequately provided for. The attraction of working in an organization with high professional standards is, unfortunately, not without its disadvantages for those whose performance may not measure up to the standards applied.

These conclusions of the present study, which arise directly from findings in the Marie District, also apply to education generally and represent a significantly different and quite unconventional approach to staff development. However, the process suggested does not seem particularly difficult or expensive to establish. If it could be done, the improvement in teaching effectiveness could be substantial.

Creating a Process of Development

Realizing these opportunities for the strengthening of staff development would require the creation of a process involving multiple professional appraisal of performance with respect to individual teachers, development of an inventory of possible action steps, and selection and prescription of such steps on an individualized basis. It seems important to set forth the requirements that would have to be met if the approach to staff development implied by the conclusions set forth above is to be realized in practice.

The district should determine that it does wish to take a positive and individualized approach to staff development. Although the costs are not believed to be great, a considerable innovation will be required as well as investment of time on the part of both teachers and administrators. The process of appraisal and prescription should be recognized as far more important than specific criteria or forms.

The need to appraise performance as a basis for prescribing action should be recognized, and every effort made to overcome the inherently threatening character of evaluation, especially in school districts likely to experience enrollment declines. The process should be specified in an open, explicit way so that it can be widely understood, and challenged by the professional staff where they are so inclined.

Performance appraisal and diagnosis phase should involve multiple views as a hedge against inevitable variations in educational style and philosophy among professional educators, and the appraisal should focus heavily on educational performance rather than personal traits.

Information relevant to teacher performance appraisal such as that specified in the preceding chapter (test data, student and parent opinions) should be developed and provided in a systematic way and coupled with adequate safeguards and analysis. In other words, the appraisal process should be based on objective information rather than exclusively on subjective judgment, recognizing that in practice the balance will always favor the latter.

The action steps resulting from this diagnostic and prescriptive process should focus heavily on the desirability of teachers learning from other teachers in a practical situation. And while the district should have a positive staff development program, fundamental responsibility for individual development should be recognized as resting initially and primarily on each professional employee of the district.

Recommendations

Recommendations for staff development to meet these requirements are outlined below, in four sections: diagnosis, prescription, organization, and information.

Diagnosis

The most essential requirement for an effective staff development program is the first step of diagnosis, i.e., teacher evaluation of performance.

Teachers are surprisingly knowledgeable in appraising their own performance, and are necessarily the starting point for any diagnosis of development needs. The nature of professional development requires that responsibility for it should rest heavily on each individual. Furthermore, teachers, based on observations during this study, are very knowledgeable about their own performance and are the obvious best source for an initial effort to define and understand current classroom situations.

It is possible in this aspect of diagnosis to build upon the approach that the district has already taken in encouraging teachers to appraise their own performance. The key difference, however, is that at the present time there is no adequate opportunity for teachers to express opinions about their own performance to an appropriate individual or group. Without this step the opinions and judgments of professionals other than the teacher cannot be incorporated. And the teacher loses any benefit of the perspective that would come from outside observation. Nor is it possible to develop a plan of action for further development and to authorize whatever actions or expenditures may be required to implement it.

In effect this requires inserting someone, or a group, into the role of teacher, coach, or supervisor in the staff development process. Doing so will permit individualizing the staff development process, starting with the teacher, but also providing support in diagnosing and planning how best to meet development needs.

A group is needed to review performance with each teacher. It appears essential to have a group involved in helping each teacher review performance, in a professional field where style and philosophy can differ significantly from one individual to another. Any performance appraisal system that depends on a single observer is, in our experience, unworkable. It appears essential that the members of this group meet at least these primary criteria: (1) they must be thoroughly competent professionals in the teaching field; (2) they must be personally able to develop a counseling relationship with the teachers of the district; and (3) they must be respected by teachers for their professional competence and skill in helping others develop.

These requirements clearly point toward a group whose character is primarily professional rather than administrative. Therefore, a good deal of thought and discussion has been devoted during this study to whether the group should be comprised of teachers or administrators. The conclusion, although advantages and disadvantages can be found in both directions, is that such a task is properly an administrative function and ought not to be expected of teachers with respect to their colleagues, since their base of information and comparison would be inadequate and decisions might be required that would go beyond those that should be expected of teachers.

The conclusion of this study is that a team comprised of balanced representation from district, school, and team levels would be most appropriate. Logically, this suggests that the team leader, the school principals, and the district administrator most concerned with staff development should comprise the group. Its membership would therefore be different for each of the teams in the district, with the principal of each school providing continuity across all teams within a school, and the district administrator providing continuity across the district as a whole. It also seems logical that the district administrator would provide a role of staff support to the group in two respects. First, the administrator should record findings, conclusions, and recommendations and maintain records. Second, he should collect and develop the experience of the district in appraising performance, identifying development needs, suggesting action programs, and appraising whether these have in fact proved useful in improving teacher effectiveness.

This performance review group would be expected to become a vitally important element of the management process in the Marie District, and is perhaps the keystone of the staff development recommendations in this survey.

The steps, timing, and procedures for diagnosis of staff development needs should be specified. This portion of the report provides a general outline of the policies and approach to staff development for Marie.

A process is envisioned in which the performance review group would meet with each of the district's teachers on a regularly scheduled basis several times each year. While experimentation and further discussion are also needed, it is suggested that perhaps three meetings would be an appropriate balance between the relatively time-consuming nature of the process and the need for an initial starting point, interim check, and final review. The timing for these meetings logically seems to be approximately September, January, and June.

Some observation of each teacher concerned would be required on the part of each of the members of the performance review group. In the case of the team leader and principal this would be expected to occur within the normal course of their responsibilities without necessarily having to be provided for separately. In the case of the district administrator, classroom observations at least in advance of each of the meetings are probably essential. Although such observations are widely regarded as highly inaccurate as a complete basis for understanding teacher performance, they appear essential as at least a part of the appraisal process.

For the district administrator to spend at least one hour in each classroom three times a year will amount to something on the order of 200 hours, or as much as 10 percent to 15 percent of the time available during the year. Such observations are already intended to be a part of the responsibility of the director of curriculum, but it has not been possible to implement them in practice. This investment of time on the part of a district administrator in observing individual teachers in the classroom seems well justified, though obviously it would have to compete with other requirements for administrative activities.

The meetings of the performance review group would be expected to last at least an hour and perhaps somewhat longer, and would probably have to be scheduled at the end of the working day. Obviously they would require at least an hour or two approximately three times a year on the part of each teacher. The meetings would also require time from the team leader, principal, and district administrator, roughly totaling on the order of 300 person-hours per year for three individuals. Again the time required is significant but is considered to be an appropriate and indeed essential allocation of administrative effort.

While the steps and procedures in the process are expected to require definition in some detail, as suggested by the preceding paragraphs, it is at the same time suggested that the structure of the discussion itself should be left in a relatively flexible format. Exhibit 11.3 outlines suggestions for the teacher's recording of personal performance, a record of classroom observation, and a summary of the performance review group discussion with the teacher. The primary organizing theme is around the three categories of: (1) factual description of the situation; (2) conclusions reached from these factual observations or evidence; and (3) recommendations that are based on the conclusions.

EXHIBIT 11.3
Suggested Actions of Performance Review Group

Description of the Situation
(Factual observations that provide a basis for conclusions and recommendations
– utilizing present room visitation form, or following general categories for
recording findings and observations.)
- Teacher Behavior
  - Management
  - Information
- Classroom situation, learning environment
- Appropriateness of teaching activity to district curriculum
- Extent of individualization
- Evidence of student learning
- Information resulting from analysis of test data and from feedback opinions
  of students and parents
- Teacher contribution to team and school

Conclusions
Conclusions about teacher performance as well as development needs and opportunities, based on description provided by teacher and/or observer(s), individually and, after the performance review group meets, in composite form.

Recommendations
Action steps recommended by observer and, collectively, by performance review
group.

Source: Compiled by author.

This relatively simple format is believed to have advantages over
any more complex structuring of the discussion itself. Furthermore,
it should accommodate some of the present forms now in use, both
those peculiar to the individual schools and the room visitation form
in use on a district-wide basis.

While everything possible should be done to divorce staff development from the threat of evaluation, it must also be understood
inherently to involve performance appraisal, if there is to be an
adequate basis for diagnosing development needs. Multiple appraisal
views, explicit steps and responsibilities, and the development of
information are believed adequate to provide teachers an opportunity
to challenge and at least tolerate the diagnosis process that is suggested.

Objective information should be developed as fully as possible so that the performance appraisal process has as much of an objective basis as is possible, but it must also be recognized that judgment and subjectivity are inevitable in a field as inherently unmeasurable as education. If the opinions and views expressed are those of professionals and reflect a fair balance of knowledgeable opinion at team, school, and district levels, then a basis for fairness seems to be built into the system.

Prescription

Although some suggestions for the inventory of techniques and action that seem likely to prove most useful in practice can be made as a direct result of this study, it should be recognized that further development based on experience is expected to be substantial. All members of the performance review group should be encouraged and expected to develop their skills in identifying development needs and recommending practical steps that result in improving teacher effectiveness. The district staff person on the team in particular should develop an inventory of techniques and a record of their effectiveness, including both specific steps and the success of various individuals in the district in implementing them. Included in the inventory should be at least the following elements:

- Providing the opportunity for teachers to observe other teachers within the Marie District.
- Providing counseling of individual teachers by other designated teachers, either during school hours or after school.
- Arranging for team composition so that teachers are in a situation where they can obtain coaching and counseling from other teachers within the team.
- Arranging for teachers to have the opportunity to observe classrooms and teachers in action in other districts.
- Organizing small courses for teachers within the district to be taught either by other teachers in Marie or teachers elsewhere.
- Sending teachers to seminars organized outside the district, either specifically for Marie or in general.
- Sending teachers to college courses.

In the case of both seminars and courses the district may well find it advantageous to expand upon the knowledge it already has of courses available and practical benefits that are derived from attending them.

In several of these cases some allocation of funds will probably be necessary, either to arrange for substitutes or to provide for tuition payments. Although cost estimates have not been made, it seems unlikely that these expenditures will be beyond modest levels. In part they might be recovered by a reconsideration of present district expenditures for staff development activities, both in terms of inservice days and in the additional compensation provided teachers for college credits accumulated.

The district will probably wish to be more precise as to how development authorization, whether cost is involved or not, is to be allocated among the various categories of problems that seem likely to develop. For example, a few teachers may be having acute problems, the remediation of which may be critical to district performance and worth the allocation of whatever resources may be required. Other minor problems may warrant a lesser expenditure. On the other hand, satisfactory or excellent performance ought not, it would seem, to preclude the allocation of resources for further development. Therefore a policy decision is required as to how the district's staff development program resources should be allocated between the further enrichment of performance for those teachers who may already have achieved excellent levels, and remediation for those relatively few who may be having serious difficulties.

Organization

The organization implications of these conclusions are important, although they do not require any substantial change in the district's present structure. The primary implication is that under the recommended approach to staff development it appears that the team leaders must fulfill a critical role in team supervision and leadership as well as performance appraisal/diagnosis. To do so will require that they be selected on a basis that recognizes this role, rather than the present liaison function. It appears that team leaders will need to be selected by the superintendent in the future, subject to review by the teachers on that team.

In addition, the desirability of a team leadership rather than liaison role is strongly supported by other findings of this study as a highly advantageous move. It should be recognized that to impose these responsibilities on individuals may require some additional compensation.

Finally, the composition of membership on individual teams is an important factor in positioning teachers needing developmental aid with others who are able and willing to provide that assistance. In this sense, the reorganization of teams which may arise from recommendations of the performance review group should at least be recognized as a possible longer run organizational implication of these staff development conclusions.

Information

The opportunities to expand teacher performance information described in the previous chapter – namely the utilization of test data as well as opinions from students and parents – obviously provide an important supporting element in the staff development process. However, because the information will be of little value or relevance until the process is developed, it need not be a first priority. Nor is it a prerequisite of moving toward the staff development approach suggested here.

Finally, it would be inappropriate not to point out explicitly that the present structure of teacher compensation in Marie as in education generally is not functional in terms of the staff development approach discussed in this chapter. While it is not necessarily a prerequisite of moving toward this staff development approach that the compensation policies of the district should be changed, it would appear to be highly desirable that they be reconsidered in an effort to find a more constructive approach, without in any way suggesting that teachers should be paid less than is now the case. The findings of this study, apart from this approach to staff development, are highly critical of present compensation methods and promotional opportunities available to teachers. The combination of this critical view by teachers themselves with the dysfunctional character of present compensation practices with respect to staff development argue compellingly for an effort to develop better policies.

These findings, conclusions, and recommendations point in the direction of a staff development process that is significantly different from common or traditional practices in education. The suggested process – perhaps best described by the phrase "individualization" – seems quite compatible with the teaching philosophy of the Marie

District. That such a distinctive approach to staff development should have evolved out of a study rooted strongly in the opinions of teachers themselves is not surprising, since teachers are outspoken in their criticism of staff development programs today. If these conclusions provide the basis for a program that can improve teacher effectiveness through staff development, it seems obvious that there is little that could be of greater benefit to the educational performance of the district.

12

FINANCIAL PLANNING
AND COST CONTROL:
To Build Support
and Improve Performance

The three case studies in this chapter present examples of a number of political issues on the structural and financial side of district operations.

Case Study Twelve on financial planning and cost control outlines a general conceptual scheme of school finance and cost control as a framework for board decision making. The model and accompanying description are generally applicable to any district. It is designed to enable school boards to focus on a few simple factors critically important to effective cost control, to know what information they should expect in order to provide for sound financial planning and projections, and to appreciate the uncertainty and complexity of financial decision making in a political context.

Case Study Thirteen presents a related but broader set of questions regarding school closing, integration, and the general structure of a district. The complexity of both financial and unquantifiable factors involved in these decisions has been very challenging to schools during the past decade. This complexity is revealed in the outline of issues considered by one district.

Case Study Fourteen ties together both the financial and people sides of school management in terms of board responsibilities. It contains a comprehensive model of evaluation that provides a framework from the board's perspective for tying together the whole organization at board/superintendent, administrative, and teacher levels. And it shares a management model applicable to both business and public services.

CASE STUDY TWELVE
Financial Planning and Cost Control Model

INTRODUCTION TO CASE STUDY TWELVE

Case Study Twelve presents a financial planning and cost control model designed to simplify school finance and help school boards focus on key factors to make sure they exercise effective control and make sound decisions.

Over the past several decades cost control in schools has generally been quite effective. The business management side of school administration has been fairly well developed with competent, responsible people attracted to this small but important aspect of school management. By contrast to management on the instructional side of things it seems fairly efficient. But more recently it has been overtaken by the growing complexity of financial planning and cost control in schools, by problems surrounding the general economic circumstances of the country, by much more complicated school finance plans (particularly involving complex state aid formulas not always thoughtfully developed with a view toward their overall consequences), and by an era of inflation in which awkward property assessment practices have proven inadequate to sustain confidence today.

Obviously these issues raise a host of serious problems for schools. One is that some school boards have lost control. Not knowing what data to focus on for cost control purposes, they have allowed their districts to get out of line. This accounts for the adverse trends of costs relative to inflation and enrollment that are frequently noted in national media attention to schools. I believe one of the most important underlying reasons is that school boards have not had a simple focused model to point them toward the most critical factors in this control, the main one of which is staffing ratios relative to enrollment.

Equally difficult has been the problem of school boards facing their public, or school administrators facing their boards, and trying to explain and defend a system of school finance that is inherently more complicated and less effective for confidence-building than is needed. School finance in most states has grown up over a period of years in which the complexity of organizational responsibilities for setting property assessments and tax rates and deciding state aid formulas has never been thought through as a single system designed to build confidence, to be comprehensible to the public and boards, and to encourage effective staff support of school administrators for boards. Consequently many school boards find themselves unable to understand school finance in the limited time available to them, especially with the requirement for amateurs on school boards that is appropriate to democracy. They have trouble explaining school finance and costs to the public. They have difficulty controlling costs effectively. They don't know what to ask their staff for. Equally difficult is the position in which this puts school administrators, causing them difficulty in trying to explain to board members who don't know what questions to ask and who may not appreciate the uncertainty involved in school finance today.

The attached description and model are designed to help overcome these problems. They don't do the whole job; some of the changes needed are in the overall structure of school finance. A more simple model that builds confidence and encourages understanding is needed. The place to begin is with the simplicity of the corporate accounting field in which earnings and dividends can easily be related to overall corporate sales and profits and to stock prices. The purpose of this model was to build the confidence of investors and to make cost control and financial analysis feasible. Applying these standards to public finance is equally important. The state of the art of school finance is far behind industry in terms of the effectiveness of cost control and the building of confidence.

The model was developed for a highly cost-conscious school district in a relatively affluent suburb. In this district effective financial planning and cost control had already been established. But the absence of an overall model and the desire of the district to act upon its projections and analysis required some fine tuning. Placing the projections in the context of an overall concept of board responsibilities, decision-making and their essentially political character was needed. The model was developed for these purposes.

CASE STUDY TWELVE

Many school board members today are understandably confused about financial planning and cost control. School finance is complicated. In an era of declining enrollment and resources school boards naturally feel under pressure to demonstrate that they are spending the public's money wisely.

Described in this part of the case study is the model of school financial planning and cost control. I use it as the basis for discussion seminars with school boards, to help them understand and focus on the most important factors for successful financial planning and cost control. The model is based on consulting with more than 100 school districts, developing and teaching the Northwestern School Management Case Study Course, directing the School Performance Research Project for the Illinois Association of School Boards, and serving as a local school board member. The model is shown in Exhibit 12.1

Cost Control – Key Board Policy Decisions

For cost control purposes, concentrate on staffing rations, salaries, and supporting services.

Focus on Staffing Ratios

Make sure your staff presents a clear analysis and historical comparison of staffing ratios. They are the primary determinant of total costs.

Many boards may be surprised to find that staff/student ratios have increased significantly over the past decade. This is one of the reasons that national average school costs have risen more rapidly than inflation during this time period. You'll find that research evidence on the correlation of performance with class size leaves a wide range for board discretion and judgment.

Control requires not only monitoring what has happened, but an administrative team willing to take the sometimes difficult steps needed to control these ratios as enrollment declines. For example, eliminating positions, restructuring classes, or sharing teachers among schools, grades, or programs may need to be considered. At secondary

EXHIBIT 12.1
School Financial Planning and Cost Control Model

This model is designed for discussion with school boards, superintendents, business managers, and other administrators. The objectives:
- To provide a conceptual framework identifying key components of financial planning and cost control.
- To recognize the inherent complexity and uncertainty of school finance, and to focus on the most important factors.
- To highlight important board decisions and information.
- To help boards and administrators work together to deal responsibly with these difficult issues.

COST CONTROL: KEY BOARD POLICY DECISIONS (SEE DETAILS BELOW FOR EXPLANATION)
- Staff/student ratios.   1
                                                          x
- Salaries policy.   2
                                                          +
- Other costs.   3
                                                          =
- Tax rate (referendum timing).   4
                                                   cushioned by
- Cash reserve/debt policy.   5

FINANCIAL PLANNING: PROJECTIONS AND ASSUMPTIONS
- Enrollment.
- Assessed valuation.
- Timing of tax receipts.
- State aid.
- Inflation.
- State school finance policy; taxpayer revolt.

DECISION GUIDELINES AND CAUTIONS
- High level of complexity and uncertainty.
- Staff support from superintendent and business manager.
- Positive rather than negative morale implications.
- The political/financial equation — parents, teachers, taxpayers.
- Cost control and financial planning versus program and resource allocation decisions.
- School performance information to support board confidence and delegation.

continued

EXHIBIT 12.1, continued

COST CONTROL: KEY BOARD POLICY DECISIONS

Considering community needs, desires, and resources, and the educational program to be provided in response, these are the key financial policy decisions that must be made by the board:

Staff/student ratios.

- Primary determinant of total costs.
- Control important; cost implications, public sensitivity, impact on staff.
- Research evidence limited, often conflicting: a judgment call.

Salaries policy.

- Teachers, administrators, others.
- Relating compensation to performance.
- Internal equity, external comparisons.

Other costs.

- Less important than salary, but must be considered.
- Aggressive identification of possible cost reduction opportunities.
- Program options.
- One-time gains or expenditures – sales of assets, maintenance, facility requirements.

Tax rate (referendum timing).

- First three components total to district budget, indicating tax rate required.
- Timing of referendum to increase tax rate: when funds are required, risks of defeat, local circumstances that might affect the likelihood of success.

Cash reserve/debt policy.

- Outside the basic equation.
- Could cushion uncertainties of financial projections, avoid short-term adjustments in other elements of the equation.
- Need to establish a cash reserve policy.
    - Considering debt capacity.
    - Holding of working capital by district versus citizens.

FINANCIAL PLANNING: PROJECTIONS AND ASSUMPTIONS

These are the key factors in developing school financial projections:

Enrollment.

- Rolling forward prior enrollment experience usually produces fairly accurate projections, at least in the short run.

Assessed valuation.

- Assessment practices appear mysterious; contrasting trends in similar communities inexplicable.
- Past accuracy of local projections should be monitored as an indication of how predictable this factor may be.

continued

EXHIBIT 12.1, continued

Timing of tax receipts, and allocation of revenues by tax year.
- Might use cash reserves to hedge against variations in the timing of tax receipts.
- As much as six months operating budget might be needed.

State aid.
- Projections can be based on historical funding or formula projections — both subject to uncertainty.
- Changing economic circumstances, or adverse political decision making at state level, can have a major impact.

Inflation.
- Obviously difficult to project.
- Range of alternative possibilities seems essential, e.g., 5 percent, 10 percent, and 15 percent.
- Risk of a self-fulfilling impact on teacher expectations.

State school finance policy; taxpayer revolt.
- Most uncertain area of projection.
- Potential swings up or down can be substantial.
- Obviously Illinois' position in the national taxpayer revolt is extremely hard to predict, although it has been relatively uneventful to date.
  - Local initiative.
  - State initiative.

DECISION GUIDELINES AND CAUTIONS
These are some considerations that may affect board financial decision making:
High level of complexity and uncertainty.
- Inherent complexity, in some respects artificial.
- Several components of assumptions unprojectable; quantifying them may mask the real uncertainty that exists.
- Judgment, and differentiating between short- and long-run, essential.

Staff support to board decision making from superintendent and business manager.
- General strategy for financing the district, with contingencies.
- Analysis and supporting information, in all areas identified in this model.

A positive rather than negative impact on public confidence.
- Challenging human dimension of financial planning; more difficult under some circumstances than others.
- Public and staff sensitive to financial issues, potentially compounding negative impact.

Rationalizing financial decisions to the public and staff.
- Inherently conflicting interests of teachers, parents, and taxpayers without children in school.

continued

EXHIBIT 12.1, continued

- Political and financial equation; difficulties of decisions involving both qualitative and quantitative factors.
- Strategic leadership from superintendent and board.

Separate cost control and financial planning from program and resource allocation.
- Frightening and confusing to deal with all at the same time.
- Natural defensiveness can be damaging to morale and teamwork.

School performance information.
- Evidence to show that expenditures were worthwhile.
- Analysis of test data to indicate student learning.
- Surveys of parents and teachers, to understand their perceptions.
- Strategy of good performance and cost control.

Source: Compiled by author.

level, analysis should extend to each department, analyzing present enrollment and future projections in detail. At elementary levels, specialist staff in areas like music and art will need to be monitored carefully, especially if enrollments are declining. At both levels, special education warrants separate attention, because high costs and staffing ratios often presenting significant cost control opportunities, within legal requirements.

Establish Policy on Salaries

Consider both internal equity and external comparisons in deciding salary policies for teachers, administrators, and others. In most areas, salaries in nearby districts follow a very similar pattern. You will need to decide how your salaries should relate to the prevailing pattern in your area.

If possible, relate compensation to performance. This strengthens staff recognition and reward for good performance, adds to board and public confidence, and improves staff morale, satisfaction, and performance (if coupled with fair and effective evaluation and communication). Note that these evaluation and communication prerequisites are challenging, and will take most districts several years to achieve, before you can consider performance-based compensation.

You'll probably want to develop performance-based compensation for administrators before teachers. But be wary of most merit pay plans that have been tried in school districts. Only a handful have worked successfully in practice, and many have done more harm than good. A good plan will produce better school performance at lower cost.

Analyze Other Costs Periodically

The combination of staff ratios and salaries will account for the majority of district expenditures. However, it is also important to analyze other possible cost reduction opportunities.

You might want to ask your administrative team to target one area each year for detailed scrutiny — to identify possible cost reduction opportunities, and consider levels of service and overall cost effectiveness — e.g., transportation, the lunch program, office organization, and staffing including word processing and computer applications, supplies, books, and materials.

Total Budget Indicates Tax Rate

These three factors will add up to the district's total budget, and thus indicate the tax rate required. Depending on how you are required to seek public approval of tax rates, this will obviously have implications in a number of areas. Demonstrating effective cost control is virtually certain to be essential, whatever you decide to do. The timing of tax rate changes is likely to be especially important

It will also be substantially affected by your cash reserve and debt policies. These policies can cushion tax rate changes from short-run fluctuations in costs and revenues. You'll need to consider both the extent to which you are willing to draw upon debt capacity and/or to accumulate case reserves. Both should serve to cushion you against unexpected changes in costs or, more likely, in revenues. Most schools operate with a highly predictable and fixed cost structure, because of annual contracts with teachers, whereas revenue fluctuations can be substantial.

Financial Planning — Projections and Assumptions

Make sure your administrators project the district's financial situation several years into the future, in spite of complexity and uncertainty.

One of the surprising things to many new school board members is the complexity and uncertainty of revenues. These characteristics can also make school administrators uneasy about making projections. You may even find yourself being told that this is impossible. You will need to express a sympathetic understanding and appreciation of the complexity and uncertainty involved, if your administrators are to be comfortable in making projections. They will have to make assumptions, which should be specified, with an indication of the range of probable outcomes and rough probabilities involved. It makes sense to place more credence on short-term than long-term forecasts. What follows are the key elements of school financial projections that you should be concerned with.

Enrollment

Many districts have found enrollment projections of a decade ago that are off by as much as 100 percent. Yet actual enrollment projections should be fairly straightforward for most districts. Unless your community is changing dramatically, rolling forward your enrollment in a simple calculation based on retention rates from grade to grade should provide accurate short-run projections. Also take account of construction plans and progress in your area, and other indicators such as birth rates and in-migration.

Assessed Valuation

In many communities assessment practices are mysterious and difficult to project. Look carefully at your past history, but be cautious because assessment practices were designed before today's inflation and economic uncertainty. In many states you will also be affected by state-applied factors, such as multipliers of local assessments to equalize them across the state, subject to inexplicable change and political influences that make them difficult to predict.

Timing of Tax Receipts

This can vary substantially from year to year, based on local county administrative practices, law suits arising out of the taxpayer revolt, or other situations. Because most school district expenditures are not subject to modification during the year, and are committed by contract, the need to hedge against unexpected shifts of timing is important.

State Aid

While most states have established formulas for funding the state's contribution to local school districts, in many cases these are subject to uncertainty of funding availability and/or modifications in the formula from time to time. Changing economic circumstances or adverse political decision making at a state level can have a major impact. Still, forecasting is essential.

Inflation

Obviously from the pattern of the last decade this is difficult to predict, and the current climate of economic uncertainty doesn't help. Be sensitive to the risk of a self-fulfilling impact on teacher negotiations.

Taxpayer Revolt

This is perhaps the most uncertain area, obviously subject to shifts in national attitudes and political trends. Some states (such as California and Massachusetts) have been hard hit. But every state and community is potentially subject to these pressures today.

Decision Guidelines and Cautions

Be cautious and positive in your decisions. Given the cost control and financial planning factors described in the first two sections, these are some decision-making guidelines and cautions that we have found helpful in practice:

Recognize the High Level of Complexity and Uncertainty in School Finance

In some respects this complexity is artificial, resulting from archaic fund accounting. An iterative process of state decision making seems to have resulted in a school finance system that is very complicated. It is genuinely difficult for a local district to project its financial future and plan soundly. Especially in an era of inflation and public concern with schools, the system tends to invite suspicion and make it unnecessarily difficult for school boards to understand school finance and explain and defend costs to the public. Recognize that some assumptions are largely unfounded, and be prepared for a range of possible outcomes. Judgment and differentiating between short- and long-run projections are both essential.

Use Staff Support from Your Superintendent and Business Manager

Your superintendent should present a general strategy for financing the district, including contingencies to account for major uncertainties, and updating at least annually or where any major change occurs. This strategy should make sense both politically and financially. This is a real challenge. The board will make the final decisions, but you should have clear-cut recommendations, alternatives, and an explanation of circumstances and implications from your superintendent.

Equally important is the analysis and supporting information from the superintendent or business manager. Use the key factors described in this article to review the information with which you are provided, to help assess whether or not you have sufficient data. The greater complexity and uncertainty of school finance today, as well as such political factors as the taxpayer revolt, are increasing the demands on school business managers.

Consider the Impact of Financial Decisions on Public Confidence and Staff Morale

Minimize the negative impact of financial decisions on the staff and public. How these decisions are explained by the board and administration is crucially important. Rationalize effective cost control in ways that make the staff feel that they are being more productive and the public feel that they are getting better value for money. The staff is also likely to appreciate careful planning and control that avoids abrupt changes resulting in lost jobs or wasted effort. Without due regard for the human impact of school finance, the same decisions can initiate a downward spiral of confidence and morale that in the long run will cost more than the original budget cut.

Appreciate the Political Aspects of School Finance

The need to rationalize financial decisions to the public and staff is an especially challenging aspect of school management, one that boards and their management teams must deal with together. It is a political *and* financial equation, especially when public approval through referendum is needed, with all of the especially challenging difficulties of decisions that involve both qualitative and quantitative factors. Of course you'll appreciate the inherently conflicting interests of teachers, parents, and taxpayers without children in schools that also must be taken into account. Leadership from the superintendent and board is essential and challenging. The difficulty of rationalizing such decisions successfully is obviously more challenging under some circumstances than others.

Separate Cost Control and Financial Planning from Program and Resource Allocation Decisions

One way districts get into trouble is by combining decisions about programs and resource allocation with cost reduction. Good financial planning should put you in a position to consider these things separately. Otherwise, as you consider which programs to cut, fear and apprehension will overtake the district. Every group interested in a particular program will feel threatened and defensive. Finding sensible compromises becomes very difficult. Try to keep these issues separate, by dealing with them at separate times and by anticipating the need to cut costs well in advance. Once you have resolved the cost control issues identified in the first section of this article, you may want to consider across the board cuts if financial resources won't fund as full a program as you wish to have.

Use School Management Techniques to Encourage Board Support, Public Satisfaction, Staff Morale, and Student Learning

Use of these techniques is more important to the overall cost effectiveness of schools than cost control and financial planning. They make possible board confidence in district performance that is essential to sound decision making, and support staff and parent satisfaction as well as student progress. An overall board strategy of good performance and cost control is essential, with evidence that expenditures are worthwhile.

Such evidence includes: (1) analysis of test data to indicate student learning; (2) surveys of parents and teachers to demonstrate their satisfaction and build confidence, to understand perceptions and concerns, and to identify improvement opportunities; (3) administrative evaluation and compensation that demonstrates and rewards good performance; and (4) teacher evaluation and development based on participation, communication, and fair and effective evaluation.

These suggestions should help boards and administrators work together more successfully and responsibly to plan, finance, and control school costs.

CASE STUDY THIRTEEN
Decision-Making Model

INTRODUCTION TO CASE STUDY THIRTEEN

A second critically important dimension of school financial planning and cost control is decision making with regard to specific issues. It isn't really possible in this book to cover this subject in adequate detail. But an example of the complexity and the kind of issues involved in such decisions is feasible.

This example deals with school closing in the context of declining enrollment and state mandated integration requirements. I think you will find that it helps to understand the kinds of factors involved in such decisions, and their inter-relationship. One particularly difficult aspect that becomes clear from this brief document is the challenge of balancing financial aspects of such a decision with the feelings and attitudes of those involved.

While many school districts have successfully calculated and handled decisions about school closing (many of the more successful ones deciding not to close schools as a result), others have either miscalculated and in the process lost the credibility and trust of their public or failed to appreciate how strong and important the emotional attachment of communities is to their schools. Some districts found to their dismay that board elections hinged on these factors, superintendents were fired, and closed schools reopened.

Background on the District

This report was developed for the board and a citizens committee of a medium-size district in Michigan. It faced the need to consider school closing both because of declining enrollment and to meet state mandated integration requirements. The report was prepared as a framework of factors to be considered by the board and committee, and was found to be quite helpful. It identified a large number of factors that needed to be considered, and helped to assure that none was overlooked in the course of deliberations or forgotten at the time of final decision making. District administrators gathered data and presented reports against the "table of contents" set forth in the outline. The report seemed particularly helpful in indicating the number, complexity, and overlapping nature of the many issues and factors involved, some highly quantitative and related to cost and physical facilities, and others highly emotional and social such as the feelings and attitudes of parents about neighborhood schools and integration.

CASE STUDY THIRTEEN

The district is faced with a need to make several difficult decisions regarding a variety of complicated issues including the basic structure of educational programs and facilities. In doing so, the board retains responsibility for considering and deciding from a general management and public interest viewpoint — in a context of complicated local opinions, facts, and feelings as well as specific mandates and the broader legal framework of state and nation. The possible implications for the district and community are obviously significant, including the risk of damaging currently functioning schools and communities.

As an aid in organizing the process of consideration leading to these decisions by the board, Exhibit 12.2 outlines the issues and factors that seem relevant to the decisions that will be required. The pages following the outline discuss in somewhat more detail the information required regarding each issue.

EXHIBIT 12.2
Outline of Restructuring Issues and Factors

Issues	Factors
DISTRICT PERFORMANCE	Satisfaction with school programs and
1. Parent survey	performance, general as well as by
	school, grade, and area
2. Evaluation	Continuing future monitoring of per-
	formance
EDUCATIONAL PROGRAMS AND	School clustering
ORGANIZATION	Departmentalizing
1. Educational options options	Staffing Patterns
	Educational alternatives
2. Neighborhood schools	Values, attachments
3. Intermediate, junior high, high	Educational options
school grades	Facility options
4. Split classes	Problems, concerns
EDUCATIONAL FACILITIES PLAN-	Satisfactions and concerns
NING	Possible changes
1. School boundaries, communities	Transportation costs
2. Facilities planning	Problems if any with sites, size, needs,
	maintenance cost
	Alternative use values
	Capacities versus enrollment and pro-
	jections
	Alternative school configurations
	Long-range facility plans
3. Possible school closing	Candidates, savings, feelings
INTEGRATION	Satisfaction with present arrangements
1. Bilingual program	Quality and effectiveness
2. Mandate	Legal obligation for racial balance
	State and national trends
	Local community uniqueness
	Formula defects and mechanics
	General management, community, and
	public interest versus special man-
FINANCIAL PLANNING	dates
1. Circumstances	Resources, projections, cost control
2. Plans	Alternatives, strategy

Source: Compiled by author.

This section is intended to provide a way of organizing the process of consideration for the board and committee, assuring balanced attention to all relevant issues and factors in a thorough and thoughtful decision-making process. During the process, the outline of this plan should be subject to change, and obviously considerable detail will be filled in with respect to each issue involved. Later, decisions to be made and options to be considered will also probably need to be specified more precisely.

Outline of Information Requirements

District Performance

Parent Survey. Results of the parent survey currently being conducted will be available by late summer or early fall. They should provide the board and committee with an overview of parent satisfaction with school programs and performance at the present time, and an indication of concerns according to school, grade, or subject area. This information is considered likely to be valuable as a general base of information on district performance against which other issues can be considered, and as one component of a larger effort to strengthen evaluation.

Evaluation. Also resulting from the current work will be a plan for strengthening evaluation that will improve future monitoring of performance in the district. This is likely to include attention to: teacher evaluation, development, and reward; administrative evaluation and compensation; board policies for evaluation; evaluative information including student learning, surveys, and cost analysis; and noncertified personnel evaluation. Although recommendations for strengthening evaluation will be made later this summer, obviously neither implementation nor operation of these evaluation systems will be available in time to be taken into account in decisions to be made this fall.

Educational Programs and Organization

Educational Options. The possible alternatives available to the district along with their educational advantages and disadvantages should be documented and reported to the board and committee in some detail. Clear-cut research findings supporting one alternative or the other are unlikely to be available, but it may be advantageous to review literature to identify alternatives and summarize evidence on their effectiveness. Responsibility for this aspect of information might focus on the assistant superintendent for instruction. Certainly to be considered are all of the options thus far identified in consideration of the restructuring issue, including the clustering of schools, alternative staffing patterns, and other educational alternatives that are feasible and worth consideration.

Neighborhood Schools. It has been evident from our discussions with parents as well as teachers, administrators, and board members to date that the attachment of the people of Martins to neighborhood schools is unusually high. Undoubtedly this reflects the nature of the community and what appears to be a relatively high level of neighborhood and community identity in spite of the changing ethnic composition of the population. The values of neighborhood schools in terms of parent involvement, community focus of identity, convenience to parents and children, retention of children from one family in the same school for a reasonable number of years, established expectations that may have been factors in purchasing a home and selecting a neighborhood, knowledge of school location, travel patterns, faculty, procedures and personnel, and the inevitable uncertainty of change are important factors that need to be taken into account. They apply particularly to children at lower grade levels. It seems clear that the board should consider the possibility of a different policy for the organization of schools at lower grade levels than in intermediate and higher grade levels. A board policy committing the district to neighborhood schools at primary grade levels might enhance flexibility to restructure intermediate and junior high school grades.

Intermediate, Junior High, High School Grades. Both educational and facility options at these levels seem to afford more flexibility and less attachment to and value in neighborhood schools than at lower levels. The district has recently restructured itself in these areas, and further change should be considered in this light. It certainly seems feasible that at the fifth, sixth, and seventh grade levels, the possibility of other configurations is realistic, based on patterns being successfully operated by other districts today. At least three options deserve consideration:

- K-4, 5-6, 7-8, 9-10-11-12
- K-5, 6-7, 8-9, 10-11-12
- K-6, 7, 8-9, 10-11-12 (present)

Other alternatives are likely to be identified.

Split Classes. Problems and concerns about split classes expressed by parents during preliminary discussions were not conspicuous. Certainly from a teacher point of view the challenge of functioning effectively in classes with more than one grade level is recognized to require an above average capability and work load on the part of the teacher, and to be feasible only with teachers who are prepared to accept such responsibilities. Given these limitations, it seemed to be felt by teachers participating in our discussion that split classes do not disadvantage the children in terms of learning. However, the trade-off between flexibility in class size and placement of youngsters with teachers in larger schools, and the probable need for split classes in smaller schools, deserves to be thoroughly explored.

Educational Facilities Planning

School Boundaries, Communities. School boundaries have not been subject to change in recent years in Martins. Such stability has many advantages. However, the possibility of boundary changes for any reason ought to be identified at this time. Areas in which school boundaries may be out of line with neighborhoods or disadvantageous in terms of traffic or transportation patterns should be considered.

Facilities Planning. Considerable information seems to be available with regard to each of the school sites — capacity versus enrollment and projections, maintenance needs and costs, and general adequacy of property and facilities. Information on these matters should be developed and explained to the board and committee. Alternative use values should be considered, in terms of the possibility of more advantageous economic utilization of sites and facilities. Alternative school configurations should be considered. The facilities implications of alternative educational plans, and the facilities requirements that impact upon these plans, should be made clear. This would logically seem to fall within the responsibilities of the assistant superintendent for business affairs.

Possible School Closing. Although logically a part of the facilities planning question, the importance and complexity of school closing warrants addressing this as a separate issue. Candidates, potential savings, and community and educational impact should be assessed. The emotional side of this issue tends in most districts to far outweigh the cost calculations in ultimate impact. Even though no further schools may be closed, the desirability of thorough exploration of this issue while restructuring is being considered seems clear.

Integration

Bilingual Program. Description and evaluation of the bilingual program based on the considerable evidence available within the district should be made available to the board and committee. It would appear that the quality and effectiveness of this program may be exceptional, and that there is widespread satisfaction in the community with present arrangements.

Mandate. The district's legal obligation for racial balance as established by the State Board of Education and national Constitution and laws obviously needs to be taken fully into account. State and national trends in the enforcement and interpretation of these complicated matters should be considered. The uniqueness of Martins in its bilingual racial situation and in the character of its community and schools is also relevant.

The formulas that have been developed and applied in Michigan and elsewhere are rather mechanical, and appear defective in certain respects, for example, applying the same formula to quite different communities and local circumstances, failing to recognize different requirements and characteristics at lower grade levels as opposed to higher ones (for example, the importance of neighborhood schools to parent involvement and community identity discussed above), and not taking into account the experience of children as they proceed through the grade levels. (In Martins, for example, approximately half of each child's educational career is spent in an integrated setting.)

The committee and board should recognize that they are charged with a general management, community, and public interest decision that must take into account all of the many circumstances and factors and issues that are relevant, rather than just responding to a single specialized requirement outside of this larger context.

Financial Planning

Circumstances. Projections of resources and expenditures several years into the future should be available, with evidence of cost and revenue trends in the past.

Plans. The district's future financial alternatives and strategic choices will need to be set forth, particularly as these will interrelate with some of the other issues discussed above. As with facilities, these subjects seem appropriately the responsibility of the assistant superintendent for business affairs.

The complexity of the information with which the committee and board must deal is obvious. The possibility of a series of meetings in which information, factors, and issues would be presented and discussed in an organized fashion along the lines of this outline would seem advantageous in assuring attention to all relevant issues and affording a framework within which thorough consideration can be given.

CASE STUDY FOURTEEN
School Board Responsibilities

This last case study consists of three exhibits that provide models of school board responsibilities, a comprehensive approach to evaluation encompassing all levels of the organization, and a description of management responsibilities applicable to both business and public organizations.

Exhibit 12.3 shows school board responsibilities on both the human and financial sides of school management. The financial side parallels the model for financial planning and cost control described

EXHIBIT 12.3
School Board Responsibilities

Relationships and Performance	*Financial Planning and Cost Control*
The human side of good school performance and management – practical, positive accountability to improve morale, confidence, and learning.	The financial side of good school management, for positive, constructive board decision making.
1. *Board confidence*, support and delegation.	1. *Cost Control*
2. *Performance information* – e.g., test data, parent/teacher surveys.	• Staffing
	• Salaries
3. *Relationships*, communication, trust, and confidence.	• Other costs
4. *Organization* and responsibilities – teamwork and performance.	• Tax rate
	• Cash reserve
5. *Program* planning and evaluation, reporting and participation.	2. *Financial Planning*
	• Assessed valuation
6. *Administrative* evaluation and compensation.	• State aid
7. *Teacher* evaluation and development.	• Enrollment
(details in the School Performance and Management Model)	• Inflation
	• Facilities
	3. *Decision Guides and Cautions*
	• Complexity and uncertainty
	• Staff analytical support, and strategy
	• Morale
	• Political equation
	• Program and resource allocation
	(details in the School Financial Planning and Cost Control Model)

Results

Typical range of performance ± 20 percent.

- Student learning.
- Parent satisfaction.
- Public confidence.
- Staff morale.

Typical range of performance ± 20 percent.

- Reasonable costs.
- Justified to public and staff.
- Sound planning in spite of uncertainty.
- Positive effect on morale and performance.

Source: Compiled by author.

271

in Case Study Twelve. The human side ties together the subjects discussed in earlier case studies. The emphasis is on building confidence, support, and delegation through performance information; on defining organization thoroughly and carefully with responsibility for performance and teamwork as well as relationships, communication, trust, and confidence; on a process of program planning and evaluation as well as reporting and participation that is sound and effective; and finally on the two key components of good school management discussed in the two preceding chapters: administrative evaluation and compensation, and teacher evaluation and development. All of these subjects have been addressed in earlier chapters, and this exhibit may help you tie them together with the financial side of school management discussed in this chapter. At the bottom of this exhibit are indicated the impact of these responsibilities in terms of performance – the plus or minus 20 percent range discussed in the first case study.

Exhibit 12.4 is a comprehensive model of evaluation applicable to board/superintendent, administrative, and teacher levels of the organization. It parallels the model shown in Case Study Eight regarding superintendent evaluation. It is the underlying assumption for the administrative and teacher evaluation approach described in Chapters 9 and 10. Collecting these concepts in a comprehensive model that includes the planning and evaluation process, performance information, and personal development helps to show how all of these things tie together to build communication, effectiveness, and performance at all levels of the organization.

Finally, a model of management responsibilities that applies to both business and public organizations is shown in Exhibit 12.5. The techniques described in these case studies on school management have implications for the broader development of public management in government and other nonprofit organizations as well as education. There are important parallels in business and public management requirements. Both sides would benefit from a more aggressive exploration of similarities as well as differences. The model is designed to improve communication between business and public management and to integrate the management disciplines as they apply to both business and public services.

EXHIBIT 12.4
School Evaluation Model

Communication Process	Performance Information	Personal Development
Reporting of objectives and results. Planning and analysis by teachers and administrators. Regarding program performance: district, school, department, subject, grade, and classroom. The process of setting objectives and reporting results, and the planning and analysis that supports it, should help to link together the organization with commitment and participation. A simple, practical process should avoid excessive paperwork or time.	Student learning. Parent satisfaction. Staff morale. Cost control. Information is essential: • To support board confidence and delegation. • To document good performance. • To build confidence and support as the foundation for positive, constructive relationships. • To identify improvement opportunities.	Board/superintendent relations. Administrative training. Teacher development. This component differs on each of the three levels: • For board and superintendent: personal behavior and relationships. • For administrators: career planning and personal development including management training. • For teachers: positive individualized development and growth.

Source: Compiled by author.

EXHIBIT 12.5
Public Management Model

1. Monitor Performance
   - What business are we in?
     - Mission and purpose.
     - Planning and reporting.
     - Goals and objectives.
     - Trends and circumstances.
   - How well are we doing?
     - Performance concept.
     - Information and indicators.
     - Evaluation, standards, and expectations.
     - Analysis and judgment.
   - Cost control.
     - Key factors.
     - Financial planning.
     - Decision making, reporting, political equation.

2. Develop People
   - Communication and participation.
     - Planning and reporting process.
     - Performance information.
     - Impact of collective bargaining.
   - Organization.
     - Structure.
     - Responsibilities and relationships.
     - Concept of management.
   - Personnel.
     - Talent required.
     - Evaluation.
     - Compensation.
     - Development.

Source: Compiled by author.

CONCLUSION OF CHAPTER 12

These three exhibits deal quite briefly with critically important aspects of school management in terms of board responsibilities, stressing the importance of board attention to purpose and performance as well as people and their development. The implications of these management responsibilities of course extend well beyond education to business and government as well. If we are to regain the U.S. reputation for successful management, founded in agriculture and business and now being extended to public services as well, we will need to be much more insightful to the requirements and techniques of good management and how they relate to performance in all fields of endeavor. I hope these exhibits convey some sense of the importance and nature of these responsibilities, albeit in a rather short form. Those interested in school board responsibilities will find a somewhat longer discussion in my first book on school management, *Effective Schools Through Effective Management*, listed in the bibliography and published by the Illinois Association of School Boards.

CONCLUSION OF PART II

In total these fourteen case studies represent all of the major components of good school management essential to good school performance today. I hope you find these examples to be practical and, while you may have to modify them for application in your own situation, I believe they are all relevant.

Collectively, they add up to a model of school management that I believe will achieve good performance in every district. Individually, I know that they represent successful applications of management techniques that work in schools to improve performance, build morale, raise learning, develop confidence, and control costs.

Implementation is of course challenging and will require the best talents and efforts of school administrators, teachers, and board members working effectively together. I know that the talent of these people is adequate to the job to be done, but they will need the encouragement and in some cases the assistance of other elements of our society. Parents and taxpayers in local communities as well as universities and foundations all have important contributions to make. The responsible support and participation of teachers internally within the district and through channels of collective bargaining will be essential. The active support and assistance of various associations, perhaps especially those of school boards and administrators, will be critically important.

The final section of the book turns to the roles these various groups should play in helping to improve school performance through better management.

PART III
WHAT TO DO

Evaluates what action educators and others should do to strengthen school management and improve performance.

13

WHAT EDUCATORS SHOULD DO:
School Boards, Administrators, and Teachers

Taking action to strengthen school management and improve performance is obviously important. That is, if management is indeed one of the important reasons contributing to the decline of school performance during the past decade, and if the new techniques described here are essential to turn it around. If by now you agree that this is the case, and that these techniques do offer promise for a turnaround on a much broader scale than has yet been accomplished, then these two chapters should help to focus on what needs to be done. In such a huge institution as education, many people must be involved. There is ample room for contribution on the part of virtually everyone.

This chapter describes the action required on the part of those inside education and responsible for its performance and management — school boards, administrators, and teachers. In the next chapter, opportunities for outside help are described — on the part of parents, taxpayers, and citizens as well as universities, corporations, and foundations.

School Boards

One of the lessons I've learned from my own service as a school board member is how limited the impact of such a position is, and yet how important it can be. School board members serve on a part-time basis, usually meeting in the evenings after a full day of work or other obligations. The time available to them is extremely limited. For both the instruction and management of the districts for which they are technically ultimately responsible, they are in fact highly dependent on their teaching and administrative staffs.

Yet school boards can still have a vitally important impact. The way in which they make decisions, and the decisions they make, can mean the difference between a district that is performing well and managed well, and one that is spiraling downward in conflict and fragmentation. The following paragraphs give steps that school boards must take to successfully fulfill their responsibility for good school management and performance.

Take the decline of performance and your responsibility to turn it around seriously. I believe school boards today should receive fairly good marks for this. They have become more aggressive than in the past, quite willing in many cases to pay attention to national indicators of decline and to seek out similar indicators within their own districts. But school boards are by no means perfect in this regard; many have not yet really considered what to do. That is why the techniques in this book should be helpful. Most boards already have taken public concern and their responsibilities seriously.

However, don't overdo your sense of responsibility by becoming excessively involved in district operations, or fighting internally within the board or with the staff. One common mistake school boards make is to become overinvolved in the operations of the district, seeking to make personnel decisions with respect to administrators or teachers, or to direct specific program changes in an effort to improve performance. Worst of all are boards who have become so oriented to conflict that they spend most of their time fighting among themselves. This only contributes to demoralization of the staff and internal fragmentation.

An even more important "don't" concerns collective bargaining. Too many school boards have fallen into a pattern of adversarial relationships with the staff, sometimes spurred on by associations, lawyers, and collective bargaining experts who see financial opportunities in this conflict. If more school boards had understood the benefit of good staff relations and fair and effective evaluation, unions would not have moved in so quickly on education, and their impact would be more positive and constructive. Every board must recognize that bargaining is a tough business, one in which defining the public interest and then bargaining effectively for it are essential board responsibilities. Nevertheless good staff relations, communication, participation, trust, and confidence are also essential today. Their place cannot be taken by adversarial bargaining, yet some school boards seem to behave as though this were the case.

Take the management suggestions in this book and see that they are carried out by the administrators in your district. You are likely to find a high level of interest on the part of both administrators and teachers in these practices. But you may find in some cases that insistence by the board is required. Here are some specific suggestions of what to look for, and if necessary insist upon.

First, your board meetings should not take too much time. A substantial part of each of them should be spent on receiving program descriptions and evaluations from your staff, including both teachers and administrators. If this is not your pattern of operation, consider changing. To do so, you may have to ask your administrators to change the format of information they're providing to you, and to bring forward presentations to the board on programs.

Be sure to consider management capabilities and orientation when you're hiring a superintendent. Remember the most important job of the superintendent is to build a management team and faculty that can perform successfully together. The management techniques described in this book should give you a good sense of what is required. Take them into account in looking for a superintendent.

Be sure you are receiving performance information that is understandable and acted upon by your administrative team. Specifically, be sure that you receive a soundly analyzed and summarized report of test scores at least annually, as well as reports on the results of surveys of parents and teachers and occasionally students and the community. Make sure this information is used inside the district to actually analyze performance, make decisions, and take action. And look for evidence of improvement the next time the information is provided.

Expect your superintendent and management team to be able to explain to you in some detail how communication and participation are provided for in the district. The participation of teachers in committees, the channels of communication available for teachers when they have problems and concerns, and how these are provided for within the district should be described by the superintendent and administrators.

Be sure your district has formal, well-defined, positive, and constructive programs for the evaluation of administrators and teachers. Don't be misled by assertions that this can't be done in education. Your management team should be able to describe in detail for you how these things are done. And you may well expect some feedback from those concerned as to how they see the process working and whether or not it is satisfactory from their point of view.

Of course you should have a good feeling for the levels of satisfaction and concern on the part of parents and teachers from your day-to-day contacts in the community. Be cautious that you are not overreacting to these, and consider them in the context of broader evidence such as the test score analysis and parent and teacher surveys described in this book. While there will never be a district in which some parents and teachers are not dissatisfied, in a community where schools are functioning successfully there should be a widespread feeling of satisfaction, appreciation, support, and confidence based on personal observation and experience as well as participation and communication.

Administrators

Of course the overall job of the administrative team in the district is primarily to achieve the good management and high level of performance described in this book. Many of their day to day tasks will focus on specific parents, teachers, children, programs, and other things that are not directly a part of this management process. But the central importance of good management in their thinking and its preoccupation of a substantial portion of their time should be evident.

Recognize the importance of management and do everything you can to develop and apply successful techniques in your own district. Historically some superintendents have not felt that they should have responsibility for performance and management. The concepts and techniques required for successful acceptance of this crucially important responsibility have not been well developed. You should understand the need to depart from traditions of school administration that were successful and effective 20 years ago.

As you look around to those districts that are most successful today, you should be able to find techniques worth emulation. But be careful because many of the most sophisticated and complicated management techniques have proven more costly than effective. And you should understand that the application of management in any setting is extremely challenging. The traditional values of integrity, honesty, and good intentions on the part of superintendents are still important today.

Of course most of this book is directed toward administrators, and understanding the concepts and considering the techniques in this book represent a major challenge that need not be further discussed here. If administrators take these techniques seriously, adapt and apply them to their own situation, and build upon them to further refine and develop school management, that leadership will make the greatest possible contribution to the future of U.S. education.

Everyone on the management team will need to bring leadership qualities to management development if the district is to be successful in it. This will take understanding of the concepts and techniques of performance and management described in this book, and the opportunity for discussion and consideration of these ideas at some length. This is why the seminars I conduct seem useful in giving administrators an opportunity to step back from the immediate pressures and tasks of their jobs to consider some of these issues.

In my experience, you'll need some outside help to develop management in the district. As a school management teacher and consultant, I appreciate that I may not be 100 percent objective in this regard; nonetheless, it seems important to share the conclusion with you. A district that tries to learn management on its own risks internal disruption and less effective performance than might otherwise be achieved. Like learning to swim or play the piano, management is something that greatly benefits from guidance and counsel. Until schools of education are able to catch up with these management requirements, and the techniques are more fully developed, widely documented, and readily available, I think outside help is essential.

Teachers

Good management is as important to teachers as to administrators. Now that teachers have won the right to participate in management through collective bargaining, it is extremely important that they exercise this prerogative responsibly and successfully. Therefore my approach to defining school management has started with teachers — their concerns, problems, needs, and desires — as well as the nature of education and what is required for effective performance and the success of each teacher.

It is especially important for teacher union leaders to recognize the need for good management in schools and bargain toward it. I hope that the policies and practices suggested in this book are equally appealing to teachers and administrators, and that teachers would be as likely to bargain for them as administrators. I have found this to be the case in practice.

Teachers should also keep in mind that their bargaining position is likely to be greatly enhanced if they can demonstrate that the public would benefit from these techniques; this is also a point of view maintained in this book. While this should not discourage unions from aggressively defining the interests of teachers and working to achieve them, it also requires a somewhat broader view of the public interest. Balanced and responsible consideration in teacher union bargaining of the interests of students and parents and the responsibilities of board and administrators — as well as teachers — is needed.

Certainly one would hope that those responsible for education would take the initiative in seeking to develop management. Even if they do so, they will need help from those outside of education. And if they don't, the outsiders may need to take the initiative themselves.

14

OUTSIDE HELP:
Parents, Taxpayers, Citizens,
and Universities, Corporations,
and Foundations

This chapter looks at the help that can be offered, and where required the initiative that can be taken, by those outside of education to improve performance and management.

Parents

Parents should expect open channels of communication and active opportunities to participate in school districts. This might be through local chapters of the National PTA or similar local organizations.

They should expect school districts to listen to their concerns and respond to their suggestions. While no school district will ever be perfect in meeting every need and desire of every parent, by and large a widespread feeling of satisfaction with school performance should be evident in the community. If it's not, and the district isn't responding, then parents should be as aggressive as they need to be to get the situation changed.

The accessibility of school board members will affect parents' ability to bring about such changes. In most smaller suburban school districts and in smaller cities and towns board members are readily available. In large urban areas the scale of school districts means that boards are relatively inaccessible to local community residents. I believe this is a persuasive reason for decentralizing these school districts back to neighborhoods, on the model of suburban organization at the present time. In my opinion the boards of such large districts cannot effectively provide a channel of communication for public concern.

Parents should expect periodic surveys like those described in this book, to provide more formal channels of communication. They should expect some feedback to the community from these surveys as evidence of good performance. And they should expect to have similar opportunities afforded to the staff in the district.

As these questionnaires suggest, parents should expect to be satisfied with the progress of their children and the performance and programs of their schools in general and in regard to many specific areas. Specific categories I have found most helpful are indicated in these surveys.

As parents you should also expect a good deal of communication from the district in regard to such quantitative indicators of performance as the analysis of test data, cost control, and financial planning. If you don't receive regular information of this sort from the district, you should take the initiative to find it. And of course you should be told at some length personally as well as in written form about programs and activities of the district and programs of your own child.

TAXPAYERS

It seems clear that taxpayers should expect and demand accountability of their local governments and school districts. The evidence of cost control and financial planning suggested in Chapter 12 should be available and used in every district. It is equally important for taxpayers to be assured that schools are gathering and using performance information such as the test data analysis and parent/teacher surveys described in this book. Where this evidence is not available, and school districts are unresponsive to the need to demonstrate good performance and sound cost control and financial planning, taxpayers may well be justified in their revolution.

UNIVERSITIES

Universities have been hampered in responding to the new management needs of schools by a number of factors. One is that their own enrollments have been declining, and thus they've been financially constrained during the past decade or so. In addition, most of the experimentation and development of new management techniques in education has occurred on the firing line, where the needs are most evident and immediate. Progressive superintendents, administrators, and teachers have taken the initiative to solve problems and meet needs even though techniques and traditions of management have not been fully developed in education. Universities have not always been in a position to have access to the techniques that are proving most successful in practice.

Now, however, many schools of education are recognizing the need for new management techniques. They should look to the development of business management education for some clues as to what might be effective and successful, without expecting to duplicate those programs exactly.

One important need is for practical management education seminars for current school administrators. This will have the most immediate impact on the development of management and improvement of performance. And consideration should be given to how best to prepare school administrators. It does not appear that the traditional programs are the best way. And universities should reconsider the continuing education requirements for teachers, especially in light of the staff development and evaluation findings, conclusions, and recommendations discussed in Chapter 11.

Another important requirement is for practical school management research to help develop and define techniques such as those described in this book. Universities should stimulate and coordinate such research in order to help build the school management profession. This should include a better conceptual framework for understanding the rationale and philosophy of management as it applies to education. More examples of successful management techniques need to be developed, with evidence of their successes and hazards, and a variety of techniques appropriate to different circumstances and districts. Case studies to be used in school administration courses and seminars are needed.

An example of the kind of school management education that is relevant, and an indication of the kind of research and development that is needed, is my School Management Course at Northwestern.

ASSOCIATIONS

Education is well served by many associations ranging from school boards and administrators to research, curriculum, reading, and a host of other areas. All of them should consider more seriously the implications of the performance and management concepts and techniques in this book. And they should be more aggressive in research and communication in this regard. Certainly this would not replace or put aside their many other worthy activities. But it would add an important element to them. Some associations such as the Illinois Association of School Boards have already been quite aggressive in this regard. The benefits in better performance and management in the districts they serve have been substantial.

CORPORATIONS AND FOUNDATIONS

The concepts and techniques described in this book have benefitted from contributions of a few corporations and foundations to funding school management research. However, for the most part their contributions fund additional activities that only add to the productivity problem of public services rather than helping to solve them. This is unfortunate.

Corporate and foundation giving could provide an extremely important source of leverage, incentive, and funding in the development of public management for local governments and schools as well as other public services. To do so would be especially appropriate since these funds arise out of the quality of business management; for that success to contribute to improvement of the quality of public management would seem quite fitting. These sources of funding and incentive could help to channel more attention to this important national need. This would help to encourage recognition of the need to strengthen public management on the part of those directly responsible — governing boards, administration, and professional staff.

CONCLUSION

If the suggestions in this book can be followed even in part, I believe a substantial improvement in the performance of education will result. It seems hardly necessary to comment on the importance of this to our future national well-being. Education is vital as we seek to carry forward the economic success of our country in spite of a changed world situation, with the risk of following in England's pattern of industrial decline after early success. And it is equally important to our continued political success as we seek to carry forward our great accomplishments in eliminating unfair treatment and segregation. The potential further contribution of education seems at least equal to its successful history. If we are to forestall the decline said to await all successful societies, turning around the performance of education would seem perhaps the first and most important requirement. I hope the ideas in this book will help to do so.

BIBLIOGRAPHY

This book is based primarily on my own personal experience interviewing school board members, administrators, and teachers in more than 100 districts. Consequently, there are relatively few footnotes in the text of the book referring to the specific sources. However, a reading list prepared for my School Management Course at Northwestern University was designed to relate the case studies as well as the concepts and rationale of school management to the current literature.* Particularly emphasized are the changes and characteristics of education that I believe are extremely important as a foundation for defining and understanding the kind of management required for education to maintain and improve performance. This list is not a comprehensive survey of educational literature relevant to management, but only highlights of that field. The bibliography is organized into several sections to facilitate its usefulness.

Changes in the Organization of Education, Content of Programs, and Responses to Accountability Demands

Cresswell, M., Murphy, M., and Kerchner, C. *Teachers' Unions and Collective Bargaining*. California: McCutchan, 1980.

Erickson, D. A., and Reller, T. L., Editors. *The Principal in Metropolitan Schools*. California: McCutchan, 1979.

Harnischfeger, A. "Curricular control and learning time: district policy, teacher strategy and pupil choice." *Educational Evaluation and Policy Analysis* 2 (November-December 1980): 19.

Lutz, F., and Iannoccone, L., Editors. *Public Participation in Local School Districts*. Massachusetts: Lexington Books, 1978.

---

*I am particularly grateful to Barbara Schneider, Assistant Dean of the School of Education, who helped develop portions of this list as a part of the syllabus for my School Management Course at Northwestern University.

Millman, J., Editor. *Handbook of Teacher Evaluation*. California: Sage Publications, 1981.

Changes in the External Environment Impacting on the Educational System and Policy

Kirst, M. "The changing politics of education: actions and strategies." In *The Changing Politics of Education*, edited by E. K. Mosher and J. L. Wagoner, Jr., pp. 145-170. California: McCutchan, 1976.

Rubin, L., Editor. *Critical Issues in Educational Policy: An Administrator's Overview*. Boston: Allyn and Bacon, 1980.

Thurston, P. "Is good law good education?" In *Review of Research in Education*, edited by D. Berliner. American Educational Research Association, 1980: n. p.

Timpane, J., Editor. *The Federal Interest in the Financing of Schooling*. Massachusetts: Ballinger, 1978.

Wise, A. E. *Legislated Learning*. Berkeley: University of California Press, 1979.

The Goals of Schooling — Diversification and Changes

Atkin, J. M. "The government in the classroom." *Daedalus: Journal of the American Academy of Arts and Sciences* (Summer 1980): 85-97.

Fiorina, M. P. "The decline of collective responsibility in American politics." *Daedalus: Journal of the American Academy of Arts and Sciences* (Summer 1980): 25-45.

Firestone, W. A. "Images of schools and patterns of change." *American Journal of Education*, 8 (August 1980): 459-487.

Graham, P. A. "Whither equality of educational opportunity." *Daedalus: Journal of the American Academy of Arts and Sciences* (Summer 1980): 115-132.

Lightfoot, S. L. *Worlds Apart: Relationships between Families and Schools*. New York: Basic Books, 1978.

Wood, R. "The disassembling of American education." *Daedalus: Journal of the American Academy of Arts and Sciences* (Summer 1980): 99-113.

School Performance

Copperman, Paul. *The Literacy Hoax: The Decline of Reading, Writing and Learning in the Public Schools and What We Can Do About It*. New York: William Morrow, 1978.

Kozol, Jonathan. *Death at an Early Age: The Destruction of the Hearts and Minds of Negro Children in the Boston Public Schools*. Boston: Houghton, Mifflin, 1967.

Mitchell, Richard. *Less Than Words Can Say*. Boston: Little, Brown, 1979.

n. a. "A Kappan special section on teacher education." *Phi Delta Kappan* 63 (October 1981): 106-133.

Rutter, M., Maughan, B., Mortimore, P., and Ouston, J. *Fifteen Thousand Hours*. Cambridge: Harvard University Press, 1979.

n. a. "The 13th annual Gallup poll of the public's attitudes toward the public schools." *Phi Delta Kappan* 62 (September 1981): 33.

n. a. Special issue on collective bargaining. *Phi Delta Kappan* 63 (December 1981).

Education cover story. "The plight of U.S. secondary education: why are today's high school students learning less and disliking it more?" *Time*, November 14, 1977, pp. 62-75.

Education cover story. "Help! Teacher can't teach: the multi-faceted crisis of American public schools." *Time*, June 16, 1980, pp. 54-63.

School Management

Allen, J. L., and Genck, F. H. "Management education: the school of management concept." *American Assembly of Collegiate Schools of Business Bulletin* 6 (April 1970): n. p.

Genck, F. H., and Hay, D. W. "Local government reorganization in England." *Local Government Chronicle*, (England). (Serialized in 17, 24, 31 July and 7 August 1971 issues): n. p.

Genck, F. H., and Klingenberg, A. J. *Effective Schools through Effective Management*. Springfield: Illinois Association of School Boards, 1978.

Genck, F. H. "Public management in America." *American Assembly of Collegiate Schools of Business Bulletin* 9 (April 1973): 1-13.

_____ . "The school board's role." Presentation to the 1980 National School Boards Association Convention, San Francisco, California. May 1980.

_____ . "Improving performance." *The School Administrator* 39 (January 1982): 14-15.

_____ . "Make your school system accountable." *The American School Board Journal* 169 (February 1982): 34.

_____ . *Northwestern School Management Course Case Study Book* (Fredric H. Genck, 1982).

Both individual case studies and the complete book are available from the Institute for Public Management, 550 West Jackson Boulevard, Suite 365, Chicago, Illinois 60606. (312) 559-0515. Included are the following case studies:

Introductory Case Study, and Description of a Well-Managed School District

How To Improve School Performance — Report of the School Performance Research Project

Test Data Analysis To Improve Student Learning

Parent and Teacher Surveys To Improve Public Confidence and Staff Morale

Administrative Compensation and Evaluation

Teacher Evaluation and Development

Financial Planning and Cost Control with School Structure, Closing and Integration

INDEX

ABOUT THE AUTHOR

Fredric H. Genck is a prominent Chicago-based management consultant who has helped to pioneer the development of public management. He is managing director of Peter Warner Associates and the Institute for Public Management.

His management experience spans nearly two decades of counsel to hundreds of education, government, and business clients in the United States and Europe. This has included helping to reorganize English local government and redirecting U.S. business schools into schools of management embracing public as well as business concerns. In public schools, he has worked with more than 100 districts and presently serves as a local school board member. He has also directed the School Performance Research Project and developed the School Management Course at Northwestern University, which he currently teaches. Prior to forming his own consulting firm in 1973, he was with Booz, Allen and Hamilton in Chicago as assistant to the chairman and in London heading general management, corporate planning, and organization work.

Mr. Genck has published widely in the field of management. His first book on school management, *Effective Schools Through Effective Management*, was written with Allen J. Klingenberg and published in 1978 by the Illinois Association of School Boards. He has written more than 20 articles, which have appeared in many periodicals including *The School Administrator*, *American School Board Journal*, and *Local Government Chronicle* (England).

Mr. Genck holds an AB in economics from Cornell University and an MBA from Harvard University.